wissen & praxis 135

A Training Manual for Theatre Work in Social Fields

Edited by
Bernadette Cronin
Sieglinde Roth
Michael Wrentschur

In Cooperation with
Gerd Koch
Florian Vaßen

Finanziert von:

 Europäische Kommission, Sokrates-Programm GRUNDTVIG, Projekt "TWISFER: Theatre Work in Social Fields" – European Research" (Contract No. 110497-CP-1-2003-1-AT-GRUNDTVIG-G1)

Unterstützt durch:

Bundesministerium für Bildung, Wissenschaft und Kultur, Österreich

Fachabteilung für Sozialwesen des Landes Steiermark

Land Steiermark, Abteilung für Wissenschaft und Forschung

Kulturamt der Stadt Graz, Wissenschaftsreferat

A Training Manual for Theatre Work in Social Fields

Edited by
**Bernadette Cronin
Sieglinde Roth
Michael Wrentschur**

In Cooperation with
**Gerd Koch
Florian Vaßen**

Brandes & Apsel

Auf Wunsch informieren wir regelmäßig über das Verlagsprogramm:
Brandes & Apsel Verlag, Scheidswaldstr. 33, D–60385 Frankfurt am Main
E-Mail: brandes-apsel@t-online.de
Internet: www.brandes-apsel-verlag.de

wissen & praxis 135

1. Auflage 2005

© Brandes & Apsel Verlag GmbH, Frankfurt am Main

Alle Rechte vorbehalten, insbesondere das Recht der Vervielfältigung und Verbreitung sowie der Übersetzung, Mikroverfilmung, Einspeicherung und Verarbeitung in elektronischen oder optischen Systemen, der öffentlichen Wiedergabe durch Hörfunk-, Fernsehsendungen und Multimedia sowie der Bereithaltung in einer Online-Datenbank oder im Internet zur Nutzung durch Dritte.

Lektorat: Ann Barry (Cork), Bernadette Cronin (Cork)
Gestaltung: Karin Pütt (Berlin)
Foto Umschlag Vorderseite: Karin Pütt
Druck: Tiskarna Ljubljana d. d., Printed in Slovenia
Gedruckt auf säurefreiem, alterungsbeständigem und chlorfrei gebleichtem Papier

Bibliografische Information der Deutschen Bibliothek:
Die Deutsche Bibliothek verzeichnet diese Publikation in der Deutschen Nationalbibliografie; detaillierte bibliografische Daten sind im Internet über http://dnb.ddb.de abrufbar

ISBN 3-86099-335-6

Contents

Introduction 9

BASICS AND PRINCIPLES 13

Theatre Work (in Social Fields) 14
Manfred Schewe

Theatre Work and its Target Groups – 21
A Reflective Approach
Sieglinde Roth

Social Fields 30
Michael Wrentschur

MODULE PROJECTS 41

Coming Together in Bärnbach
Theatre Work with the Elderly – Promoting Health 42
Katharina Grilj, Martina Pusterhofer, Gabriele Skledar

- Structure of the Module 43
- Competencies and Learning Objectives of the Facilitators ... 46
- Module Project: *Coming Together in Bärnbach* 54
  - How the Project Progressed 54
  - Exemplary Working Instructions 55
  - Particularly Successful Segments 64
- Target Groups: Aims and Competencies 68
- Evaluation 71
- Bibliography 74

Theatrality and Everyday Life
Theatre Work with People with Special Needs 75
Matthias Bittner, Gerd Koch, Annetta Meißner, Florian Vaßen, Tina Wellmann

- Structure of the Module 76
- Competencies and Learning Objectives of the Facilitators 77
- Module Project: *The People with Special Needs from the Theatre Group "Confetti"* 87
  - How the Project Progressed 88
  - Exemplary Working Instructions 93
  - Particularly Successful Methods 96
- Module Project: *The Lord of the Theatre* 100
  - How the Project Progressed 100
  - Exemplary Working Instructions 108
- Target Groups: Aims and Competencies 109
- Evaluation and Theoretical Reflection 111
- Bibliography 125

Transforming Desire into Law Legislative Theatre as a Tool for Transitive Democracy with Migrants and Homeless People 128
Roberto Mazzini, Armin Ruckerbauer, Martin Vieregg, Michael Wrentschur

- Preface 129
- Structure of the Module 132
- Competencies and Learning Objectives of the Facilitators 134
- Module Project: *Legislative Theatre with Migrants* 138
  - How the Project Progressed 138
  - Exemplary Working Instructions 143
  - Particularly Successful Segments 144
- Target Groups: Aims and Competencies 146
- Evaluation and Reflection 148
- Module Project: *Legislative Theatre with Homeless People* 159
  - How the Project Progressed 160
  - Exemplary Working Instructions 169
  - Particularly Successful Segments 173
- Target Groups: Aims and Competencies 175
- Evaluation 179
- Bibliography 183

No Fear Theatre for Wicked Kids
Theatre Work with Young Offenders — 185
Jennie Hayes, Henrietta Ireland, Roger Sell

- Structure of the Module — 186
- Competencies and Learning Objectives of the Facilitators — 188
- Module Project: *No Fear Theatre for Wicked Kids* — 196
  - How the Project Progressed — 196
  - Exemplary Working Instructions — 198
  - Overview of the First Six Weeks — 201
- Target Groups: Aims and Competencies — 209
- Evaluation — 212
- Bibliography — 220

Creative Models of Communication (KREMOK)
Theatre Work with Children and Young People with Special Needs — 222
Zlatko Bastašić, Jelena Sitar-Cvetko

- Structure of the Module — 223
- Competencies and Learning Objectives of the Facilitators — 225
- Module Project: *KREMOK* — 229
  - How the Project Progressed — 229
  - Exemplary Working Instructions — 239
  - Particularly Successful Segments — 245
- Target Groups: Aims and Competencies — 249
- Evaluation — 252
- Bibliography — 254

APPENDIX — 257

List of Authors and Editors — 258

TWISFER Partner Institutions — 263

Photos and Translations — 268

Introduction

I can take any empty space and call it a bare stage.[1]

After Peter Brook, the word "stage" considered in its broadest sense - this image of the naked stage – can serve as a symbolic starting point for theatre work in social fields. Social fields are not empty spaces, but they are indeed 'empty' or free of classical theatre conventions. Anyone who begins to undertake theatre work with those social groups who feature in this book will scarcely encounter the conventional ingredients listed by Peter Brook such as, "red curtains, spotlights, blank verse, laughter, darkness, [...] box office, foyer, tip-up seats, footlights, scene changes, intervals, music"[2]. Theatre work in social fields is more concerned with interventions in living spaces marked in equal measure by their artistic, socio-pedagogical as well as their socio-political dimensions. Theatre work in social fields is understood as theatre work "with people in difficult life situations" and "as a means of intervention, prevention, participation and empowerment in social life"[3].

This book concerns itself with the approach outlined above. It has emerged from a European Cooperation Project under the title "TWISFER: Theatre Work in Social Fields – European Research", whereby twelve institutions from nine European countries joined together to set up this project, which was coordinated by uniT, Graz. All are concerned, albeit with varying emphases, with the intersection between culture, education and social issues. The objective of this project was to bring together the practical experience from various countries with a view to establishing a common European terminology. Five pilot module projects about target group-specific theatre work investigated the possibility of developing personal, social and communicative competencies and skills through the medium of artistic work with the following target groups: elderly people, people with special needs, immigrants, homeless people, young offenders, children, adolescents and their families threatened by marginalisation. This project culminated in a three-day conference under the heading of theatre work in social fields with an accompanying work-shop programme for people involved in adult education, theatre practitioners and those involved in social work.

The idea for this book emerged in the preparatory stages of this project and was suggested by a former colleague from the Austrian National Socrates Agency.

We departed from the idea that while theatre work as a means for educational work, particularly with those regarded as fringe groups in society, was indeed a well-known concept, this concept was not well researched. Despite the fact that there is quite a wide range of theoretical material/books available as well as books describing concrete projects in the form of empirical reports, there are hardly any "textbooks" in the narrower sense of the word.

Out of this realisation the idea was born to describe the model-projects in such a comprehensible manner as to render them transferable to other social and national contexts. Consequently, the presentation, theoretical elaboration and modularisation of the projects form the core element of this book.

Following on from this the editors came up with the idea of developing a common structure, with the help of which the various model projects should be so transparent that, divorced from the social and artistic realities of their conception, they should be comprehensible and applicable to other contexts.

The subsequent attempt to "modularise" the projects creates the link to the curriculum-orientated way of thinking. In keeping with the Declaration of Bologna, which is aimed at synchronizing the European education systems, a further step was taken and envisaged with regard to the pilot projects: considering the projects as modules, i.e. as teaching units aimed at instructing in how to carry out theatre work with the respective target groups, they should serve at the same time above and beyond the immediate context of their conception as training models. Connected to this is the question the requirements of such a model.

The following structure of the module descriptions emerges from the above: it begins with the description and explanation of the content as a teaching unit (=module) on the respective theme. The contributions adhere as much as possible to a synchronized and modularised format in order to render requirements and content comparable. Furthermore, they outline the necessary competencies of the facilitators so that (module-) projects can be carried out by the appropriate.

This is followed by a description of the respective individuals project including exemplary working instructions in the form of examples, which highlights the textbook-character of this book. These instructions are intended to serve as tools and ideas or suggestions for people with a basic practical experience in the area of theatre work and teaching.

The attempt to structure these two parts by providing clear guidelines led to numerous discussions and deliberations as a consequence of partly quite different preconditions, approaches and thought traditions. The texts, therefore, adhere to the proscribed structure while at the same time retaining a very individual quality. This is due to a large extent to the individual social, artistic, pedagogical and societal differences and traditions in the various countries. At the same time it is a reflection of the cultural range within Europe and its multi-faceted colourful character.

A third part outlines in each case the competencies and skills that the respective target groups can acquire by working on the project. Additionally, it gives a summary of the backgrounds of the participating organizations and institutions.

The fourth part of the module descriptions leads back again once more to the starting point since the evaluation of and reflections on the initial projects vary in their structuring and at times can have rather the character of a reflection on the project.

Preceding the module descriptions are three articles concerning the main focus of this book: Theatre Work (Manfred Schewe), Target Groups (Sieglinde Roth) and Social Fields (Michael Wrentschur). The three writers of these articles do not claim to provide an all-inclusive and comprehensive definition of the respective subject matter they focus on; they regard their contributions, rather, as leading into the spirit of the project and as signalling the dialogic approach to the work in question.

The contributions on the projects should be regarded as impulses for planning and carrying out similar interventions and furthermore as an appeal for increased willingness to reflect and to acquire qualifications in the area of theatre work in social fields. Dialogue and reflection hereby take into account the needs and living situations of all participants. As inspiration to all those striving to work in this direction allow me to offer a quote from the Romantic poet Bettina von Arnim:

> The wise gardener provides shade, coolness and hard ground for some and for others sun and fertile earth, as each requires in order to blossom.[4]

The Editors   Graz/Cork, June 2005

Footnotes

[1] Peter Brook: The Empty Space. New York: Touchstone 1996, p. 9
[2] ibid
[3] Definition of theatre work in social fields coined by the curriculum-group of the Sokrates-project TWISFER, November 2004
[4] Freely translated from: Bettina von Arnim, Die Günderode. Quoted from: Bettina von Arnim: Ein Lesebuch. Stuttgart: Reclam 1987, p. 117

Basics and Principles

Manfred Schewe

Theatre Work (in Social Fields)

As the term "theatre work" figures prominently in the title of our European research project and I am not aware of any definition as yet of this specific word combination, the following reflections might help to initiate a broader discussion of what exactly we mean when we speak of "theatre work".[1] So let's get to work!

Work

"Get to work", according to the Oxford Advanced Learner's Dictionary of English, is an equivalent of the verb "begin". However, equivalence is not sameness. A difference remains. The difference is that when I say "get to work" I purposely emphasise the actual *effort* I am going to invest in writing this short article rather than merely indicating the start of something. According to the dictionary, "work" can be defined as the "use of bodily or mental powers with the purpose of doing or making s.th. (esp. contrasted with play or recreation)." Thus while I am now writing this text (with the purpose of making a contribution to a TWISFER publication) I am primarily using my mental powers, whereas half an hour ago I was turning over the soil in my garden (with the purpose of making a new vegetable bed), using my bodily powers.

When we say "work" we tend to highlight the aspect of bodily and/or mental effort, doing and making. And, consequently, if we say "theatre work" we especially tend to stress the aspect of effort, doing and making in the context of theatre-related activities. To which degree mental or bodily powers are used will naturally vary from activity to activity. For example, warm-up exercises might use up a lot of bodily power, while primarily mental powers are called upon for a practitioner to make a detailed plan for a series of workshops. However, given the complexity of theatre work, it is often not possible to distinguish that neatly, as mental and bodily powers merge in most of the activities. If a workshop participant, based on Boal's concept of statue theatre, is forming a statue s/he is usually doing both, physically forming a statue and simultaneously reflecting on the meaning of what s/he is creating.

Although the Oxford Advanced Learner's Dictionary definition seemed to be a good departure point, I hesitate and have my doubts where the writer suggests a distinct contrast between "work" and "play or recreation". In the case of our word combination (theatre work) it is in fact quite the opposite. The areas of play and work are actually not contrasted. On the contrary, work and play seem to be purposely joined together here, "play", "player(s)", "playhouse" etc making up the connotative field of theatre.

We note that the concept of "theatre work" challenges the notion of such separateness and, instead, emphasises the productive relationship between "work" and "theatre / play". Those who are involved in "theatre work", we could say, are playing while at work and, vice versa, they are working while at play.

Another dictionary on my shelf (Oxford English Dictionary) contains a definition which adds a further level of meaning (see underlined) to the reflections above: "activity involving mental or physical effort done *in order to achieve a result*". Therefore, in the specific case of "theatre work", the elements, tools, techniques etc. of theatre are being used in order to achieve an outcome. This outcome can be very visible and concrete (a group of prisoners perform a play they have devised and worked on over several weeks at 8 p.m. in room 2.892 in prison X) or less so in projects where the emphasis is on the working *process*. Even if the outcome will not necessarily show immediately in the form of a concrete product and might be difficult to measure, the individual participant may nevertheless go through a personally important and rewarding learning experience, which can have a lasting impact on his / her (social) life.

Theatre

In theatre we are looking at the full complexity of human life or, as Erika Fischer-Lichte (1999, 3; transl.) puts it: "In the theatre, society observes its own actions." According to her theatre is a "social institution" in that a group of actors present symbolical actions to an audience which are of high significance for society at large or important groups in society, because they address questions of individual, social and historical identity. Thus "theatre work", in a very broad sense, aims at addressing questions of identity which arise in different (social) fields with the intention of working towards a diagnosis and ultimately a solution for identity-related problems. The term itself signals a hands-on approach to these problems.

Hans-Thies Lehmann – in a theatre dictionary edited by Manfred Brauneck and Gérard Schneilin (1986) – traces the origin of the term to the Greek word 'theatron', meaning "space for spectating" and distinguishes broadly between five different meanings which are briefly paraphrased here: 1. Technical term for the audience part of the building, later for the whole building, 2. Generic term for the dramatic works of an author (for example "the theatre of William Shakespeare"), 3. "Theaterbetrieb" (Betrieb = factory, works), a place of work where a high diversity of professional skills are represented, 4. "Theater oder Szenen machen / theatralisch sein" used in everyday language (in German:) to express exaggerated, passionate behaviour (English adjective: theatrical), 5. Artistic practice based on the basic elements of actor, role, spectator and the use of specific signs – acoustic, visual, olfactory etc.

"Theatre" as part of our word combination "theatre work" would be primarily linked to meanings 3 and 5. Theatre projects in/for a specific social field[2] usually require a variety of hands-on professional skills (organisational, social-interactive, leadership-related, or in more closely theatre-related areas, costume design, sound, lighting etc.). It goes without saying that these practical (theatre) skills need to be learned, for example in specially designed degree programmes (footnote 3).

The success of such projects ultimately hinges on the project leaders', but also on the participants' understanding and of the elements of theatre as an art form and their capacity for and skills in applying these.

In his dictionary entry Hans-Thies Lehmann also proposes a number of criteria to distinguish further between different categories of theatre, including, for example, professional versus amateur and commercial versus state-subsidised. From the perspective of "Theatre Work in Social Fields" it is noteworthy that he also differentiates on the basis of the underlying *purpose (motives, intentions)*, using political theatre, pedagogical theatre and therapeutic theatre as examples.

Applied Theatre

This brings us to the concept of Applied Theatre.[3] I propose that this term be used as an umbrella term for all the different forms in which theatre is applied to a field of practice, including the specific form of "Theatre Work in Social Fields". The following quotation from an article by Judith Ackroyd (2000)[4] in which I highlight some key aspects, might serve to illustrate this further:

> The term Applied Theatre is relatively new. It brings together a broad range of dramatic activity carried out by a host of diverse bodies and groups. Many of those who would fall under the umbrella title of Applied Theatre may not be familiar with or even aware of those with whom they huddle. The dramatherapist sees her work as distinctly different from that of the group who employ drama to enhance the skills of a company sales team. The prison theatre practitioner will not necessarily relate to those using drama to support the elderly. *The practitioners in each group will see themselves working with specific skills appropriate to their work and not therefore the same as those in other fields.* ...
> In the face of this plurality I suggest that it is an *intentionality* which all the various groups have in common. They share *a belief in the power of the theatre form to address something beyond the form itself.* So one group use theatre in order to promote positive social processes within a particular community, whilst others employ it in order to promote an understanding of human resource issues among employees. The range is huge, including elements such as theatre for education, for community development, and for health promotion, and dramatherapy and psychodrama. An intentionality is presupposed in all these examples. The intentions of course vary. They could be to inform, to cleanse, to unify, to instruct, to raise awareness. ...

We note that practitioners are expected to have a range of specific skills. A practitioner in TWISF needs specific practical theatre skills but also specific skills relevant to social fields and related to disciplines such as Applied Psychology, Social Studies, Education etc. It would be desirable to compile a catalogue of such basic and advanced skills as part of a curricular structure for an international MA Programme in Theatre Work in Social Fields.[5] Within such a curriculum skills related to theatre as an art form would have to figure prominently, if we accept Ackroyd's view that the *"appropriate use of theatre form is essential in order for the intentions to be achieved"* (ibid). She furthermore suggests that, in addition to intentionality, *"audience participation* may be a further distinguishing feature of applied theatre" (ibid).

Sieglinde Roth (2004, 22), freely translated here, confirms the central importance of active group participation and sees it as an important and distinguishing feature of "Theatre in Social Fields", prioritising social and political learning processes over a concern with (public) performance.

> In contrast to a traditional perception of theatre the production itself is never the central point of interest in TWISF. What is important is the group of players with their needs, problems, questions. These are not primarily of a theatre-related or artistic nature. At the centre are two aspects, social and political: *the learning processes for the players and the potential for change in relation to the environment they live in*.

While the issue of how much the focus of the work should be on theatre as an art form and how much on social and political learning might require further discussion it is interesting to note how Roth's statement from the perspective of "Theatre Work in Social Fields" is similar to Taylor's (2005, 2) description of the general aims of Applied Theatre:

> Applied theatre is becoming a more frequent description of theatre work conducted outside of conventional mainstream theatre houses for the purpose of transforming or changing human behaviour. Applied theatre is characterised by its desire to influence human activity, to raise issues, have audience members problem solve those issues.

Key Concept Change

We note that "change" seems to be a key concept in the discourse surrounding "Applied Theatre", including "Theatre Work in Social Fields". This kind of work wants to make a difference by "intervening in people's everyday life" (Roth 2004, 22) and ultimately aims at effecting change which results in improving an individual's and/or group's social situation and overall quality of life.

Perhaps it is appropriate in this context to remind readers of a definition which I developed together with my colleague Bernadette Cronin and which

was presented and positively received by the participants at TWISFER's 2nd Partner Conference in Berlin (December 05):
> Theatre in Social Fields aims at reaching a new and deeper understanding of what it means to be a social being through collaborative exploratory theatrical activity in the space and in the moment, thus paving the way for change.

To conclude I wish to refer to a literary text, "The Stage by the Sea" (1998), by Austrian writer Christoph Ransmayr. The author, who has chosen to live in Ireland, seems to be fascinated by how Irish people in the past developed great improvisation skills in order to enjoy life and deal with its hardships. In this excerpt he reflects on theatre and the community and, in more general terms, on coping with human life. The focus is a "platform" which is a marked space in the middle of a field somewhere in the countryside of 19th century Ireland owned by a village man Liam O'Shea. The poetic quality of the text appeals to me. It reassures me of how little it actually takes (one stride) to get involved in theatre and what it can mean to us and others. Also, I like the author's measured assessment of what theatre can and perhaps cannot achieve: some change yes, but perhaps not miraculous change?

> O'Shea's stone stage had no roof, not a single wall that might shelter it from wind and rain, no curtain, no flight of steps. Hardly raised above the pasture surrounding it, performers could step onto it simply by clambering over gorse and grass, and with this one stride could leave a whole world behind them: they entered a melody, a ballad, a burst of applause or laughter in which their lives suddenly seemed new and different, transfigured into chords and words. This did not make their life any easier, but at least it became a story that could be told and understood – and ... perhaps even changed. (1998, 234 - 235)

Perhaps practitioners who are using theatre in order to work towards "change" in social fields should begin to address the issue of "evaluating change – what change exactly and where is the evidence"?

Footnotes

1 Given the time and space constraints for this publication I will not attempt a profound academic analysis of the term "work". This would require to look at the perspectives of social history, political economy, anthropology, intercultural studies etc. However,

sociologist Iring Fetscher's Arbeit und Spiel (1983) might be a first step in this direction.

2 "Project" here does not necessarily mean a complex (public) performance project but is understood as a very loose term which can be applied to all forms theatre-related activity in social fields, including distinctly process-based activities. For a definition of the term "social field" see the contribution by M. Wrentschur in this publication.

3 A term which has been introduced more recently into the subject debate in English speaking countries (I am not aware of any equivalent in German or indeed any other European language). Note, for example, that the universities of Griffith/Australia and Manchester/GB offer special degree courses in Applied Theatre. For a description and evaluation of such courses which aim to develop articulate practitioners who are capable of applying theatre in a wide variety of disparate fields, see Millet (2005) and Taylor (2005).

4 I would strongly recommend reading the full article to those, who intend to develop a solid theoretical framework for their specific approach to theatre work in social fields.

5 A draft proposal with a concrete modular structure for such a programme has been presented by the curriculum working group of the project at the 3rd TWISFER partner conference in Bucharest in July 2005.

Bibliography

Ackroyd, Judith: Applied Theatre: Problems and Possibilities. In: Applied Theatre Researcher 1, 2000, p. 1.

Fischer-Lichte, Erika: Geschichte des Dramas. Epochen der Identität auf dem Theater von der Antike bis zur Gegenwart (1990). Two volumes. Tübingen/Basel 1999.

Lehmann, Hans-Thies: Theater. In: Brauneck, Manfred / Schneilin, Gérard: Theaterlexikon. Begriffe und Epochen. Bühnen und Ensembles. Reinbek bei Hamburg 1986, p. 880 – 881.

Millet, Tony: Applied Theatre Taught and Caught: a Program Review. In: Applied Theatre Researcher 4, 8, 2003, p. 1 – 16.

Ransmayr, Christoph: The Stage by the Sea. (Transl. by Eoin Bourke) In: Gruber, Marianne / Müller, Manfred / Niederle, Helmuth A.: In anderer Augen. Die Staaten der Europäischen Union in der österreichischen Literatur. Klagenfurt/Celovec 1998.

Roth, Sieglinde: Theaterarbeit in sozialen Feldern/Theatre Work in Social Fields. In: Koch, Gerd/Roth, Sieglinde/Vaßen, Florian/Wrentschur, Michael (Eds.): Theaterarbeit in sozialen Feldern/Theatre Work in Social Fields. Frankfurt/Main, p. 21 – 26.

Taylor, Philip: Afterthought: Evaluating Applied Theatre. In: Applied Theatre Researcher 3, 6, 2002, p. 1 – 10.

(http://www.griffith.edu.au/centre/cpci/atr/journal/article6_number3.htm)

(http://www.griffith.edu.au/centre/cpci/atr/journal/number4_article8.htm)

(http://www.gu.edu.au/centre/cpci/atr/journal/article1_number1.htm)

Sieglinde Roth

Theatre Work and its Target Groups – A Reflective Approach

"No target group" –these three words, framed in a red and black box, jump into your field of vision during a Google search as you click on the first link under the term "target group" in German. What follows is an insight into the wishes of an 'anti-consumer' who fights for his right to be an individual that thinks independently and it insists on choosing for himself rather than having those choices made for him – and he does not mince his words.[1] He does not want to be pressed into a mould and he resists any attempt at categorisation in the truest sense of the word as he maintains that all his decisions are unique to the situation and circumstances and therefore resist any attempt at categorisation. And above all: "In order to reach me one has to make an effort."[2]

This sentence could serve as a motto for the discussion of the term target group. What else do theatre people do if not make an effort? Effort is associated with work and strain but at the same time with a serious attempt to debate with people with whom or for whom theatre is made. Effort is also associated with play, fun and creativity.

Part of the current discussion about theatre work and its target groups is in fact couched in advertising jargon even though this results now and again in contradictions. Advertisers define and single out their target groups for the purposes of selling products. Firms and clients aiming to sell a product to a consumer do so with the product in mind. Consumption, in this sense, is passive even though the products being sold suggest activity. The relationship between consumer and producer is merely an act of barter. 'A' gives an object to 'B' and 'B' hands over money in exchange for the object. Interaction in the personalized sense of the word does not take place. The nature of the exchange is determined by the two sides entering into the deal. On the money side is the type of person who desires to purchase something, either because of a real need or simply to create a certain image connected with the product – not everyone buys golf clubs whereas everyone probably buys potatoes. On the side of the object of exchange (which might include a trip, club membership, any type of service) a certain expertise in the manufacture and use of the object is customary. This has, in the strictest sense of the word, the character of an interaction, i.e. "an interrelation between people, groups and actions"[3] since the action of one person provokes the reaction of the others. Nevertheless, the relationship is determined by the object at the centre of it – the product, the object, the mental construction. One party wishes to sell something; another party wishes to acquire something. Influence is mutually exerted, which is not oriented towards a common experience but at enrichment for both parties – a relatively clear matter, functional and more or less independent of the individuals involved. Each of the two parties wants something that they can attain together but the objects that each side is looking for are of a completely different nature.

The process of making acquaintance is basically a one-sided affair: it is important for the manufacturers to get to know the needs of the consumer. What exactly is the consumer looking for? Or to put it another way – and it is here that advertisement comes into play – which needs can be engendered in the consumer? These needs do not constitute real needs in the sense of an independently perceived necessity but are actually needs of which the consumer is not yet aware.

In the context of theatre work target groups are treated very differently and are seen in a different light. The question of FOR whom or WITH whom theatre is created does not as a rule enter into the discussion in the early stages. In "professional" theatre, that is, any kind of institutionalised theatre work, the question regarding the audience and their expectations is – at least in the German speaking world – very one-sided. Even in this context a product needs to be promoted and sold – in this case a theatre production. Generally speaking it will be a performance of a text that has already been chosen and rehearsed over a number of weeks with professional actors under technically and – in terms of equipment – equally professional conditions. The play will most likely have been written independent of the social situation in which it is to be performed and will normally have been translated into a number of different languages. It will contain artistic statements about life in the abstract, which are far removed from the reality of everyday life. This concept of theatre is driven by a consumerist culture, often to be found in the context of financial support and promotion of art and culture. Any theatre projects outside of the establishment, which may include writing and developing a play based on the real-life experiences of its protagonists, produced and staged by people who also practice a profession outside of the theatre, most certainly cannot be defined as art in the professional sense. Any projects of this nature are conveniently relegated to the realm of amateur theatre or therapy.

For our purposes one thing must be clarified: distinctions drawn between what is or is not art and between what is or is not theatre is based on a certain professionalism in terms of input. The concept of professionalism however is not based on the issue of whether or not all participants are in possession of a university degree. It has been well-documented that drama / theatre / art schools – in German speaking and other European countries – do not really prepare their students for a theatre scene that is socially relevant but rather for a one-sided municipal theatre. This kind of Theatre sees itself as a well-established institution for the middle / upper middle classes or as a cool scene for the youth to hang out in (such as in the HAU in Berlin or formerly in the Volksbühne). This would appear to be standard in Western Europe. This kind of theatre is exposed to seemingly provocative but ultimately affirming criticism. It is not just light-hearted in tone, but also thoughtful, politically reflective and aware of its mission and its audience. Ultimately, however, it might provoke change at the level of artistic taste but not at the social level.

Central to the kind of theatre work, which TWISFER seeks to research, to carry out and to promote, is a field of activity free from prejudice and in which theatre has an important role to play Different traditions exist in various countries. The JSKD (state foundation for the encouragement of amateur art of Slovenia) for example looks after the free theatre scene as well as supporting (since the establishment of the country) theatre projects for socially marginalized groups. Giolli in Italy intervenes directly in everyday life by employing the methods of Augusto Boal and involves the spectators and politicians, who are concerned with the problems addressed. At Dartington College of Arts, Britain, it has long been the tradition to look at and produce art in a social context. Art here constitutes a means to analyse and discuss current affairs, to get close to the realities of the lives of those people for whom and with whom one is making theatre. Thus theatre is clearly an artistic medium but it is not in the sense of the "l'art pour l'art" concept of art. On the contrary, it intervenes in reality. As such it becomes a true-to-life political and educational tool. It not only descends from the ivory tower but also moves beyond and outside traditional theatrical realms by conducting research, encouraging contact and even in its approach to performance.

In this context theatre work is orientated towards artistic processes and results but it is also used, sometimes even predominantly, as a medium for psychosocial processes. This is quite a legitimate approach as long as the line between art and therapy is clearly marked. Theatre work cannot replace therapy although theatre can have a therapeutic impact. Therefore any cooperation at various levels between bordering subject areas is as necessary as it is useful. If one approaches social issues and issues from everyday life in an artistic manner, the fear threshold typically encountered in therapy and adult education becomes less significant. Through play – a senses-oriented and seemingly harmless starting point – the individual opens up sufficiently to enable him / her to engage with essential life issues.

The term "target group" plays an important role in dealing with potential sponsors but it also aids the process of concept development of artistic practitioners in the social field, a term which can come to define one's own objectives and which reinforces one's thought processes and actions.

When it comes to the target groups, financial sponsors are generally concerned with the question of concrete results. In this regard they are not that far removed from those in the advertising domain. Here the exact description of the target group is as important as the number of individuals that can probably be targeted. One is often forced to outline one's objectives – objectives which can be measured, counted and weighed. This may cause problems for those working in the area. Recent accusations of a lack of professionalism can only be countered by referring to and describing concrete cases. Difficulties in defining objectives and the absence of any methodological approach to achieve this stem from the fact that the objectives are of a heterogeneous nature. If we take the example of teenagers who are regarded as difficult, the institution responsible for them – which employs drama teachers – could aim to generate alternative approaches in how objectives are defined. Examples might include: simple leisure activities, performing plays, which train the young people in socially acceptable behaviour, or simply encouraging self-reflection through the medium of the theatre. An increase in self-confidence may (eventually) ensue and the newly developed ability for realistic self-assessment may in turn lead to more reflective and therefore more appropriate behaviour in social situations.

To avoid labelling theatre work in social fields as purely charitable, institutions also need to address and examine social realities and needs, as they could also constitute a "target group". This quickly provokes categorization of identities. Theatre work in social fields has to engage with institutions even though it tends – in keeping with the Freire tradition – to side with the underprivileged in the existing hierarchy. The current political context in Europe – at present the modules in this book only concern Europe – provides a different kind of context. While in many ways individuals experience more freedom, there are now more subtle mechanisms of suppression at work, ones that are not governed by totalitarian regimes but rather by the workings of a market, which also demands top performances from the same individuals. To intervene in this reality and to question the criteria of market performance, and with it of course the mechanisms of the market, is still a worthwhile objective for a pedagogical approach. It is not the intention of this article to discuss in detail how change and improvement in the living circumstances of the participants could be achieved. Rather the modules contained within this publication espouse a common ethical, pedagogical and socio-political approach, one that could be described as the motto (partly implicit and partly explicit) of the TWISFER project.

The "target group" are the people with whom and for whom one makes theatre. The search for them is determined by their needs, which on the other hand tie in with the needs of society. This type of "selection" is diametrically opposed to the kind of selection that occurs in a performance-driven society. The focus of attention here is not the high echelons of society, not the hit-list leaders of image-conscious wealthy individuals who are professionally very competent, but rather those who for various reasons find themselves in difficulty. It is of utmost importance to move mentally from the former (inadequate) approach to an approach, which takes into account the needs of the individuals in question. This development parallels a development within social work, which is a re-defining of its role; the old image of "caring" has given way to the new image of "accompaniment" – a deviation from a latent patronising attitude.[4]

This has created – in theatre work with target groups (as well as in other fields) – different hierarchies and has attempted to abolish old ones: there is no longer a teacher-pupil relationship in the traditional sense of the word but rather cooperation between equals. A hierarchy is permitted to come into play only when it is in relation to work issues and where competencies and abilities differ. These obviously fluctuate in accordance with individual situations. In addition to dividing the group into facilitators (project managers, coaches, drama teachers) and people with special needs, attention should be paid to the various competencies. The facilitators are more competent as they have been systematically trained and have professional experience with group work methods as well as pedagogical and theatre skills. People with special needs should have confidence in the facilitators in relation to dramaturgical logic, aesthetical means of expression and methodological approaches. During the process they will learn many of these skills and gain experience but they may never have the ability and insight to place the work in progress in a wider methodological and artistic context, which can be essential for rehearsing and staging a production. They are, however, experts when it comes to their own lives and their own needs. They contribute to the theatre work by providing personal knowledge in the shape of experiences, aspiration and in terms of their potential for development, that is, they bring a uniqueness to the work, a uniqueness which in the context of their everyday existence is regarded and experienced as a handicap, deficit(s) and/or limitation(s). Although the facilitators are trained (to a degree) in this field and have gained practical skills they lack the range of personal experience, which consequently inhibits their scope for action. The vocal skills of the two parties in theatre work are not called upon as much as their ability to take practical action. A certain sensuousness and direct body language can help to overcome possible barriers to participation and fear of social contact and in turn promote direct communication. Mutual teaching and learning takes place It involves effort and exchange, both of which re-define everyday "normal" habits of communication and which make up for deficits, for example, a lack of vocal expression can be balanced by body language and gestures/facial expression; sounds and music can depict moods which cannot be expressed either verbally or by body language. The common objective is to integrate real-life issues and experiences into theatre work.

Mutual exchange is essential at all levels. Hierarchical structures do not really exist or if they do they fluctuate – in a balanced manner if possible.

Everyone takes on certain responsibilities for him-/herself, for the group and the work according to his/her skills and abilities. This should not detract from the fact that in certain target groups the ability to take on responsibility can be partly impaired, for example, groups in a psychiatric hospital. In such circumstances it falls to the facilitator to take on the bulk of the responsibility beginning with the choice of exercises. It is always essential to assess the different constellations of people with whom one is working and not to assume that each individual should be able to take on the responsibility. Each new phase of the training or exercise can help to find answers to this. Supporting any acquired helplessness should be avoided. On the other hand it is important to provide support and encouragement that could help the individual to fully develop his/her potential to cope with everyday life and last but not least, to develop his/her artistic talents. It is also important that the unique personal and professional qualities of the facilitators are recognised.

"Target groups" are consequently not just the people with whom one is working but also the people who work with these groups and who interact and collaborate artistically. To develop this idea further, it can also apply to the potential audience and the other participants in the project, regardless of their role in the work processes. Interpreting the term "target group" in this way it loses any military connotations. During a brief discussion in the TWISFER-project the question as to whether one should replace "target groups" with "client groups" was raised. If the implicit hierarchy is turned upside down then one wonders whether anything would actually be gained by this substitution. The term "client groups" does indeed focus more on the needs and desires of the clients, however a new issue arises: the clients would have to articulate precisely their needs so as to avoid a situation whereby their needs are suggested to them, needs that have not yet occurred to them. The sales aspect, which distorts rather than clarifies communication, suggests itself here and interferes with the terminology. One would also have to examine further the legal and therapeutic connotations of the term.

If on the one hand "target" denotes an objective one should aspire to and on the other hand the word "group" implies a joint effort based on the needs and skills of each participant, the working term "target group" should be retained. "Target group" describes a mutual exchange between facilitators and participants and also involves interaction with the audience and other participants. The term should be thus understood in the subsequent chapters of this publication. The parties move towards one another and a growth in awareness takes place for all concerned. It does not entail a hierarchical passing on of knowledge but rather a process of learning from one another on the artistic, human and communicative level. Qualities such as respect, interest and enthusiasm, support, curiosity and a good deal of fun and enjoyment, born out of the satisfaction achieved in getting to know others and in working with others on a common project, govern all activities in this context.

"No target group" from the aforementioned web site can be downloaded free of charge and utilized. This should also be possible in the context of theatre work with certain target groups in social fields – "I am a target group!" – in terms of the public's willingness to engage with unusual circumstances and to deal with these artistically on the basis of an acute awareness of authentic needs.

Footnotes

[1] http://www.shesaiddestroy.org/keine-zielgruppe/
[2] ibid.
[3] http://www.sociologicus.de/lexikon/lex_geb/begriffe/interak1.htm
[4] Wrentschur, Michael: Theatre Work in Social Fields Meets Social Work: Connections, Associations and Ideas, In: Koch, Gerd / Roth, Sieglinde / Vaßen, Florian / Wrentschur, Michael (Eds.): Theaterarbeit in sozialen Feldern / Theatre Work in Social Fields. Frankfurt am Main: Brandes & Apsel 2004, p. 38 - 48

Bibliography

Finkelpearl, Tom (ed.): Dialogues in Public Art. Cambridge and London: The MIT Press 2001.

Freire, Paolo: Pädagogik der Unterdrückten. Reinbek bei Hamburg: Rowohlt 1970

Gallagher, Kathleen and Booth, David (ed.): How Theatre Educates. Convergences & Counterpoints. Toronto: University of Toronto Press 2003.

Gallagher, Kathleen: Drama Education in the Lives of Girls. Imagining Possibilities. Toronto: University of Toronto Press 2001.

Galuske, Michael: Methoden der Sozialen Arbeit. Eine Einführung. 4.Aufl. Weinheim und München: Juventa 2002.

Girtler, Roland: Methoden der Feldforschung. 4. Aufl. Wien, Köln und Weimar: Böhlau 2001.

Goffman, Erving: Wir alle spielen Theater. Die Selbstdarstellung im Alltag. München und Zürich: Piper 2003.

Kwon, Miwon: One Place after Another. Site-Specific Art and Locational Identity. Cambridge and London: The MIT Press 2004.

Koch, Gerd/Roth, Sieglinde/Vaßen, Florian/Wrentschur, Michael (Eds.): Theaterarbeit in sozialen Feldern/Theatre Work in Social Fields. Frankfurt am Main: Brandes & Apsel 2004.

Michael Wrentschur[1]

Social Fields

A theatre project takes place in a high security prison.

A performance in an old people's home depicts everyday life in such an institution; with the participation of its occupants.

Homeless people perform scenes from their everyday existence at the train station, in the underground stations and in the town hall.

During a festival in a public park a play is staged interactively in which conflicts and tensions between the park users are dramatized.

These brief examples highlight theatre work with and for social groups. They also create links to different social fields as locations for theatre work.

Theatre work in certain social fields always interacts with the environment in which it takes place. (Roth 2004, p. 22)

Key questions include: What exactly are social fields? How are they characterized? How does theatre / drama work establish contact with social fields?

The term "field" alone suggests a wide variety of meanings. The Longman Dictionary of contemporary English offers – among others – the following explanations: magnetic field, snow field, corn field, study/work field, lab, class room in terms of physical manifestations and thematic areas, and in the figurative sense: battle-field, sports field etc. The variety of ways in which the term is used points to numerous social contexts. The term 'playing field' leads directly to the theatre and the social stage, the playing field for social protagonists and social drama.

In the following I will endeavour to portray sociological perspectives, which can and do serve as links for theatre work in social fields.

Within this publication Sieglinde Roth discusses the relationship between the target groups in question and the attitude of those who are working with her. For my part I will ask and discuss the following questions: in which social fields and surroundings is theatre work taking place and furthermore what theoretical and practical knowledge of social fields could be useful for this?

I will begin with society and its social fields, then move on to public places and locations and finally look at the fields of activity of social work. I begin with the assumption that theatre work constitutes intervention in social fields, which can consequently contribute to prevention, empowerment and participation; particularly if theatre work develops an awareness of structures and processes within social fields and is able to find a suitable point of access.

The Field Theory – Society and its Social Fields

I would like to begin with the idea that society consists of social fields, which provide a framework for the behaviour and action of people. The French sociologist Pierre Bourdieu[2] (1985, 1987, 1999) has devised an approach departing from Marxist class theory, Luhmann's system theory and subjectivist perspectives, whereby he seeks to combine subjective and objective elements, e.g. the structure of objective relationships and the concrete forms of lifestyles and interactions, thus explaining how social practice comes about. In contrast to subject theories and the corresponding habitus theory, it is not the isolated individual that is at the centre of his field theory but rather the socially initiated, acting individual.

The plural "social fields" hints at the variety within and heterogeneity of the respective society formation. These fields can be compared to sports fields, which are subjected to certain rules. While these have developed historically, with every human exchange and interaction they are constantly being renegotiated. The fields resemble magnetic fields, and the players within a particular social field have access to specific resources, which Bourdieu calls capital. The most essential forms of capital - which cannot always be neatly distinguished and which are sometimes interdependent – in terms of objects, abilities and talents are: economic capital (e.g. material possessions), cultural capital (e.g. possession of works of art), and figuratively speaking: social capital (i.e. social networks, belonging to a certain group, place etc.), and finally symbolic capital: reputation, prestige, status etc. The volume of capital means the amount of economic, cultural and social capital typically owned by a social class, i.e. in terms of statistics. The opportunities for profit and the scope for action of a social agent are linked to his / her position in a particular social field and are therefore dependent on the amount of capital available to him / her. The various kinds of capital represent investments, which are consequently at stake and which are fought over by agents in social fields, serving essentially as weapons. Unfortunately, capital is distributed unevenly within society. The groups that have successfully fought over the capital and have as a result accumulated a huge amount of it try to hold on to it with various defence strategies. Fighting over capital inevitably leads to situations of oppression / dominance and dependency between social groups.

Questions of 'taste' and life-style are used to legitimize social discrepancies. The respective 'habitus' – the socially conditioned part of the human being with the corresponding modes of perception/thought and action – defines these discrepancies and serves as a basis for social orientation in society.

The habitualisation process marks the human being for life and singles him / her out as a member of a certain social group. Deeply engraved social and cultural patterns and habits based on the existing power structures, become second nature, i.e. the habitus. Neither the social order nor the existing balance of power is questioned. They are accepted as they are even though they may lead to negative consequences and suffering. These structures are part of the habitus and delineate, among others, the line between possible and impossible practices / procedures. As previously mentioned, these lines are drawn and cemented by the type of capital owned by a social group or class, that which feeds the human habitus. The habitus is the starting-point for social procedures /practices within the respective social field and the field's position in society. This is due to class-specific factors. The external and objective structures of social fields relate to and compliment the habitus of the protagonists.

The social field is as much a product of historical developments as is the habitus. The relationship they form is dialectical in nature. They are mutually influential and are therefore in constant motion. Paradoxically, the freedom of the human being lies in his/her habitus since the habitus also establishes the framework within which each individual can develop his/her abilities. The habitus defines the framework within which the social protagonist has scope for action and scope for improvisation. The more resourceful and more able one is to act and improvise within existing boundaries, the greater the scope for creativity and activity becomes.

The theoretical basis for theatre work in social fields needs to be grounded in this context. Intervention in social fields using theatre work means that power structures and capital distribution must be addressed. One must also ask how existing resources and capital can be increased and how the protagonists can be equipped with more 'capital to play with' for their respective social fields – thus widening perspectives and the scope for action.

Just as the acquired habitus limits thought processes and opportunities for action – as social conditioning also reflects itself in body language and gestures – playing and experimenting with gestures, body language, actions and social masks can increase the habitus' scope for action. The social structuring of the social space, as suggested by Bourdieu, can also help us to better understand the basic social positions and capital situation of the respective target groups[3] – particularly with regard to their historical make-up and their resistance to change – and to make the dialectical process between 'objective' structures and their 'subjective' interpretation and analysis the basis for theatre work.

The Social Environment – Public Places

Social conflicts and contradictions are often reflected in public spaces. The latter are characterized by the fact that they are open to and they are accessible for everyone.
To what extent do they constitute a social field for theatre practitioners?

In his famous study on changes in public life, Richard Sennett (1986) draws our attention to the fact that for a long time public life in the streets and squares was understood as a stage, as theatre, in which normal people took part as 'actors'. Aesthetic action in a culture of play and performance was a component of social processes that progressively fell into oblivion during the last two centuries. The history of streets and squares has always been and is still accompanied by social conflicts, battles and cleansing procedure, to which a number of modes of existence associated with various social groups have fallen victim. The bourgeoisie eventually managed to successfully "keep the masses at bay" (Sennett 1991, p. 53). The monofunctional, economically orientated principle of exploitation, which gives priority to consumerism and trade, asserted itself in many instances over multifunctional uses. The urban public space, which had originally functioned as a market square and a place of contact and interaction, was turned into a transit and storage space (Wrentschur 2004a, p. 138ff).

The public space became empty and people began to behave less expressively. Nevertheless, it has remained a living space and a place of residence for different groups. Theatrical interventions can bring this space to life again and create public spheres in which social conflicts and inequalities can be played out, thereby raising issues, which are currently suppressed by prevailing political and media discourses. Theatre work in public spaces has the freedom to voice opposing views publicly, thereby enabling socially underprivileged groups to have their voice and opinions heard in public, which can lead to the re-possession of public spaces (Wrentschur 2004b, p. 45ff).

Theatre work in public spaces can also be regarded as a socio-spatial issue in that it takes its cue from a community, a housing estate, a residential quarter, a section of a town or a parish, thus taking into consideration the interests and needs of its inhabitants and encouraging and fostering participation and interaction. There is a close link between biography, identity and social space (Böhnisch 1999, p. 286) and these consequently have to be understood in terms of how they might be interpreted and used by the addressees. How can a socio-spatial theatre project attempt to establish contact with the psychological make-up of the inhabitants? How can resources and capabilities, ideas and spaces of a community or a part of town be activated and employed through theatre projects? Furthermore, how can a particular performance practice, oriented towards the public, move and activate the environment and stimulate reflection and thinking? Access to public spaces can be gained through observation and inspection or by making contact with people in public places, in parks and in pubs etc. Story-telling cafes (e.g. Koch 2005) or public breakfast buffets (El-Monir / Wrentschur 2002) can even lead to more intensive field research in relation to aspects of staging a production.

Institutions – Enclosed Spaces in Social Fields

Access to public and social spaces is in stark contrast to institutions such as prisons, psychiatric hospitals, hospitals, schools, homes and social care institutions, to which there is very limited access or no access at all. These constitute essential fields for theatre work. They are characterized by the fact that they function like a small, enclosed social field within the social fields of society; they follow their own rules, have their own structures and culture and are governed by access and exit criteria and by internal power and status discrepancies, which in turn significantly affect everyday routines and procedures.

The sociologist Erving Goffman (1984) coined the term "Totalitarian Institution" to describe this phenomenon. Totalitarian institutions such as psychiatric hospitals, prisons or monasteries check and control every move of their inmates thereby placing drastic constraints on their personal freedom. An institution is classified as totalitarian if it is all-embracing, if it is governed by a person or persons of authority, if every detail of everyday life is meticulously planned and governed by explicit rules which are implemented and enforced by the staff of the institution. All of these features are supposed to culminate in a rational plan, which ensures that the objectives of the institution are met. A similar idea is present in the works of Michel Foucault. In his book "Discipline and Punish – The Birth of Prison" (1976) he discusses the concept of the disciplinarian society and points to the structural similarities between the architecture and discipline of monasteries, military barracks, schools, prisons and hospitals. Their course of action is to press people and their bodies into moulds - thus rendering them useful – with as little effort as possible. In order to achieve this, time and space, movement, gestures, activities, procedures and the hierarchical establishment of power are structured and controlled.

To gain access to and to enter into dialogue with these institutions is particularly challenging for the theatre pedagogue. After all, the theatre performance will create a certain amount of scope for action and freedom in an environment characterized by a lack of or complete absence of freedom, in addition to the unequal distribution of power. A precarious balance must be maintained between the objectives of the institution and the concerns and objectives of the theatre work as well as the needs, interests and wishes of the target group. Who actually are the powers that be – officially and unofficially?

What would be regarded as meddling in their affairs? What would be considered a breach of habits and customs, which could consequently lead to the failure of a theatre project? To re-phrase the question: to what extent can the theatre project encourage the institution to reflect? How can the concerns and wishes of the target group be revealed and communicated? How can the different levels of the respective institution be integrated into the theatre project? How can the theatre work contribute to enhancing, at least temporarily, a number of experiences and resources for a different culture within the institution?

Social Work – Fields of Activity

In a wider sense social fields can also be regarded as fields of activity for social work, a profession which has undergone quite a dramatic change in the "century of social work and education" (Sozialpädagogisches Jahrhundert) (Thiersch 2000, p. 235ff) and which has established a strong foothold in society. It encompasses a broad range of areas of activity and has moved from the periphery to the centre of society. A few areas that also constitute fields of theatre work include the following: after-school activities, youths centres, street work, sheltered accommodation, work with minors, child care facilities, family clinics, mobile care for elderly people, regional socio-cultural, community, development work in residential areas within towns, intercultural social work, work with the homeless, social initiatives, as well as projects to help prevent problems such as poverty, unemployment, migration, crime, addiction and violence etc.

All of the areas mentioned above are of interest in the context of theatre work as there is a strong link between the paradigms and concepts of those fields of activity and potential theatre projects. Social work and social education (in addition to their primary tasks of helping, caring and educating) had for a long time as their main objective the reintegration and readjustment of those who were classified by the prevailing bourgeois social norms, as "asocial", "neglected", "deviant." Discipline and control were seen as the key to achieving this. A number of bureaucratic administrative institutions were in place to help enforce disciplinary measures. In keeping with changes in society and the consequent trend towards greater diversity in life styles and in ways of living discourse in the field of social work now concerns itself with subjective experience, the interpretation of conflicts and coping with the (biographical) vicissitudes of life within the tension of social structures and individual resources. It concerns itself with empowerment, managing everyday life, prevention, integration and participation. One could draw all of these approaches together under the umbrella term: 'social work oriented to the living world' (Thiersch 2000, Wrentschur 2004b).

This creates links between the objectives and attitudes of social work and theatre / drama work even though the methodological approaches associated with each may differ substantially. One thing is certain: theatre work often 'needs' social work. Moreover, the contact established by social work with clients and target groups can provide the basis for developing a framework for conditions and vice versa. In working with socially underprivileged groups or individuals in conflict situations social work 'needs' theatre work as its partner. The reason for this is that the social welfare state, in the current atmosphere of neo-liberalism and global capitalism, has come under pressure more and more – social services are increasingly being questioned and undermined as they represent a counterbalance to the increasing tendency in society to favour liberalism and individualism.

An essential prerequisite for cooperation is learning about and discussing the respective objectives, concepts and working methods employed by social work, thereby clarifying the kind of relationships and the type of cooperation that can and should be built up between theatre work and social work.

Implications for Theatre Work Arising out of Theory – Grounded in the Field

What, therefore, are the implications for theatre work that is founded on theory relating specifically to the field? In order to address this question we look back briefly to the last century. The dramatist Bertolt Brecht observed the following while in exile in America early in 1943: "New acquaintance: Kurt Lewin, trains scouts and workers in the art of 'leadership-behaviour' and invites me to come along." Kurt Lewin, the well-known founder of experimental social psychology, lived, like Brecht, in exile and in 1939 wrote the essay "Experiments on the Social Space", in which he discusses solutions to social conflicts:

I am convinced that it would be possible to carry out experiments in the area of sociology and social psychology and that these should be regarded as having the same scientific nature and justification as any experiment in physics or chemistry. I am also convinced that there is a social space containing all the essential elements of a real empirical space. This space deserves just as much interest and attention from scientists in the field of maths or geometry as the physical space, although it is not of a physical nature. The perception of the social space and the experimental and conceptual research on the dynamics and laws of what happens in the social space are of fundamental importance both theoretically and practically […]. (Lewin 1985, p. 52)

Theatre work in social fields makes a contribution to research into social fields and spaces. It would be the task of theatre work – through practical experience – to systematically describe and define further the various social fields, such as the marginalized, underprivileged and ostracized as well as the various ways of life (urban and rural, sub-culture, petite bourgeoisie, single, intercultural aspects etc.) This also implies an analysis of and preoccupation with cultural, religious, political and economic fields in accordance with the homologies of the fields. In the case of action research – that is carrying out the research while doing the work – theatre work intervenes in such fields by activating and changing them and also documenting their processes and results. Theatre practitioners are very similar to social field researchers, who enter into dialogue with ways of life and fields of life. They are equipped with fine sensors and aesthetical tools similar to those employed in the approach referred to as socio-cultural animation, which "operates in open situation fields":

Any intervention in a socio cultural environment requires knowledge of how that system functions. Whoever wishes to initiate and to effect changes needs to be aware of phenomena of resistance and how to deal with them. (Moser 1999, e.g. p. 127)

This requires meticulous research and knowledge about social fields, an inquisitive and open-minded attitude and a willingness to analyse and conceptualize in cooperation with those being addressed. Theatre workers are far from 'distant' researchers in this process; on the contrary, by employing the tools of the theatre they enter into direct contact with the field. Bertolt Brecht saw the process of activating a social power field as "the liberation of the productivity of human beings from all chains. The products can include bread, lamps, hats, music pieces, chess moves, watering, complexion, character, games etc. etc." (Brecht, 1941)

Theatre work, therefore, grounded in field theory gives rise to a new field quality.

Footnotes

[1] I would like to thank Gerd Koch and Florian Vaßen and acknowledge their input into this article by putting material at my disposal, which gave me interesting points of departure.

[2] I refer to the Schwingel's valuable discussion (1995) when I am discussing Bourdieu.

[3] In his thesis on the project, "wohnungs/Los/theatern" (Homeless People Make Theatre), Martin Vieregg has attempted to place the capital equipment / resources of homeless people on the social 'map' and to describe those in the group itself; He also uses it as a reference for the assessment of the educational processes of the participants (Vieregg 2005).

Bibliography

Böhnisch, Lothar: Sozialpädagogik der Lebensalter, Weinheim und München 1999 (1997)

Bourdieu, Pierre: Die feinen Unterschiede. Kritik der gesellschaftlichen Urteilskraft. Frankfurt am Main 1999 (1982).

Bourdieu, Pierre: Sozialer Sinn. Kritik der theoretischen Vernunft, Frankfurt am Main 1987.

Bourdieu, Pierre: Sozialer Raum und <Klassen>. Lecon sur la Lecon. Zwei Vorlesungen, Frankfurt am Main 1985.

Bourdieu Pierre: Sozialer Sinn. Kritik der theoretischen Vernunft, Frankfurt am Main 1987.

Bourdieu, Pierre: Die feinen Unterschiede. Kritik der gesellschaftlichen Urteilskraft. Suhrkamp Verlag, Frankfurt am Main 1999 (1982).

Brecht, Bertolt; Journale I, in: Ders., Werke, Bd. 26, Berlin/Weimar/Frankfurt amMain 1994 (1941).

Brecht, Bertolt: Journale II, in: Ders., Werke, Bd. 27, Berlin / Weimar / Frankfurt am Main 1995 (1943).

El-Monir, Karin / Wrentschur, Michael. Quartierfrühstücke im Gries 2001. Endbericht eines Projekts von InterACT und IGGries, Graz 2002.

Foucault, Michel: Mikrophysik der Macht. Über Strafjustiz, Psychiatrie und Medizin, Berlin 1976.

Foucault, Michel: Überwachen und Strafen. Die Geburt des Gefängnisses, Frankfurt am Main 1977.

Goffman, Erving: Asyle, Frankfurt am Main 1984.

Koch, Gerd / Schmidt, Birger / Stephan, Wessling: ErzählCafes. Herstellung narrativer Situationen im Felde einer Hochschule, in: Steinweg, Reiner (Ed.) in Zusammenarbeit mit Gerd Koch: Erzählen, was ich nicht weiß, Berlin 2005.

Kurt Lewin: Experimente über den sozialen Raum, in: T. Brocher / P. Kutter (Eds.): Entwicklung der Gruppendynamik, Darmstadt 1985.

Moser, Heinz / Müller, Emanuel / Wettstein Heinz / Willener, Alex: Soziokulturelle Animation. Grundfragen, Grundlagen, Grundsätze, Luzern 1999.

Roth, Sieglinde: Theaterarbeit in Sozialen Feldern, in: Koch, Gerd, Roth Sieglinde, Vaßen, Florian & Wrentschur Michael (Eds.): Theaterarbeit in sozialen Feldern / Theatre Work in Social Fields. Frankfurt/Main, 2004, p. 21 - 26.

Schwingel, Markus: Pierre Bourdieu zur Einführung, Hamburg 1995.

Sennett, Richard: Verfall und Ende des öffentlichen Lebens. Die Tyrannei der Intimität, Frankfurt am Main 1986 (1983).

Sennett, Richard: Cicitas. Die Großstadt und die Kultur des Unterschieds, Frankfurt am Main 1991 (1990).

Thiersch, Hans: Lebensweltorientierte Soziale Arbeit. Aufgaben der Praxis im Wandel der Zeit, Weinheim/München 2000 (1992).

Vieregg, Martin: Diplomarbeit "Wir sind da ... und haben etwas zu sagen!" Emanzipatorisch – partizipative Bildungsaspekte von "wohnungs / LOS / theatern" – einem soziokulturellen Theaterprojekt mit wohnungslosen und ehemals wohnungslosen Menschen in Graz. Institut für Erziehungswissenschaft der Universität Graz, Graz 2005.

Wrentschur, Michael: Theaterpädagogische Wege in den öffentlichen Raum. Zwischen struktureller Gewalt und lebendiger Beteiligung, Stuttgart 2004a.

Wrentschur, Michael: Theaterarbeit in sozialen Feldern trifft Soziale Arbeit: Anknüpfungen, Assoziationen und Anregungen, in: Koch, Gerd, Roth Sieglinde, Vaßen, Florian & Wrentschur Michael (Ed.): Theaterarbeit in sozialen Feldern / Theatre Work in Social Fields. Frankfurt/Main, 2004b, p. 38 - 48.

Module Projects

Katharina Grilj, Martina Pusterhofer, Gabriele Skledar

Coming Together in Bärnbach
Theatre Work with the Elderly – Promoting Health

Structure of the Module
Context-Specific Theatre-Pedagogical Project with Elderly People

Qualification on Completion of the Module:
Gerontology Theatre Pedagogue

Format and Minimum Timeframe

Participatory teaching modes and methods are employed.
The module is comprised of the following units:

1. Theoretical units:
Seminars and small group work on the following topics;
Age and aging, biography, theatre pedagogy with elderly people.

2. Practical units:
- Workshops on theatre work with elderly people
- Presentation of concrete projects located in this field
- Interdisciplinary exchange with individuals working with the elderly in various contexts
- Discussion and reflection with project leaders

3. Planning and realising a theatre-pedagogical project with elderly people:
Preparing and carrying out a concrete theatre-pedagogical project with practical guidance.

4. Reflection on the theatre-pedagogical work:
Reflection on and evaluation of the theatre-pedagogical project; Writing a report.

Minimum Timeframe

Theory input	150 hours
Practical input	150 hours
Theatre-pedagogical project	250 hours
Reflection	<u>150 hours</u>
Total	700 hours

Evaluation Criteria

The following entails a list of criteria that the authors consider to be of general importance for theatre projects with the elderly:

- Paying attention to participants' needs
- Highlighting the potential, special qualities and abilities of participants
- The product is a group outcome, the result of cooperation
- The process is enjoyable, and encourages motivation for group work
- Undermining stereotypical ideas concerning elderly people
- Review of the project in the public sphere
- Project documentation
- Reflection on and, ideally, evaluation of the project

The needs, abilities and special qualities of the participants are discovered and brought to light. The theatre work is perceived as a basis for multiple possibilities. Applied methods and approaches are chosen in accordance with the needs and abilities of the target group and the project context is closely examined. The working mode is developed in the course of the process whereby issues are raised without being forced, participants are challenged without being over-challenged and attention is paid to the individual without losing sight of the group. The individual participants identify both with the process and the product. The project is understood as a political statement; it is seen and discussed in the public sphere. On completion, the project is documented and reflected upon, and, ideally, evaluated internally and externally.

Admission Requirements

Existing knowledge of the following areas is a pre-requisite in order to undertake the module:

- Devising theatre
- Forum theatre
- Project management
- Processing audiovisual material
- Using graphics programmes
- Research work

Recommendations for Sequencing Courses

An indepth study of different fields and methodological approaches; in the case in question, the following are recommended:

- Gerontology
- Working with biography
- Devising theatre
- Forum theatre
- Project management
- Processing audiovisual material
- Use of graphics programmes
- Research work

Competencies and Learning Objectives of the Facilitators

1 Competencies: Aesthetics

Concept Definition

In an aesthetic state the human being has the freedom of self-determination, "to make of himself whatever he will" (Schiller, 1989, 635).

In the light of Schiller's words, aesthetic competence can be understood as the individual/psychological education, an engaging with oneself, the playing out of possibilities, self-empowerment. Theatre work in this sense can give us the impulse to decipher our biographical knowledge at the level of the senses, to take cognisance of the potentialities of the unlived life (see Alheit, 1994).

On the other hand, aesthetic competence can be understood as the capacity for socio-political criticism, as the ability to question social conditions, to re-think them and to bring about change.

Learning Objectives

A heightened awareness of the needs, abilities and special qualities of participants; reflection on basic conditions in society; an examination of current and traditional role models of the elderly; reflection on the concept of theatre work as a political instrument.

Outline of Learning Content

The presentation of the results of the project in question is an exhibition in which the participants' abilities (i.e. elderly people as experts in various fields) are made visible. By organizing street parties, for instance, – an idea introduced and also carried out by elderly people – an engagement with hitherto untapped abilities can ensue. Furthermore, as a consequence of this the participants undermine current stereotypes of the elderly in the social context, and ideally generate a discussion leading to a re-assessment of these stereotypes.

2 Competencies: Ethics

Concept Definition

At the centre of theatre work with the elderly is the question of worth. The work offers the possibility of questioning stereotypical value judgements made about the elderly, of retaliating against them and refuting them. As already outlined in the context of aesthetic competencies, two goals are of major importance to the authors in the area of theatre work with elderly people: one is the making visible of life stories, experience, abilities and individual qualities. The other is the positioning of the elderly person in the public sphere. Both of these issues are concerned with the sense of worth participants should experience in and as a result of the theatre work: theatre work stimulates the senses of the participants, on the one hand and is a means to an increased sense of personal worth on the other. This is achieved by making elderly people visible in the public sphere.

Learning Objectives

Examination of one's own value judgements regarding elderly people; sensitisation towards the special competencies and the special qualities of elderly people in general and in particular; making these special qualities visible in the public sphere; the promotion of discussions arising out of the work.

Outline of Learning Content

During the city tour, which forms part of the exhibition, the tour guide announces, for example, that today he is a happy man. This event allows him to prove what he is capable of. He receives acknowledgement and appreciation for his competencies, for instance, through the participants' feedback, the announcement in the exhibition catalogue and in a daily newspaper.

3 Competencies: Methods and Application

Concept Definition

Action competence refers to the following: a specific and planned procedure based on methods that have been tried and tested, the flexibility to spontaneously adapt the plan to the unfolding process, being aware of and incorporating the needs of the target group, and the cooperation with colleagues and institutions.

Learning Objectives

Paying attention to the needs of the participants – taking as a starting point the abilities and potential of the participants; knowledge concerning and flexible employment of theatre methods in social contexts; creation of a theatre product; team and project work.

Outline of Learning Content

In the project methods and approaches were flexibly adapted to the needs and potential of the participants. In the course of the theatre-pedagogical process different methods were employed. Using the forum theatre method, for instance, research results were processed and presented in theatrical form to the inhabitants. The latter were then encouraged to actively engage with the contents of the research, to offer ideas and suggestions and to try these out.

4 Competencies: Field-Related Knowledge

Concept Definition

Field competence refers to the knowledge about the field in which one is working, both with respect to the target group and its environment. Where and under which circumstances does the target group live? how and through whom can they best be reached? who are the contact people and the multiplicators? in what kind of structure is the target group embedded?

Learning Objectives

General and specific background knowledge of the target group; knowledge of the local infrastructure (institutions, organizations, associations, groups, contact partners); making contact with key persons and multiplicators.

Outline of Learning Content

The project leaders carried out research in the area of existing groups and associations, contacted leaders, drew up a schedule and presented the forum theatre production in the various groups' spaces. To give a further example: they staged an event – "Memento" – in front of the local church, serving wine and hot chestnuts, because they discovered that a lot of people could be reached there after Sunday mass.

5 Competencies: Orientation

Concept Definition

Orientation competencies refer to the skills required to assess the sequence of effects in the theatre-pedagogical project. The concrete course of action is decided upon accordingly.

Learning Objectives

Theoretical and practice-oriented knowledge of the target group in question within a specific context; decisions regarding the employment of theatre-pedagogical means and methods;

Outline of Learning Content

The forum theatre method was employed in this project. This method offered the chance of processing themes theatrically that emerged in the course of the research. The forum theatre scenes were presented. This allowed existing groups to be drawn in and become involved in the project.

6 Competencies: Research and Communication

Concept Definition

Theatre work in social fields always takes place in a situation of conflict, which entails different points of departure, needs, interests, different group concerns, institutions and individuals. Consequently it is crucial be able to communicate one's own points of departure, needs, interests and emphases regarding theatre work with elderly people in general and also with regard to the specific project.

Learning Objectives

Reflection on and communication of one's own project goals compared to those of potential project partners; public relations work; engaging with specialist literature; examination of current projects; discussions in theatre work with elderly people.

Outline of Learning Content

Making contact with other experts in theatre work with elderly people, entering into an exchange, learning from one another and presenting the theatre work with elderly people in public are all major concerns of the authors. Consequently the authors created a homepage and organized a conference on theatre work with elderly people.

Specialist literature for this module includes research in the area of biography, concepts of aging, images of aging, forum theatre, devising theatre.

For literature related to these topics, visit the following website:
http://www.twisfer.org/module_1/TheaterAlterLebenszufriedenheit.htm

7 Competencies: Interculturalism

Concept Definition

> He who merely perceives what he already knows and feels confirmed never learns anything new (Siebert 1994, 83).

In the field of theatre-pedagogy a very broad spectrum of people and worlds intersect. Within this tension between the strange and the familiar, theatre-pedagogical work means finding a meaningful way of dealing with cultural differences. These differences do not stem solely from ethnic differences, but also include experiences of otherness within individual societies and milieus that run across ethnic boarders. Hereby a dynamic concept of culture is taken as a point of departure, which, contrary to more rigid concepts, sees culture as a process between foreign worlds. Intercultural competencies refer to the ability to move within this tension and to deal with cultural differences (see Schäffter 1997, 115 - 126). This competence in dealing with otherness is a prerequisite for theatre-pedagogical work.

Learning Objectives

Heightened powers of perception and awareness; awareness of projection mechanisms; multi-perspectivity; openness; differentiated viewpoint.

Outline of Learning Content

In theatre-pedagogical work with elderly people, the project leaders are confronted with many modes of existence, life stories and worlds that possibly differ from their own. Intercultural awareness is a prerequisite in order to be able relate to the group of participants.

In the project carried out, the emphasis was placed among other things on telling stories. In these story-circles, where personal and intimate stories were related and communicated to others, it was essential to listen with an open mind and to respond without making value judgements. Cultural differences between the individual persons arose as a result of the heterogeneity of the participants, who differed from one another in terms of background, age and personal experience. It was important to view this otherness as a productive element within the work. In the transgenerational story-circle, in which elderly people and secondary school pupils took part, the main issue was the generation gap. The exchange concerning these differences was perceived by both parties as enriching. Personal prejudice and projections were reflected upon among the members of the project team.

8 Competencies: Gender

Concept Definition

The term "gender" refers to that which is a social construct as distinct from the biological term "sex". In view of this, "gender" points to "the socially determined differences between men and women in relation to their interests, needs, competencies and life experiences" (http://www.frauenservice.at). Gender is (re)produced in everyday behaviour and is integral to social power discourses. The social gender refers to ideas of how women and men are or rather should be. By acting in a certain way, we either reinforce these expectations or reject them. "Gender mainstreaming" refers to developing a gender-sensitive perspective and to be consciously aware of social inequalities between women and men (see Weselyn 2000, p. 15).

Learning Objectives

Knowledge concerning unequal opportunities; reflection on social construction of gender, reflection on one's own ideas and construction of gender; dealing with gender differences, achieving "equal" basic conditions in the actual work;

Definition of Learning Content

The participants in the theatre-pedagogical project **zusammen_kommen in Bärnbach** ("Coming Together in Bärnbach") were elderly men and women. During the work process it became apparent that different constructions of gender, conscious or unconscious, are always present. Personal ideas concerning male and female roles were a constant theme in the stories and the theatre work. In the story-circle it was observed, for instance, that it was men, for the most part, who took up a lot of time telling their stories and putting themselves forward. In this regard the mediators were called upon to observe individual time-spans for talking and to encourage the quieter people to speak up. In the forum theatre gender-specific thought patterns were raised. One of the scenes concerned two elderly women who embodied different female roles and images. By virtue of the interactive, participatory nature of this theatre method it was possible for both women and men to engage in the context of play with the theme of women and the family. The general consensus was that women should not only take care of their families but also of themselves.

Furthermore, in the telling and writing of stories the feminine form of the personal pronoun was used.

9 Competencies: Project Management

Concept Definition

This refers to the entire complex of measures necessary to conceive, manage and carry out a project.

Learning Objectives

Making a rough plan of the project; allocating roles; clarifying the responsibilities and accountability of project partners and project leaders; making an application; carrying out the project; project documentation, presentation and evaluation;

Outline of Learning Content

It is particularly important in the case of projects that are strongly process-oriented to write frequent interim reports on the current state of the project. Responsibilities have to be continually agreed upon and distributed and work already completed must be reflected upon. Bearing in mind the timeframe and financial resources available, new modes of procedure can be gleaned from this process.

Module Project:
Coming Together in Bärnbach

How the Project Progressed

The theatre-pedagogical project *Coming Together in Bärnbach*, arising out of the EU project TWISFER, was supported by the project "Lebenswerte Lebenswelten" and the city council of Bärnbach. After initial talks with the project partners and a drawing up of the project application, a start could be made.

This project was characterized by its open, reflective attitude. The concept was developed in accordance with the needs and interests of the participants and was oriented towards the particular circumstances and the available resources. The actual concept for the project was devised. That was further developed in the course of the theatre pedagogical process, following on from meetings with key persons, with whom the content had to be clarified. Based on the methods of "Devising Theatre", the focus was on group-oriented work. People from specific target groups, the worlds they inhabit and their needs were the starting point. The work was likewise strongly process-oriented. The presentation, therefore, should be understood as a product of that which was gathered during the work process.

In the course of the work process, different approaches and emphases emerged: in order to get in contact with the inhabitants of Bärnbach activities in public places were carried out. The project was publicly advertised and made visible. The intention was to reach and stimulate people in their everyday lives. A breakfast was organised, for example, in a public place in order to establish contact and inform people about the project. Mementos were distributed as wine and hot chestnuts were being served, in order to encourage the inhabitants to share their stories and to announce further activities. With the help of the "Bärnbach TV" activity, people could be asked about their wishes and suggestions in relation to their town.

The weekly story-circle provided the opportunity of telling stories on different topics or to listen to others' stories. In the course of the process, transgenerational story-circles with school pupils and elderly participants were also held. A lost-and-found office of a different nature offered the possibility of handing in objects connected with a personal story. During the process, topics recurred that were of particular importance to the elderly people of Bärnbach. These topics were worked into forum theatre scenes by the project leaders and were presented to already existing groups.

The material gathered during the process was given artistic form and was exhibited in public. In the context of this exhibition, that was intended on the one hand as a presentation of the material gathered in the process and on the other as an incentive for cooperation, an accompanying programme was run: the inhabitants were actively involved in what consisted of a forum theatre performance, a city tour, a transgenerational story-circle and a party to round it all off.

Exemplary Working Instructions

Story-Circle

General Objectives
Biographical memories should give rise to a vivid picture of a place, shaped by the life story of its inhabitants. In the story-circle participants reminisce about a certain subject and share stories with one another. The underlying premise is that memories are helpful for structuring one's life and giving it meaning. Every life story is worth sharing with others and helps to jog the memory.

Material and Media
For the story-circle to establish itself there should be no change in the venue for the duration of the project. This space should be quiet and easily accessible. The setting should be structured accordingly with an interior design suited to the subject material, and drinks and snacks should be made available.
A recording device for documenting the stories, or a CD player for playing suitable audio material should also possibly be made available. One and a half hours have proven to be a suitable timeframe.

Account of the Proceedings

The story-circle took place on a weekly basis in the local secondary school for the entire duration of the project. This meeting point served as a means of ongoing communication with the inhabitants. Ideas such as city walks and the organisation of street parties were conceived there, taken up by the project leaders and integrated into the project. The themes of the story-circle were planned in advance and were devoted to leisure, dance, film, festivities, meeting points in Bärnbach, in the present and in former times, school and education, the significance of radio and television, Christmas etc.

The coordinator has a key role in the success of the story-circle, in ensuring that loquacious talkers are held in check and that shy people are encouraged to take part in the storytelling. Another task for the coordinator is to ensure that the participants do not digress from the theme. Coordination, however, also means utilizing the strength of the group as a whole and accompanying them in a united effort to achieve a result that satisfies everyone. This requires the ability to empathise, to create a pleasant and stimulating atmosphere, in which the storytellers can open up, but also the ability to listen closely is also required and to ask questions where clarification is necessary.

The story-circles were recorded on minidisk and a CD was made of the stories related, which people could listen to at the exhibition. The act of capturing the stories on a sound device lent importance to the stories and by association to the participants: they were presented as experts on a specific subject. Within the framework of the story-circles other transgenerational story-circles took place with pupils from the Bärnbach secondary school (see "Particularly Successful Segments").

It was important to the project leaders that the story-circle was continued after completion of the project. Therefore it was decided that the story-circle should take place once a month, under the guidance of a secondary school teacher. Meanwhile the first story-circle has taken place since completion of the project, to which many people in Bärnbach were looking forward. In this way something foreign has become part of the community, and initial fears have been dispelled.

Reflection

By means of the story-circle the project leaders were successful in integrating some inhabitants intensively into the project. Through the weekly contact it was possible to build relationships, to clarify interests and needs, and, as time went on, to make peoples' abilities manifest. The inhabitants were encouraged to become actively engaged themselves, whether by introducing and realizing ideas such as the city tour, or by taking on the running of the story-circle. This intervention also led to a weekly gathering in Bärnbach, whereby the participants formed new contacts and/or renewed old ones.

Activities in the Public Sphere

General Objectives

To enable all inhabitants to actively participate in the project, to create new opportunities on an on-going basis for people to engage with the project, to cause irritation by means of intervention, to give impulses, to intervene directly into society-related matters, to make the project visible in the public sphere, to advertise, to carry out research for the further course of the project.

Material and Media

Equipment for the breakfast, mementos, hot chestnut / wine stalls, cameras, microphone, costumes, editing facilities

Account of the Proceedings

The interventions carried out in the public sphere can be viewed as a kind of "happening", as the audience was actively integrated into the activities, and the course of events wasn't pre-planned but ensued in reaction to the audience. In this sense, art in public spaces is not aimed at a specific audience but at society in general. "Art located in public spaces per se works in a concrete way in society-related contexts, by virtue of its choice of location alone it intervenes in social contexts that contain corresponding conflict potential" (Köttering 1997, p. 7). The activities are designed to encourage questions, to promote conscious awareness of the habitual and to broaden horizons, "to enrich our functional reality with additional values" (Hoet, in: Köttering 1996, p. 38).

1. Activity: Breakfast at the Bärenbrunnen

Inspired by "Permanent Breakfast – Breakfast in Public Spaces", we invited everyone for coffee and "Topfenstrudel" (cheese cake) in the town square. This intervention marked the starting point of the project and was designed to promote the project and make it visible. The nature of the activity was intended to clearly demonstrate that this project was directed at all of the inhabitants of the town. In addition, we wanted to get into dialogue with the inhabitants at this breakfast, become acquainted with their needs and interests and forge links for further interventions. By means of this breakfast in the town square, we took up space in the public sphere, occupied it (with tables and benches) and thereby tried to sensitise people towards the use and usefulness of this concrete space. We wanted to promote the notion of "conquering new open spaces and turning them into living spaces" (http://www.permanentbreakfast.org/).

2. Activity: Mementos over Wine and Hot Chestnuts

What the authors mean by memento-gifts are objects holding a special value for the giver and which are connected to a particular story or memory that is told while presenting the gift.

The project leaders erected hot chestnut and wine stalls at several points in the town. They approached the inhabitants, gave them gifts of mementos and invited them to the stalls. While serving hot chestnuts and wine, they informed the inhabitants about the project *Coming Together in Bärnbach* and invited them to the story-circles and the special lost-and-found, which were starting up in the following days. With this intervention we wanted to give information by means of personal contact about the forthcoming activities and to issue a personal invitation to the inhabitants. Furthermore, we wanted to use this occasion to awaken the inhabitants' curiosity about the project, to get them interested in the idea of telling stories and listening to others as well as dispelling fears and shyness.

3. Activity: Bärnbach TV

For the purpose of this activity, we founded "Bärnbach TV". We dressed up as a camera team – two project leaders were equipped with cameras, one with a microphone – and we approached inhabitants in different parts of the town to interview them on the following subject: "If you were the lord mayor of Bärnbach for one day, what would you do?" With this activity we tried to garner information about the inhabitants' needs and desires. We also wanted to use it as an impulse to think about the place as well as individual responsibility for possible changes. A further aim of this intervention was to get in contact with people who were not yet informed about the project, to provoke and cause irritatation.

Reflection

By means of the aforementioned activities in the public sphere, the project leaders managed to reach many inhabitants and to inform them about the project. One participant in the story-circle, for example, was sourced through the event: "memento – gifts over wine and hot chestnuts". For the most part, unfortunately, it did not go beyond brief interactions.

By means of the Bärenbrunnen-breakfast the project leaders managed to provoke irritation, but for many inhabitants the activity was too high-risk and they didn't dare to sit down. It was amazing how little irritation the "Bärnbach TV" activity caused; scarcely anyone questioned the existence of this fictitious TV station. Impulses for the further course of the project could be gained from these interventions, and courses of action already adopted proved to be viable.

Forum Theatre

General Objectives

To create awareness about conflicts and to put various strategies to the test by acting them out, thereby making it easier to solve everyday problems; to confront as many inhabitants as possible with the results of the project work.

Material and Media

Research material for editing scenes; stage set; costumes; props; video camera for documentation; making contact with group leaders; scheduling performance dates; sourcing suitable spaces.

Account of the Proceedings

Forum theatre is a public theatrical discussion in which the audience can try out various courses of action. Forum theatre removes the "fourth wall" between actors and spectators; the audience members become participants and carry responsibility for the dramatic, theatrical actions. A scene is presented that depicts an experience of social reality. Its ending is unsatisfactory and unresolved, leaving one person powerless and at a loss or oppressed. After this performance the audience is invited to consider possible changes to the situation concerning the oppressed person and to try them out in play. Spectators get on the stage, enter into the scenes and try out different solutions to the conflict presented. In this way the consequences of the action are made transparent, action and insight unfold and are reflected on altogether in a "drama laboratory". The intensity and imaginative dimension of the action give rise to a dialogue with the audience, whereby exchanges take place more through actions than through language.

The result of the project research was that the town of Bärnbach did not develop organically, given that this rural place was swiftly transformed into an industrial town (coal and glass), attracting workers from various parts of Austria and the surrounding countries. Many inhabitants moved there from elsewhere and do not feel like "true Bärnbachers" even if they have lived there for a long time. A lack of integration into and identification with Bärnbach was the subject of the first scene, in which the project leaders questioned the audience in a humorous manner about the characteristics of a true Bärnbach woman.

A complaint frequently heard during the research phase, "It's very difficult to find participants or an audience for events in Bärnbach", was the starting point for the second scene. Two older women meet, the one, motivated and socially active, tries to motivate the other, reserved and lacking in confidence, to engage in social activities with her. The audience was challenged to try out ideas and suggestions about how to motivate this woman, that is, they were called upon to think about motivating others as well as reflecting on their own social behaviour.

Reflection

The forum theatre performance, which was presented to several groups, allowed the project leaders to successfully make the project and its contents visible, and to reach a lot of people. Unlike with the rest of the project, here the project leaders could make contact with existent groups and reach people who take an active interest in shaping the town without any further ado. Making contact and cooperating with existent structures at the beginning of the work would have been beneficial: it is recommended that intensive cooperation with these groups should be given more emphasis.

The performance gave rise to discussions: after initial hesitation the participants developed many different ideas and had lots of fun trying them out. The content mostly concerned models of the elderly, which are not characterized by a life of sacrifice for the family, but rather by the right to a self-determined life.

Exhibition

General Objectives

The aim of the exhibition was to bring together the material garnered and present it to the public for the purpose of creating a basis for transgenerational community thinking and action in a continually evolving context.

Material and Media

The body of material produced during the process, artistic work produced via installations, creation of audio-, video- and visual material.

Account of Proceedings

The project leaders conceived of the exhibition as a town within a town. A cardboard Bärnbach was constructed that visually presented possible perspectives on the town, possible changes and activities. The purpose of the exhibition was to do justice to the project, which, comprised of many different elements, is a product of those people who worked on it and contributed to its formation. The contributing parties should be foregrounded for their input of ideas, suggestions, life stories and actions and should experience a sense of worth as a result. It was also important to the project leaders that the visitors could actively contribute to the exhibition, that the exhibition was also seen as a participatory activity within the project, and that its success depended largely on the participation, the attendance and the efforts of the local population.

All of the activities carried out in the course of the project are represented in different ways in this town. Visitors are invited on a city tour. The open windows of a house, for instance, reveal the favourite spots of the inhabitants. Explanations for why these are favourite spots are written on the walls of the houses, for instance, "Billa, because their bread rolls are so good". Documented on traffic signs are the results of the various forum theatre productions. At the end of the traffic-sign-labyrinth stand two puppets in the costumes of the forum theatre protagonists. Comic-strip balloons with suggestions for solving the conflicts presented are placed, so to speak, in the mouths of the protagonists. Tables and benches set up in the street invite you to spend some time there. Behind them on a blackboard the guidelines for a possible street festival can be read. On the tablecloth the visitor can leave his/her name and street address, thereby indicating that he/she will also organize a street festival in the near future.

The results of the "Bärnbach TV", that is, the inhabitants' suggestions for changes in the town, are presented in the Bären citadel. Instead of hearing the suggestions the visitor hears the questions asked in the interviews. This stage of the tour is not intended for listening and consuming, but rather for generating ideas, suggestions and desires concerning changes in the city. These can then be noted on the board, which will be handed over to the mayor on completion of the exhibition. Mementos hang from the church steeple, the emblem and pride of the city. Everyone is invited to take a gift and to replace it with another one. In a comfortably furnished corner, with a table and chairs and a coffee machine, the story-circle has been set up. A picture belonging to one of the inhabitants, which depicts a historic Bärnbach, is hanging on the wall; a local woman's radio adorns a trunk. While drinking self-made coffee, the visitor can listen to a CD of stories recorded from the story-circle. Fortune cookies containing an invitation for the next story-circle are ready for consumption. At a computer terminal the visitor can scroll through a picture presentation, a documentation of the entire project, possibly discovering him-/herself, his neighbours and acquaintances. An exhibition catalogue documenting the project and introducing the project leaders and partners can be taken.

It was important for the project leaders to highlight the importance of all those who participated in the project at the opening of the exhibition, to present them as co-creators and put them in the spotlight.
Also highlighted was the fact that the exhibition was interactive, depending largely on the active participation, the openness and willingness to contribute ideas of the visitors, the fact that the project leaders saw themselves as

animators and coordinators, but that the active application and the responsibility for realizing all the ideas gathered lay in the hands of the inhabitants.

The end of the exhibition, which likewise marked the end of the project, was organised as a celebratory event. We wanted to celebrate a street party with the inhabitants of the exhibition town, and saw ourselves as the organizers of the 1st Bärnbach Street Party, thereby opening the season of Bärnbach street parties and realizing the ultimate goal of the project, *Coming Together in Bärnbach*.
On completion of the project, we wanted to hand over the results of the exhibition to the inhabitants. Therefore, we organized a tour through the town in the town, visiting the various stops, making gifts of the photos of favourite places, for instance, or the mementos with their accompanying stories, or the CD, a compilation of stories told in the story-circle; the lord mayor was given the list of suggestions from the blackboard, and, finally, all visitors were given comic-book balloons containing the results of the forum theatre, with ideas of how to motivate others to get together. The inhabitants that had volunteered to organize a street party were given rolls of paper tablecloth.
This tour was intended to highlight once again possibilities for change in the town and to make it clear that the responsibility for these changes lies with each and every inhabitant of the town.

Reflection

The exhibition succeeded in presenting the project as the sum of various activities and in making visible the many people who took part and helped to shape the project. In the authors' view the interventions succeeded in giving rise to transgenerational community thinking and action, for instance, by means of the intergenerational story-circle and the performing of the forum theatre for school pupils and elderly people. Furthermore, those participants that were intensively involved throughout the entire course of the project are now motivated to actively intervene in community life, to realize intergenerational community thinking by means of concrete action. Hopefully their behaviour will encourage other inhabitants to think differently and to become actively engaged. The path towards realizing this aspiration is without doubt a rocky one.

Particularly Successful Segments

Tour of the Town

General Objectives

The aim of this event was to reinforce the ideas of the inhabitants, making competencies, interests and abilities visible, initiating get-togethers.

Material and Media

Provision of infrastructure (a space where a start could be make, flip chart, folding chair - Mr G. had been discharged from hospital shortly beforehand and had difficulties walking); advertisement of the event in the exhibition catalogue, on exhibition flyers, in daily newspapers, over the community server, via personal calls; documentation of the activity (photos and video).

Account of the Proceedings

In one of the weekly story-circles on the subject of "Where do people from Bärnbach meet each other", one participant suggested the idea of taking the project leaders on a tour of the town, with which they were not yet familiar. A tour of the town, therefore, took place in the context of the story-circle, which was so enriching not just for the tourists but also for the guide that an additional tour was organized as part of the exhibition. The tour guide, the 82-year-old Mr G., who takes great interest in the history of the town, entitled the tour "Bärnbach then and now". The ten participants, all over the age of 70 – some born there others who had moved there –, partly knew each other and partly became acquainted with each other during the tour.

    At the beginning of the tour Mr G. drew the route he had meticulously planned on a flip chart, and the group set out on its way. Other pedestrians were informed of the tour along the way and invited to come along. At several stages of the tour Mr G. handed over to experts, for instance, his friend at the train station, who had been working as the stationmaster for a long time. At the kindergarten – especially included in the tour as one of the participants used to work there – he handed over to a mother who was just collecting her son. Other participants frequently shared stories, anecdotes and personal associations with the various places. At the end of the tour the tour guide invited us to a café.

Literature he had brought along about the town and/or the old times was passed around and commented on, personal photos were shown and stories were told. Mr G. led the group discussion, in which all participants were asked to relate something about the town then and now.

One participant was so taken with this event that she wants to organize further tours under the guidance of Mr G. for a group she leads. Mr G. himself announced: "today is the best day of my life as a senior citizen".

Reflection

This activity fulfils on a small scale what the project leaders had in mind for the project. Inhabitants of the town demonstrate their abilities and special qualities and experience appreciation from the public. The project leaders simply set up the framework for the idea and its realisation. The activity receives positive feedback with the result that it will be repeated and has on-going impact.

This was not just a great day for Mr. G, it was also one of the best days of the project for the project leaders.

Transgenerational Story-Circle

Basic Objectives

Conversations with people of various ages in a relaxed atmosphere with a thematic focus; a transfer of knowledge and experience between the generations; young people can gain a better understanding of historical connections and consequently an understanding of change in society can grow.

Media and Materials

A quiet space, suitable décor, mementos appropriate to the theme, CD player with suitable audio material, small gifts for people to take away with them, digital camera, recording device for documentation, establishing of contact with the school, advertising.

Account of the Proceedings

Within the context of the project the project leaders organized three intergenerational story-circles to which all participants of the weekly story-circle and school pupils from the local secondary school were invited. For the purpose of getting the conversation going and giving everyone a chance to talk, working with objects proved to be very effective. Everyone is invited to pick out an object that he or she particularly likes. Then each participant talks about why he / she chose that particular object. In a second round the participants choose another object and relate their memories about it.

It is important to give each generation the same amount of attention and to avoid judgement. Everyone's story is taken seriously and everyone should have the experience of being listened to and get the sense that his / her memories are of value, that others are interested in them. A pleasant atmosphere can be created by playing suitable music, singing songs together, decorating the room and serving drinks and snacks.

Reflection

The transgenerational story-circles were very well received by both generations. The older participants literally blossomed and shared their stories with great enthusiasm. The school pupils listened with fascination, asked a great many questions and confidently shared their own memories.

Forum Theatre Performance with the Sports Group

General Objectives

Communication with a large group; facilitation of an assessment of problems in the vicinity.

Material and Media

Theatrical exploration of researched material, performance space, equipment for the piece (stage, costumes, props), video camera for documentation.

Account of the Proceedings

A performance of the forum theatre piece took place for the participants of the sports group in the sports hall. There were about 30 spectators who very quickly turned into actors and took part in the performance, following new ideas over and over again with great enthusiasm. A lot of fun was had realising many of the ideas, which had to do with healthy aging as the result of physical exercise and social contacts. Men slipped into female roles with great empathy and appreciation. Throughout the entire performance enthusiasm, attention and great commitment were shown.

Reflection

The performance was marked by a potential for change in relation to traditionally defined role models in society, both with respect to images of the elderly and to images of women. The participants derived great pleasure from this activity, and the leader of the sports group told us that the performance had given rise to a lot of discussion.

We are TV Stars

General Objectives

To attribute importance and appreciation to participants as well as to the project as such.

Material and Media

Press-related work.

Account of the Proceedings

During the PR work for (the opening of) the exhibition the project leaders managed to get the ORF interested in the event. A team from "Styria today", a programme featuring reports on the region, announced before the opening of the exhibition that they would do a feature on the project. We asked a number of the project participants, therefore, to come to the shoot. They all arrived punctually, excited and nicely dressed. The 82-year-old Mr. G., who had just been discharged from hospital a few hours beforehand, had no intention of passing up on this opportunity. For one hour the project participants became TV stars, responding with calm and composure to the camera team's instructions. After the piece was broadcast, they talked proudly about the many calls they had received from relatives who had recognised them on screen. At the close of the exhibition, we all watched the report together to the audience's applause.

Reflection

Making contact with the press and TV requires a lot of work but pays off in terms of the positive effects it has. Through this media interest the project and the people involved in it experienced (additional) appreciation and importance from various sides.

Target Groups: Aims and Competencies

Competencies of the Target Group

Within the theatre-pedagocial project *Coming Together in Bärnbach* various emphases and approaches were chosen. The objectives of the project participants are chosen in accordance with these.

1 Competencies: Aesthetics

Self-assessment, self-empowerment, intensification of one's own perceptions.

2 Competencies: Ethics

Assessing one's own value judgements, recognition of one's own abilities, appreciative attitude towards others.

3 Competencies: Action

The ability to embrace the unknown, the ability to improvise, being part of a group, empowerment.

4 Competencies: Social Skills

Ability to make contacts, being cognisant of others.

5 Competencies: Orientation

Positioning oneself within a group and being able to fit into the working process.

6 Competencies: Intercultural Awareness

Openness towards strange worlds, being cognisant of differences, assessment of one's own prejudices and projections.

7 Competencies: Gender

Reflection on one's own gender role, assessment of gender-specific thought and behavioural patterns.

8 Competencies: Project Management

Active involvement in the project, responsibility for individual elements of the project.

Goals of Participating Institutions

The following introduces the basic aims of the project partners and leaders of the project *Coming Together in Bärnbach*. Further goals mentioned here were not as clear to the project leaders at the beginning of the project; they were distilled over a period of time from various models and researched at meetings.

TWISFER

The goal of the project modules in the context of the TWISFER-project is to develop theatre-pedagogical models for working with specific target groups. It is directed at educationally deprived groups or components of the population that the European Union defines as fringe groups. However, the project management wishes to stress the fact that it does not uphold this target-group definition, which is deficiency-oriented; it is much more interested in working with a resource-oriented definition. The goal of the project partner TWISFER is to initiate a project that focuses on essential life-related issues for older people. The theme should result from field research, should be grounded in results, which have emerged from the research and should be oriented to the respective life situations.

The main aim, therefore, is the development of a theatre-pedagogical project, which, in terms of its methods, contents and results, relates directly to the situation in question and is given artistic expression together with the group of elderly people involved.

"Lebenswerte Lebenswelten"

(Model project promoted by the Gesundes Österreich Fonds – Healthy Austria Fund – and undertaken by the Institute for Social Medicine and Epidemiology)

The project "Lebenswerte Lebenswelten" is generally aimed at improving quality of life for the elderly, that is, improving their living conditions with regard to social and health-related issues. Efforts are made to improve health awareness and to promote salubrious living conditions and life styles by establishing values conducive to health, living guidelines and elements of knowledge in the individual social settings.

An additional goal is community development: the idea is to motivate, encourage and support organizations and associations, elderly people and their relatives and create networks. The aim is, furthermore, to set up opportunities and structures that promote elderly peoples' activities and their social integration as well as to provide the chance to develop individual abilities and use them productively.

Community

The goals of the community institution, as regards projects initiated by "Lebenswerte Lebenswelten" and by this project, are to offer inhabitants over the age of sixty various opportunities in areas such as education, public speaking, entertainment, health, sports etc. Their main concern is to set up initiatives that are of lasting effect and that counteract the process of isolation of this generation.

The aims of the key contacts, individuals from the community who meet with the project leaders at the beginning of the project and reflect on the more concrete needs of the inhabitants, are that the key issues that emerge from these meetings, such as being not a native of the area, being a foreigner / a local person, are given due consideration.

Project Leaders

The project leaders aim to develop a project in relation to the needs, wishes and concerns of the inhabitants that is also in keeping with their own concerns. The aim of the project leaders is, furthermore, to render visible the elderly inhabitants, their life stories, special qualities and potential, and to position the participants as experts in various fields in the public sphere. The ideas and suggestions of the inhabitants should be taken up and reinforced. By means of this project the inhabitants should be motivated to become actively engaged, to make concrete contributions and to use their own initiative.

A further goal is to involve all the inhabitants of a town, if possible, in the project, to render it accessible to all and to give it an interesting form. This means operating in several locations, presenting a variety of choice and paying attention to different needs, desires and interests. The project also aims to create a basis for on-going work on different levels, to make plans for the project beyond the limits of the specified timeframe.

The concrete goal of this project is to facilitate getting together in Bärnbach, making this become a reality over and over again, both during the project and after its completion.

Evaluation

With *Coming Together in Bärnbach* a project was developed which corresponded with the needs of the inhabitants. The initially formulated theme was continually re-confirmed either directly or indirectly throughout the course of the project.

Both during the project as well as in the exhibition the town's potential, the commitment, abilities and special qualities of individuals were successfully demonstrated and made visible, for example, engaging with various questions, participating in the weekly story-circle, taking part in the forum theatre, acting out suggestions in performance, bringing objects to the lost-and-found, guiding tours or taking part in guided tours of the town.

Many inhabitants were successfully involved in the project, most, however, only to a limited extent and just a handful to a greater extent. In this regard it would have been important to utilize existing structures. It was too late into the project when the project leaders began to involve existing groups and associations. It would also have been of great importance to integrate key contacts more intensively and at an earlier date, to get them enthusiastic about the project and thus to secure them as advertisers of the project. The main concern regarding the participatory element is to make participation in the project as attractive as possible so that everyone wants to take part, and that cooperation is perceived as something of great value. At the same time it should be designed in such a way that nobody feels excluded; no hurdles should be erected that might scare away potentially interested parties.

The project leaders also managed to make *Coming Together in Bärnbach* a reality. The big street party at the close of the exhibition was emblematic of this get-together: a celebration in the town in the town. "It's actually very nice sitting down together like this, we could do it more often", one woman observed. It is to be hoped, therefore, that many street parties will take place in the summer time, as well as other small-scale get-togethers such as the story-circles and the guided tours of the town.

As regards the continuity of the project, it must be mentioned that individual inhabitants are continuing several of the project initiatives. A story-circle will take place each month, for instance; there will be at least two street parties in the summer, as well as guided tours of the town. What else will develop out of this project remains to be seen. It is to be feared, however, that the commitment will be limited to only a handful of inhabitants, and that consciousness surrounding the theme has not been raised on a broader scale. It would be very useful in this regard to utilize the results of this project for new ones initiated in the near future in the community, for example, within the framework of Lebenswerte Lebenswelten.

The project also succeeded in generating public awareness around the project and thereby reaching the elderly people of the town, by means of a television report, for instance, by means of flyers and posters that shaped the face of the town during the project, by means of regular announcements in the regional newspaper as well as advertisements in the daily newspapers. Other means employed to generate public awareness was the work in the public sphere: the exhibition itself as well as the exhibition catalogue. It has to be noted at this point, however, that despite considerable efforts to make contact with local newspaper offices very little interest was taken in the project. The events were often not announced, nor was the exhibition reviewed in any daily newspaper. A reason for this could be that the project was undertaken in a small community, that elderly people and likewise events for the elderly are of little interest to the media, which was confirmed by an ORF reporter who requested that younger people also be recruited for the shooting of the report on the project. It in not "in" to be old and does not boost viewing figures. A further difficulty in marketing the project is that it cannot be clearly categorized, a problem frequently encountered in the field of theatre pedagogy. No party wants to feel responsible for it. Generally speaking it can be inferred that more attention, time and significance should have been given to the marketing and selling of the project.

As regards the structures, the following can be said after completion of the project: The timeframe for the work should be shorter and more tightly structured, the concept more clearly marked-out in advance despite the process-oriented approach, and the resources should be more successfully utilized: what is possible given the available time, financial and infrastructure resources? The various project partners should be more closely involved in the project, and the various roles, goals and expectations should be more clearly specified. The project partners should furthermore have been given more responsibility for advertising the project; the appropriate clientele should have been contacted and informed. At least one meeting should be held where all the project partners get together and formulate the basic aims of the project. From the very beginning a stronger sense of responsibility for the (success of the) project should be created among all the participants (target group and project partners).

We conclude by invoking the ideas of Augusto Boal and affirming that theatre-pedagogical projects cannot change society but they can play a part in the formation of society. Bearing this in mind, it can be said that with the project *Coming Together in Bärnbach* the project leaders succeeded in taking up an important theme, processing it using a range of creative approaches, stimulating discussion around it and setting up a number of lasting relevant initiatives.

Bibliography

Alheit, Peter: Was die Erwachsenenbildung von der Biographie- und Lebenslaufforschung lernen kann. In: Lenz, Werner (Ed.): Modernisierung der Erwachsenenbildung. Wien/Köln/Weimar 1994, p. 28 - 56.

Köttering, Martin (Ed.): Störenfriede im öffentlichen Interesse, Köln 1997.

Schiller, Friedrich: Erzählungen,. Theoretische Schriften. Fricke, v. G./Göpfert, H.G. (Eds.): Sämtliche Werke Bd. V, München 1989.

Schäffter, Ortfried: Das Fremde als Lernanlaß. Interkulturelle Kompetenz und die Angst vor Identitätsverlust. In: Brödel, Rainer (Ed.): Erwachsenenbildung in der Moderne. Diagnosen, Ansätze, Konsequenzen 9, Opladen 1997, p. 91 - 129.

Siebert, Horst: Grundlagen der Weiterbildung. Didaktisches Handeln in der Erwachsenenbildung. Neuwied 1996, p. 84 - 89.

Wesely, Sabine (Ed.): Gender Studies in den Sozial- und Kulturwissenschaften. Einführung und neuere Erkenntnisse aus der Forschung und Praxis, Bielefeld 2000.

Online:

http://www.frauenservice.at/ (March, 2005)

http://www.permanentbreakfast.org/ (March, 2005)

http://www.twisfer.org/module_1/TheaterAlterLebenszufriedenheit.htm

*Matthias Bittner, Gerd Koch, Annetta Meißner,
Florian Vaßen, Tina Wellmann
(Task Force: coordinated and directed by
Gerd Koch, Florian Vaßen)*

Theatrality and Everyday Life – Theatre Work with People with Special Needs

Structure of the Module
Theatre Work with People with Special Needs

Qualification on Completion of the Module:
Special Needs Theatre Worker/Trainer

Modular Elements and Minimum Timeframe

Modular elements: Courses, compact seminars, workshops, aesthetic projects.

Timeframe: 600 hours of training which follows the guidelines of the German Association for Theatre Education (Bundesverband für Theaterpädagogik Deutschland) for theatre workers/trainers and refers to the curriculum Theatre Work in Social Fields (Gerd Koch, Sieglinde Roth, Florian Vaßen, Michael Wrentschur (Eds.): Theaterarbeit in sozialen Feldern/Theatre Work in Social Fields. Frankfurt am Main 2004, p. 254 ff.).

Appraisal factors: Preparation, accomplishment, analysis of and reflection on aesthetic projects. The particular training institution outlines and publishes the criteria in detail.

Admission requirements: Evidence of ongoing professional occupation in social, educational and/or artistic fields with people with special needs /a handicap; a qualifying examination in the form of a workshop.

Recommendations for professional development courses: political issues surrounding health, medical (possibly orthopaedic) training, body-oriented aesthetical training, group-educational and advanced training in meditation should be organised in as close a relation as possible to training on the job but should also take place within the framework of a self-help initiative.

Annetta Meißner in cooperation with Gerd Koch

Competencies and Learning Objectives of the Facilitators

1 Competencies: Aesthetics

Analysis of aesthetical terms, achieving an awareness of the inseparability of aesthetical and ethical aspects, facilitating aesthetical education through theatre work; art or therapy, reflecting on one's own individual style of work and personal and primary professional emphases, gaining insight into contemporary forms of theatre (e.g. post-dramatic theatre, theatre of images, performance), stage direction and dramaturgy, making the piece and the learning content comprehensible to the actors, becoming aware of actors' individual expectations regarding the practical theatre work and the theatre worker/trainer.

2 Competencies: Ethics

Examining how ethics are understood, analyzing the issue of authenticity, basic conditions and aims relating to the principle of normalisation, being able to detect the artistic potential of the actors.

3 Competencies: Methods, Decision-Making and Responsibility

Formulating one's own work scheme – thereby demonstrating the aims of the artistic and educational work, planning training units, projects and stagings, finding methods and forms that can be employed by the group, finding images, making progress in small steps during the rehearsal period, illustrating one's own working style, organizing and applying practically the units of acting, developing to varying degrees the capacity for physical expression and knowing how to use it, helping to understand acting as a special language, developing pieces from improvisations, working with styles that relate to the senses, developing the ability to use simple acting techniques, using autobiographical theatre.

4 Competencies: Field-Related Knowledge

Pursuit of aesthetic controversies (also in the practice of the professional theatre), getting to know those who are being addressed and the fields of play and theatre-educational work with the special target group, professional exchange with artists and theatre practitioners at festivals or in theatres.

5 Competencies: Orientation

Critical and reflective analysis of definitions of "mental handicap", examination of social educational competencies (such as empathy and tolerance of ambiguity), leading discussions, managing a group, accessing models of characterrisation, becoming aware of the methods of therapeutic and specialized pedagogies, being able to critically engage with and inside group dynamic processes, facilitating the development of self-awareness through elementary play and theatre practice related to body, group, language and performance.

6 Competencies: Research and Communication

Knowledge of specialist literature, media and institutions of advanced training as well as contemporary journalistic writings for the purpose of widening one's personal experience of the theatre and / or one's theatre educational repertoire.

7 Competencies: Interculturalism

Becoming aware of social and cultural fields, ability to explore ethnological aspects, being able to understand culture as a symbolically communicated way of life and not only as art, appreciating diversity and globalization in combination with localization and realising it in the context of theatre educational acting, being sensitive to difference, being able to demonstrate political engagement, being aware of one's own cultural conditioning and taking part in discourses on decolonisation (also perhaps on the world inhabited by members of the target group).

8 Competencies: Gender

Apprehending the gender perspective as a "cross-section task," responding to measures which, on the micro and macro level, deplete human beings' energy;

being against enforced standardisation and in favour of normalisation; being able to negotiate difference; acquisition of the qualifications of mediator; having the ability to differentiate.

9 Competencies: Project Management

The capacity to manage organisational issues as a matter of course rather than putting them to one side as extraneous factors, developing economical, entrepreneurial, financial, administrative and personal management qualifications, carrying out work in the public sphere with professionalism, networking with other experts, writing up reports, accessing negotiation skills to enable dialogue with potential sponsors and taking the organisational aspects of the lives of those with a handicap seriously (e.g. sheltered homes, sheltered workshops, rehabilitation centres).

Description of the Learning Content

The contents generally correspond to the curriculum framework of theatre work in social fields. The competencies are explained in terms of the learning content and reference is made to the concrete, experience-based work in Berlin and Hannover. Finally, reference is made to the theoretical reflections on "theatrality", "performativity" and "transfer". The idea behind this form of applied theatre work is to offer the target group the possibility of moving between theatre and everyday life.

1 Competencies: Aesthetics

Aesthetics and ethics cannot be separated in theatre work with people with special needs as the aesthetic perspective always gives rise to moral responsibility. When theatre productions involving handicapped people as actors are shown to a public audience, it is the theatre worker's responsibility to develop a product in cooperation with the group that is impressive because of its professionalism and aesthetic qualities rather than creating the impression that the actors are "trying hard". To undermine a perspective such as this it is very important to ensure that the actors are not presented in a way that is voyeuristic. The actors are safeguarded from this kind of staging when the trainer produces expressive images and / or text(s) and contents that fit the group's stagecraft. The moral responsibility of the theatre worker involves making the contents comprehensible to the actors at the intellectual level and at the level of the senses. Apart from accuracy and precision it is extremely important that each individual actor adopt an inner attitude on stage, so that the result is an aesthetic event which develops out of these subjective attitudes of formal aestheticism The spectator also experiences this aesthetic event and may be touched by it (Himstedt 2001, p. 190).

The focus of the artistic work should not be on the group members' various types of handicaps and their diagnoses, but rather on their capacity for playfulness, thus allowing the individual person to be seen and therby circumventing any stigma which might otherwise ensue. A developed sensitivity helps the trainer to recognise the different and specific needs each actor brings to the work and also each actor's special abilities and skills and how these can be useful in the production. As a result of this the trainer can react directly to individual needs and skills, making it easier to intervene. A piece of theatre should thus be created against the background of the group's competencies.

A fundamental requirement of theatre educational practice with people with mental and physical handicaps is to recognise the actors' conditions and to accept and integrate these into the artistic process. With the help of the tools of theatre it is possible to animate creative processes within the actor which can be developed in conjunction with the theatre trainer. This concept of theatre education requires the actor to look at himself through the medium of theatre and in this sense can be understood as aesthetic education.

2 Competencies: Ethics

Theatre educational work with mentally handicapped people should use the principle of normalisation with regard to the basic conditions and in relation to the aims of the group work. The basic conditions should be formulated in the same way as they would for people without any handicap. Theatre work with mentally handicapped people should not be viewed as adjusting to so-called "deficits"; rather it should discover the actor's artistic potential and utilize this for the group work.

Theatre work with mentally handicapped people is often peripheral to the issues of ethics and morality. Therefore it is very important to analyse whether the actors are being "used" for an effective artistic staging when it is assumed that they do not understand the play's correlation in an intellectual way. It is possible to avoid this problem if the actors are not required to fit into a ready-made scheme of staging but instead become involved in the realisation of their own ideas in the staging (Göhmann 1999, p. 142).

The key seems to be in the stage directors' and trainers' ability to find forms in co-operation with the actors that challenge them, which they can adopt and outgrow themselves during the performance (Himstedt 2001, p. 190).

3 Competencies: Methods

We can argue that there is basically no great difference between theatre educational work with mentally handicapped people and with people without a handicap. Nevertheless, the approach towards the target group is significantly different as the training is more individual and the tutor has to have a greater bank of patience (Ruping 1999a, p. 78). As a theatre trainer in this field of work one should be inclined to experiment and always endeavour to find forms and methods in cooperation with the target group which are applicable to them. This is equally true for physical/voice training and for the acting skills. As is always the case with a project that has been planned responsibly, different versions of art forms, games or exercises should be developed, which take into consideration the participants' special conditions.

Theatre with mentally handicapped people has to consider the physical condition of the actors particularly with regard to the methods employed. Many people with a mental handicap have so-called multiple handicaps. These multiple handicaps can affect the body as well as speech. For the theatre this means that the methods used on stage have to correspond to the actors' abilities, so that it is not the handicap that determines the spectator's perception but rather intensive images of people in relationship to and against each other.

The process of acting in the case of mentally handicapped people is a predominantly image-based and physical one (Höhne 1999, p.76). Acting primarily offers the possibility of using playful processes and it does not rely heavily on a differentiated demonstration or verbal expression to produce significant images. The great challenge for the theatre worker is to find these images during the work with the target group.

It is necessary to take small steps during the rehearsals and some of the exercises and games need to be repeated several times until they are completely understood. The principle of illustrative work is also recommended. To facilitate understanding the exercises can also be organized in a playful way which helps in the creation of internal images, thus making it easier to follow the moves. For example, stretching the body could symbolise picking apples.

In working with mentally handicapped people it is very important to appeal to the senses. They can learn all the necessary methods – voice and body work – with the help of concrete demands that are directly addressed to them. Those demands should not be abstract as, for example, the actors will start to train their voices when they understand why they should shout at somebody (Höhne 1999, p. 94). It can be helpful to use visual impulses like objects or teaching materials from former rehearsals to reinforce an association. On the basis of these sensory stimuli the trainer can establish which things the actors are able to retain, which things arouse attention and curiosity and to what extent the actors are able to reflect on the contents.

Theatre work with people with special needs is a very complex field with ever-changing demands. Therefore the trainers should have prior experience with people who do not have a handicap. They should be experienced in the methods of the theatre-educational sector and need to be flexible as they have to continually adapt themselves to the specific requirements which arise during the course of this work It is not unusual for the trainers' proposed ideas not to be adopted as expected or for an exercise not to take place as planned. Therefore it is necessary to be able to react appropriately. Contrary to the theatre worker's expectation, a supposedly difficult exercise can work immediately whereas a supposedly simple one can fail. Theatre work with mentally handicapped people takes experimentation as its starting point; trying out a good deal, varying the results and being flexible. The basic task of process-orientated stage direction is to observe both the process and the actors' needs in terms of methods, materials and support and to recognise how these can be integrated into the development of an aesthetic product. It is likewise of great importance to have a general socio-educational understanding because the work with this target group not only makes demands on the artistic work and the theatre-educational approach, it also requires pedagogical understanding and an ethical competence.

4 Competencies: Field-Related Knowledge

The social field of people with special needs is composed of very heterogeneous groups depending on the subjects of the field as well as the institutional structures. Practical and theoretical knowledge of the different factors should exist alongside specific and practical knowledge of the concrete field of work. Professional exchange with theatre educators, artists, actors and theatres who work with mentally handicapped people, should also be aspired to for the purposes of improving one's own professionalism (placements in art projects, theatres and art workshops). In this regard visits to festivals, symposia and further and advanced training are highly recommended. It is likewise advisable to contact supporters of further training for mentally handicapped people, relief organisations for sheltered homes and supporters of relief organisations to propose possible cooperation or to develop links within the work. For reasons of educational care and group organisation, knowledge of the group members' modes of existence and the structure of their daily work is as important as regular contact with directors, social workers and carers (time and place of rehearsals, financing, perhaps performance possibilities at festivals or public events).

5 Competencies: Orientation

The educational work with mentally handicapped people requires one to critically examine already obsolescent but still existing models of characterization and definitions of "mental handicap". It is also essential to have knowledge of current approaches as well as concepts and perspectives within special education (e.g. empowerment or the principle of normalisation). Likewise on the level of content it is necessary to engage with the concepts and models of the various institutions in which practical work is being carried out. Socio-educational competencies and a substantial capacity for empathy are necessary for theatre educational work, as are authenticity, tolerance of ambiguity, social competence and the ability to reflect upon oneself. The trainer has to have a large body of experience in elementary acting and theatre methods at his/her disposal in order to be able to direct mentally handicapped actors in a professional and theatre educational way. Furthermore, it is of great importance to be enthusiastic and to be able to draw spontaneously from a large reserve of exercises.

6 Competencies: Research and Communication

Competence in theatre work in social fields – irrespective of the target group, is a directly effective skill not only as regards technical abilities, it also involves developing competence in writing and talking about it. It is a discourse-qualification. In our case this means that a person who is working with people with special needs, limitations and special aids has to be able to talk and to write about it in a conceptual, systematic way, independent of the immediacy of the practical work. They must be able to communicate comprehensibly on an inter-subjective level, using the appropriate theoretical language. Likewise, one has to be able to engage in discussions with other professionals who work with the same target group such as doctors, psychologists, therapists, jurists, master craftsmen of workshops, social workers, officials in charge and the relatives of the people who have been exposed to theatre education (Brecht: In den Köpfen anderer denken können). Theatre work also involves the task of broader communication i.e. above and beyond what happens in the theatre. A certain amount of public relations work for theatre education has to be carried out – whether it be producing materials to accompany the performances, representing the working approach to sponsors, organizing press conferences and / or formulating press releases, evaluating theatre educational work; dialogues on the effectiveness of the work. It has to be taken for granted that it is necessary to engage, both actively and passively, in professional research conferences, with professional organisations and in festivals. The theatre worker in social fields also has the task of advocating on behalf of people with special needs and not just with regards to the immediate work surrounding rehearsals and staging.

The necessary competencies can be acquired by means of verbal exchange with colleagues, during supervision, by reading (books, magazines, internet discussions) and symposia. It is also useful to take part in advanced and further education or specialized training in conjunction with practical experience with a theatre group and also to take part in basic training programmes whether as a teacher, a student or as a person pursuing further qualifications. Life-long learning is the task of the theatre trainer as well as of the members of the group. Competence related to explanation corresponds to the profile of competencies related to methods (3) and orientation (5).

A theatre worker should have knowledge of the relevant literature with respect to both conceptual and pragmatic approaches, a general idea of media and institutions as well as current journalistic writings on this field of work. It is also important to be aware of one's own lack of knowledge and contacts, so that those deficits can be analyzed rationally thereby leading to cooperation with other professionals or working contexts and thus avoiding any sense of unhappiness at what could be construed as shortcomings. Networking abilities and communicative skills are thus required and need to be developed.

7 Competencies: Interculturalism

Whenever theatre work takes place in social fields, the competencies related to the specific field (see Competencies: Field-Related Knowledge) are necessary. These can also be understood and studied as intercultural competencies because one may be working with a target group whose cultural patterns are different to one's own. Interculturality should not only refer to what was formerly called "ethnology", the differentiated view point must also be directed towards the criteria related to different cultures within society, for example, mode of existence, milieu, self-image, interests, mode of behaviour, value systems, social groupings, classes and social strata (Michael Vester among others). Tolerance of ambiguity and empathy as qualities are equally important in order to achieve relevance of action. Intercultural sensitisation is required, which in the first instance simply means interested observation from a distance but in the second instance it is about acting on what has been observed. It is advisable to make interculturalism an integral part of the theatrical activity, in terms of how it is guided, as well as reflecting it in the entire project. As in the case of the concept of gender mainstreaming (8) and ethical competence (1), the issue of cross-section presents a task which manifests itself in concrete terms in different ways in the theatre work. This furthermore opens up the perspective on variety, globalisation and world domestic policy. Theatrical forms from various (international) cultures can certainly be offered to people with special needs and perhaps, as some believe, particularly to this group of people. If one wants to stylise people with special needs as "particularly" theatrical – as some practitioners in the theatre of the grotesque do (Peter Offermanns / Daniela von Raffay: Bouffon-Workshop mit behinderten Lesben und Schwulen) – the chance of an intercultural and inter-aesthetical exchange arises, which must be treated carefully and with sensitivity and must not be permitted to descend into the realm of the exotic or the category of abnormality. Dealing with what is perceived as ugliness and deviation in the social sphere is not an inconsiderable task of the theatre work that is concerned with the field of life of people with special needs.

8 Competencies: Gender

Being competent as regards gender issues means recognising the general task presented by a cross-section in a theoretical and conceptual way as well as in the realm of concrete action. At the United Nation's world women's conference in Beijing in 1995 gender mainstreaming was admitted to the platform for action as an instrument to be used against inequalities which weaken, defame and marginalize people – predominantly evident in the lack of equality between women and men. The theatre educational work with people with special needs is also based on this structure of gender inequality as is all theatre work or social action. Added to this is the particularly marked exclusion and marginalization of so-called disabled people. Just as so-called "women issues" need to be removed from the special and isolated "women's issues-niche" and transferred to the general discourse of gender (as a social gender discourse), so too must the marginalization of people with special needs become re-located to a general, critical and theoretical/practical discourse about standardization as an obligation, about normalization as a precept as well as an opportunity and about diversity as a pluralistic concept for living and a social structure for justice. With regards to the immediate professional qualification of the theatre pedagogue this means being "sensitized towards difference" (Heiko Kleve, Gerd Koch, Matthias Müller (Ed.): Differenz und Soziale Arbeit. Berlin, Milow 2004).

Gender mainstreaming is gender-political analysis and action, both on the micro and macro level of theatre educational work. Its participants (as trainers and members of theatre groups or individuals that are still in training for theatre work in social fields) negotiate with each other, also via conflict and on different levels of abstraction, their social roles, modes of behaviour and values. The model of negotiation (of social gender dimensions) is at the same time a democratic practice model for developing the ability to discern and promote consensus in everyday life. It can be located in the so-called "focus of the theatre work" (actors, development of the play, rehearsals, the positions of the leader, crisis management, finding aesthetic principles of style etc.) and/or in the basic conditions – as they are referred to – of the immediate theatre work (the relationship of care, medical diagnosis, needs relating to life history, age-specific matters, partnerships and friendships, violence, sexuality and eroticism etc.).

9 Competencies: Project Management

Competence in management is indispensable for cultural work, for work in projects and for dealing with the organisational aspects of educational and / or artistic processes. Theatre trainers cannot place the actors exclusively at the centre of their work; the requirements (be they economical, financial, juristic, promotional, administrative or entrepreneurial) that make the success of the immediately educating and socialising tasks possible, also have to be mastered in a professional way. This involves making applications, speaking to potential sponsors (foundations, agencies of the EU, private individuals, lobbies), devising business plans, fundraising, networking, scientific accompaniment and public relations work, factual reports and book-keeping and personnel management. The trainers have to internalise the fact that they have to act professionally in two networks at the same time that are of equal importance: in the artistic-pedagogical (aesthetic / educational) and in organisational / guarantor (custodial) network. At this point of the description of the competencies it may be particularly obvious that the work with which we are concerned with here is best achieved by a team and that division of labour is essential.

Annetta Meißner

Module Project:
The People with Special Needs from the Theatre Group "Confetti"

The group "Confetti" is the theatre group of the Wohnstättenwerk Berlin-Neukölln-Oberspree, a sheltered living complex for people with mental handicap where social workers / pedagogues are employed. The cast has changed since its establishment in 1996. There are at present eleven women and men between the ages of 34 and 65 taking part. The actors are mainly working in sheltered workshops or have retired early. Play-acting is thus a leisure time activity.

Confetti was founded in 1996 by the theatre educator Meike Herminghausen. I have been working with the theatre group for the last five years and three years ago I started the cooperation with Marion Zens (MA, theatre educator). We meet the group once a week for two hours in the gymnastic hall. In the last nine years we have staged five theatre productions with the group: "Der stumme Reiter" after Brecht (1997) and "Kirschgarten" by Chechov (1998) (stage direction: Meike Herminghausen). In winter 2000 the group performed "Leonce und Lena" by Georg Büchner (stage direction: Miriam Sennlaub / Annetta Meißner). In 2002 we performed "The abduction of Persephone" based on the Greek myth (stage direction: Marion Zens /Annetta Meißner). In 2003 the group developed the performance "Aus der Rolle fallen" in cooperation with the confirmation pupils of the Dreieinigkeit-church. This summer Confetti will present the play "Pyramus und Thyspe – ein Stück Liebe". The premieres of the plays and the stagings which follow take place in the church rooms of the Dreieinnigkeit-parish in Berlin-Neukölln. The group had several guest performances at the KREATIVHAUS e.V. Berlin and in schools in Berlin. A documentary film was also made about the production of "Aus der Rolle fallen" . In the following I will present our approach to developing plays with the actors.

How the Project Progressed

A Model: Exemplary Way of Working by the Theatre Group "Confetti"

Choosing a Working Theme

In theatre work with mentally handicapped people it is very important to find themes which are of interest to the actors as they engage more with the work when they are touched by it. The topic does not have to be limited to the subjective themes offered by the actors; themes of social or political relevance (like the search for partnership and love) can also be picked up. In the ideal case a suitable play will simply arise from the improvisation. The essential actions and emotions of a given literary work should be filtered out respectively, made concrete and improvised without being faithful in any way to the original. Themes must be chosen prudently as the actors' handicaps add a supplementary level of interpretation to the statement made by the play. Regarding the discussion of authenticity, an authentic effect can be established depending on the prevailing context of the production.

Approaching the Theme

A lot of actors with a mental handicap fall back, to a certain extent, upon their personal experiences. Transferring personal experiences from everyday life to the play's content is very often a basic requirement for slipping into the role as having a mental handicap can make the intellectual transfer of fiction and non-fiction difficult. This is in contrast to people who do not have a handicap and who find it is easier to think abstractly. Thus it is important to find methods which enable the actors to feel themselves into the roles and which support them within it. For this reason the group should become familiar with the contents and the main focus of the theme. For instance an imaginative journey can help to introduce the actors to the topic or the content can be simplified and explored by playing with others.

Collecting Materials

After the approximate content has been internalised, collection of materials should begin. Attention should be paid to the actors' questions with regard to their comprehension as well as to what they can retain; that which stimulates their interest should be worked on further. Out of this ideas for improvisations can be developed. During the improvisation on the established themes one will recognise that the actors produce improvisations, which are analogous to their personal experiences and which demonstrate their personal view on things. Improvisations on questions arising out of the working themes, can offer the group a better understanding of the content of the piece. For the theatre trainer it can suggest ideas for further work on the production.

In this phase theatre pedagogical and educational play exercises could be used to produce experiences for the actors. In the playing situation designed by the trainers the actors can transfer real experiences to the theme. They can fall back on these real experiences during the development of the play and the roles. Methods that are concerned with the art of performance can be used intensively in this way. Only when the group have memorised the theme and the content of the play and they are able to repeat it in their own words should the next stage begin.

Improvising Proposed Scenes

During this part of the process the actors should improvise a concrete given scene from the play. This should happen in a chronological way, beginning with changing roles. This produces some improvised texts or scenes that can serve the trainer as a source for the developing script. As this phase progresses the trainer will begin to recognise which roles actors prefer and which characters they identify with ... During this phase the theatre worker can find pictures which have been developed by the group through improvised pictures that will be useful later on in relation to the presentation. The search for each person's possibilities and playful expression, as well as the search for a suitable form of presentation should also be part of the development of the play. Different methods can be tried with the group and different materials, sets and equipment can be experimented on. The suitability of the methods used – in terms of realization and effects can thus be tested.

Developing a Temporary Playing Version

A temporary version of the play is then developed by the trainer. In this phase of the process the associations as developed and the accompanying pictures, texts, forms and ideas are fixed and placed within the context of the play. During this the individual possibilities of the actors have to be respected. Roles are also fixed at this point. The scenes, pictures, situation etc. are fixed in such a way that corresponds to the group and that integrates their ideas, thereby enabling the actors to express themselves. However, even though a temporary version is decided upon, it does not portray something absolutely fixed, rather the piece is continuously re-worked during the phase of correction which follows.

The trainer has the responsibility of fleshing out the material that has been produced through the improvisations. It is his / her task to dissolve the improvised scenes into pictures as well as the associations and the atmospheres that were developed during the working process. The trainer has to design pictures, which take the playing content into consideration. The pictures have to be understood by the actors and have to be in accordance with the statement of the play. It has to be meaningful for the audience as well.

Developing the Provisional Version Further

The provisional version is supplemented at the beginning of this phase. For this purpose it should be assessed for its staging possibilities and its aesthetic effects. The action is developed chronologically, roles having been allocated, thus leaving space to integrate new aspects that were developed though the actors' improvisations or to flesh out the old ones. This happens slowly, scene by scene. The actors are allocated either passages from the script or self-improvised texts in accordance with their intellectual possibilities and taking dramaturgical / aesthetical issues into consideration. It is necessary to find ways to ensure that they are not devoid of text. For people with a mental handicap it seems to be easier to repeat the text when they have developed it themselves through improvisation. If this is not possible one can continue with free improvisation after it has been arranged. The re-worked and supplemented temporary version has to be fixed in writing and serves as a model for further progress of the work.

Production Work

This part of the process concerns itself with rehearsing the play. The play is devised in small stages and repeated scene by scene. The trainer incorporates the arrangement and rhythm into the work. Building on the logic of the content, releases and reactions are becoming playable. In the course of rehearsing, the work with the role is added. It takes place under preparation of personal experiences and individual internal images. At this point the trainer is faced with the challenge of helping the actors with the transfer and with finding and showing analogies between the role and personal experiences. In spite of this fixing of roles, texts and actions, care should be taken to ensure that there is always room for the actors to improvise. It can always happen that an actor gets internally blocked because of pressure to succeed and the nervousness which accompanies this. This internal pressure may mean that the actor cannot repeat the text and action. In such cases it is agreed that he / she can improvise; another way back to the scene may be found or another actor can intervene in a way that is helpful.

To ensure that the performance runs smoothly the entrances and exits and the technical requirements should be established and integrated into the play. Furthermore, some technical rehearsals including lights need to be carried out. In working with mentally handicapped people rehearsals should take place in the relevant performance space as soon as possible because the actors find it very hard to reorient themselves. As is common for the theatre the dress rehearsal is the last one before the premiere.

The Performance for and with the Spectator

During the presentation, a state of close communication between the actors and the audience can arise on an aesthetic and on an immediate level. As the level of fiction in what is happening on stage is not continually upheld, direct interaction with the audience can be achieved. This phenomenon moves in two directions. On one side comments are directed towards the audience as one person breaks out of the role for a short period of time. The audience can also trigger developments on stage. Some actors feel animated by the audience's reactions to what is happening on stage. They use the fourth wall to become stimulated, zestfully improvising and embellishing while still staying in the role.

While the actors were more or less successful at staying in role for a longer period of time in the previous phase of working it can happen that they react differently while presenting "the play" to an audience. During the presentation it is harder for those actors to think and to act in a fictional manner. This results in different expressions. It can either happen as it was described earlier through the "play" with the audience and through loss of fiction, or from the fear of being naked on stage or of forgetting the text, or it may lead to insecurity and accordingly to loss of the role. There are also actors that fall out of role during the presentation and do not even recognise it, e.g. by waving to a friend who is sitting in the audience.

According to the understanding of how the piece developed as presented here, in the case of Confetti the experiences of the actors are primarily drawn upon. This is not only the case with role development, which would not even be possible without this, but even more the creative process falls fundamentally back on the ideas and associations of the group which arise out of their experiences, awareness and interpretations. Assuming the viewpoint that every "aesthetic action" is mainly feeding on real experiences, a play that is produced and performed by people with a mental handicapped can offer a view into how they see the world and on top of that probably explain its "aesthetic impact" on the audience.

Exemplary Working Instructions

As previously explained, performative elements that are developed out of a dramatic topic, materials or a chosen thematic focus, with regards to the content, can become an aesthetical method of production. In the following a rehearsal-sequence will explain how the actors can be lead up to a scene in a sensual way during the rehearsal process of "Pyramus and Thisbe" from Ovid's Metamorphosis and with the help of a performance with paper. In the same way they can find pictures through this that can flow into the production within the framework of a performative act.

In planning a whole course of rehearsals, the following model can be used for planning and reflecting upon the stage direction. In preparing performative actions during the process of rehearsal, a goal-orientated concept that was developed in the preparatory phase is necessary for the success of this complex way of working. The choice of methods to be used in the performance should be considered carefully in accordance with the possibilities of the group. In the same way the actions should reflect the actors' sensory experiences. Furthermore the consequences of possible symbolic associations and sensory impressions that could arise in the audience have to be considered during this period of pre-reflection.

Theme

Material-performance as a method using the example of rehearsing for "Pyramus and Thisbe" from Ovid's Metamorphosis.

Rough Target

At the end of this unit the participants should be familiar with the content of the play. The sensory dealing with paper as material should help them to experience the phenomenon of metamorphosis. Finding a personal performative expression by employing a playful approach towards the material and its creative ability to metamorphose is also a learning target.

How the Unit Progressed

	Arrangement of the Roles	Time Structure	Content	Yield	Explanatory Remarks	Refined Target
Introduction	Two trainers take it in turns to direct. As one directs the other documents the work in a written form. Explaining the content of the text / the performance background. Guiding the reflection.	One stage begins after a playful warm-up of approx. 15 - 20 min Two stages: Sensory, playful experimentation with the materials. Approx. 20 min	Presentation of the content of the play or the sequence of the scenes in an epic form; explanation of terms: e.g. "metamorphosis". Explanation of the literary relevance of Ovid's metamorphosis. Clarifying questions. General repetition of the story	Understanding the content of the scene. Finding the main focus and expressive images, refection on their effect.	Internalising the content. Learning by repetition. Finding the focuses of the group. Examining the extent to which the content has already been internalised.	Becoming familiar with the background of the performance as regards the content.
Involvement	The trainers should give impulses and ideas for testing the materials from the outside; Picking up on the ideas of several actors and feeding them back in. Gradual retreat from directing /facilitating independent processes. Leading into the theme: Formulating the requirements; suggesting objects or moods with the material that correspond to the content. Reflective dialogues about changing (metamorphosis) of the material and developing moods with the help of the material.	Requirement: Being able to use the methods in conjunction with the given text. Approx. 15 minutes	Guided experimentation with the material (paper). Making noises: tearing, folding, crumpling, shaping, transforming, figurative designing of the material. Improvising with the developed prop and the actors	Experiencing personal sensory awareness that can be released by the performative act.	Developing a way of accessing personal impulses by experimenting without guidance. Enlarging the personal repertoire of experiences by imitating the others. Connecting the content with the material. Learning a free and playful approach in a given frame.	Being able to name the sensory impulses that are developed through using the materials. Reflecting these in the background of the theme of the performance.

	Arrangement of the Roles	Time Structure	Content	Yield	Explanatory Remarks	Refined Target
Arrangement	Direction for developing a certain requisite of the production (a veil for Thispe) out of paper. Checking the clarity of the designed pictures thruogh a reflective dialogue. Checking again the plays' content. The transfer to the playing content is of a great importance for awakening the actors' awareness of what they will later present on stage.	Working freely in the form of a solo-performance with the group as the audience. Duration: until an end for the personal performance with material has been found. (Approx. 30 minutes)	The method application the dramaturgical construction of the performance as well as shape and seize of the veil are left to the actors. Experimentating with the earlier improvisations with the material. Independent development of a performance including beginning, climax and ending.	Development of a personal performance that is unique in its form, duration, expression and creation. In the performative act the actors make their own decisions about which parts of the development become part of their personal performance, what is reproduced, developed further, combined, converted or made visual.	Being present on stage; acting alone, in public and without protection through a role on stage. Realizing through the dialogue that it is possible to design concrete scenes with less concrete material. Gaining confidence in personal creativity and one's own expression.	The group is aware of the process of performance as a possibility for presentation. The final reflection clarifies whether the content can be memorised well through this playful and sensory approach.

To repeat the performance with the material as a part of the production, it has to be placed in the context of the play and has to be tested. It must be integrated dramaturgically. Therefore one has to ensure the technical support for guaranteeing repetitions and run-throughs. One can call this rehearsing but it should not be a rehearsal in the sense of fixing actions or supplementing work on the role within the performative parts of the production. Performance is not "acting as if" but action. For this reason the performative parts of a production should retain the element of chance and uniqueness to ensure that the performative character does not get lost. The intentions that inform the associations should be clear to the audience.

Material and Media

The choice of the materials required in a material-performance should emerge from a dramaturgic point of view. The most important material used for the production "Pyramus and Thispe – a peace of Love" was white printing paper. The use of this material offers plenty of possibilities for association which help to design pictures on stage, for example one can associate white paper with innocence, transitoriness or sensitivity – states that touch the content of the myth and the theme of "love". In the same way paper offers several variants of metamorphosis, as it is possible to transform it into different states; for example it can be burned, torn into pieces or shaped. This material can also be found as a part of the set or a costume.

Particularly Successful Methods

Considering a Particular Kind of Expression

The play of people with a mental handicap moves quite frequently from real experience to theatrical fiction, which creates tension. For some actors realizing the "as-if" principle of the theatre can be problematic. However this does not mean that people with a mental handicap are generally unable to get into a role. In the moments of "breaking out" of the role it can happen that they express their personal moods and thoughts or that they follow their own needs on stage. In the same way it can happen that actors break through the so-called "fourth wall" and interact with the audience. This circumstance has to be considered as the dramaturgical concept is being elaborated and has to be included as part of the staging. For example a video recording within the staging can include the private sphere or show personal statements in which the actors can take a position. The presentation of the reality can be integrated as a personal art form.

Invoking Actors' Experiences

Actors with a mental handicap often need their personal experiences, i.e. "emotional memory", for entering into the play. "According to Stanislavski 'emotional memory' is memory associated with feelings. Unlike memory for sensory impressions (e.g. optical or acoustical ones) emotional memory not only memorizes outer impressions, it acts as a reminder of the sensory appraisal of these experiences. These impressions should help the actors to develop the situation in question and to associate the experiences of the figure with their personal experiences." (Hentschel 1996, p. 168). The actors have to be able to fall back upon personal lived experiences and emotions to establish a relationship with what/who they are playing. They need more than abstract guidelines. "This is what makes the actors sometimes refuse to play or understand something. It can on the one hand be due to the guidelines which may be too abstract or logical or without fun and on the other hand it may not make contact with their personal experiences" (Höhne 1997, p. 245). For a better understanding of the action on stage comprehensible and symbolic forms of expression which are analogous to the actors personal experiences must be found.

Using Improvisation

Like all actors, people with a mental handicap have their own world outlook and imaginative expression which must be discovered and formed while working together. These skills in particular have to be teased out and supported. Improvisation is the optimal method for figuring out the actors' pictures. To offer the actor the needed feeling of safety a well-defined frame and task must be clearly available. In the same way the maximum level of freedom must be aspired to. Actors with a mental handicap seem to have a lot of fun and display much enthusiasm for the play during the improvisation of a scene. They adopt or introduce everything eagerly and in a spontaneous way that connects with their mind in the moment of playing. This happens without a guarantee of any "logic of stagecraft". Coherence is often established in a different way or processes are skipped. In the improvisation the actors react to words (or "verbal images"). With the help of single words, which within the context they do not understand, the actors develop new ideas and fantasies and improvise new unusual sequences. On a closer examination one can recognise that the ideas that seem to be absurd in the first moment often establish an association with the point of departure (Höhne 1999, p. 89).

Creating Rituals

Certain rituals make the group's orientation easier. The rehearsal structure can include ritualised units, for example beginning with a circle in which everyone is welcomed, concentration exercises, walking around the room or warm-ups that prepare the actors for the work. This procedure offers a permanent structure to many people with a mental handicap and provides the requisite safety and orientation.

Creating Space for Personal Exchange

For many people with a mental handicap it is very important for them to express their personal needs to others. This desire should be facilitated and there should be a place for it in the rehearsals so that the working process is not interrupted. The circle of welcome can be a forum for reflection for wishes or unanswered questions. In the same way an extensive break can offer space for communication. The theatre worker should use the breaks for personal contacts with the actors, as constructive teamwork needs a high level of confidence.

Guidance within the Team

For practical theatre educational work it is very useful if two theatre trainers work together with the actors in the team. One of them can concentrate on the practical realisation and the aesthetics of the production while the other can focus on the emotional part and the aesthetics of the effects. It is important to devote a lot of time to the last one because the actors' signals show which actions can be enlarged and realised for the play in a productive way. Furthermore, it is easier to explain complicated exercises when the trainers can demonstrate them to the group Sometimes it is necessary for the trainer to give little play impulses during the improvisations as well as play exercises. However, this should only happen if there is something blocking the play which needs to be torn down or for reasons of demonstration as many actors like to copy the trainers' play and as a result do not initiate their own expression.

Using Feedback Methods; Training the Eye; Motivating Others to Reflect

TThe perception of characterisation is very important in the work with mentally handicapped people. As a model for description the feedback method is very useful for asking the actor about their feelings and perceptions on stage. In the second part the members of the group who watched the play are asked about what they have seen. This method can help to describe something without interpreting it and the actors get to know what is important for their own role and presence on stage. Not only are direct and communicative situations helpful, video recordings can also help to train the senses. In the work with mentally handicapped people it is necessary to formulate concrete questions for reflecting upon exercises and plays and to give the actors a comprehensive level of reflection. It is often not enough to ask: "What did you feel?" Rather there should be concrete questions related to the moves or sensory experiences.

Written Documentation

The practical work of the theatre worker should be documented in written form and needs to be reflective. Themes might include: What is the nature of the relationship between theatre work and everyday life and how do they influence each other? How can theatre bring somebody forward without using a therapeutic approach? What did the actors like and where did they fall back? What was their posture like? When did they feel good, when did they feel bad? Where have the problems been? This transference of knowledge on the relation between the performative theatre-level and everyday experiences is part of the professional qualification of the theatre worker.

Process and Product Orientated Theatre Work with Mentally Handicapped People

Theatre educational work with people with a mental handicap requires a working method that is orientated towards the process and the product. The relevant literature shows different kinds of working models that refer to different methodical approaches for work with mentally handicapped people (Domma 1984, Schoeppe / Schellpeper 1997, Dekker 1999).

Matthias Bittner in cooperation with Tina Wellmann

Module Project:
"The Lord of the Theatre"
A Workshop Theatre / Video Project

How the Project Progressed

In June 2004 Matthias Bittner and Tina Wellmann established a theatre group with mentally handicapped people. The project's objective was to produce an imaginary play within the workshop which would be presented to an audience and which would be recorded on the last day of the project. The group consisted of eight actors from the sheltered workshop Berghoepen-Burgdorf which was specifically founded for this workshop. It was intended to be an initial point for an ongoing group at the sheltered workshop and that has already established itself. The participants have been sourced using flyers and with the agreement of the workshop director, the director of the social services contacted the candidates and formed the group. Nobody had much experience in the world of theatre. An important point in assigning the characters was each member's ability to act sociably, their personal pleasure in playing and the fact that spasticities, wheelchairs and speech impediments was not a reason for exclusion or a limiting factor to the variety of roles.

Seven of the group members had a diagnosis of mental handicap. Another member had an intellectual deficiency /a learning disability. Other handicaps included spastic tetra paresis and in one case Downs-syndrome. Before the project started, some information about the existing relationships between team members was collected. There were two couples and otherwise it was a case of relatively neutral, amicable and collegial relationships. This information was very helpful and important in the work which followed.

The theatre workshop took place in a gymnastic hall next to the sheltered workshop. The available equipment (mats, ropes, cloths etc.) was used to develop small scenes by doing sensitive exercises and interactive plays. These small scenes were worked into sequences which were more or less connected and then into a compressed play. A definitive plan to present this to an audience was not made – the reasons being that there was a tight time frame, a lack of stage and technical equipment and the fact that the group had just been founded. The freedom that resulted from this was to be used for the professional career of the group members.

Approach

At the beginning of the three-stage workshop the "play instinct" should be roused (having fun while presenting one's own themes to the group) so that it is possible later to concentrate on the work with the motives that were found through improvisation. The workshop starts with a "free modus" that is a guided brainstorming supported by warm-up exercises that lead to sequences of scenes. The actors' ability to repeat the performance is very important because "drilled memorising" is not aspired to. Instead a scenario is sought which helps the actors to produce material via improvisation which they will be able to replay.

The second step is a "secured modus," that is finding a scenario which serves as a backdrop or screen upon which common ideas can be projected. The contents can be very different, e.g. an adventure story with typical divisions of departure, initiation and return, the "holding area situation" of the candidates at the "Superstar-Show" or a patchwork carpet of fragments. The objective is to range between the "opening" and the "closing" of the theatre work because a rigid specification at the beginning would probably steer the work with a new group in a way that is directive. It is important to avoid this because this gap in the concept guaranties the space required to expand oneself. Aiming for the disappearance of a handicap, as is common in several forms of theatre with handicapped team-mates (e.g. black theatre), should be completely avoided.

Steps in the Project

Step 1: Developing one's own scenes through improvisation with an object that has been personally chosen from the training room (gymnastic hall). Replaying the scenes after the first presentation by another actor, thereby creating possibilities for enlargement.

Step 2: Developing characters on the basis of scenes; Choosing scenes, places and motives for a sequence; Beginning to play sequences and playing freely along; Feedback actually happens in the colloquium (What was good, what should be kept, what remains to be solved); Connecting different scenes and figures; continuing to run the sequences; Repetition (for consolidation).

Step 3: Preparing the sequences for video documentation, production and presentation of the film.

Planning the Days, Realisation and Annotation

Day 1

Initial hello, warm up (getting to know each other and demonstrating the "my name is-gesture" which everybody can copy). Constructing fixed places: The stage, the circle for the colloquium, the corner for protest, the memory corner (Eight strips of wall paper with the basic information about each figure). There is a "guided" inspection afterwards. Finding a name for the group: "The Lord of the Theatre" (the name was selected out of the group's proposals). No regeneration – we play "horse racing".

Figure/story 1: My precious – An object is chosen as a symbol for the new role. Presentation on stage, e.g. a girl lies tired on the floor, an old man wiggles with his walking stick, a strong man lifts weights (a paper roll). Feedback about the contents of the scene and their important parts follows; we just ask questions, the answers are provided by the group. The results are written down and hung up in the "memory corner".

Figure / story 2: Another actor replays the small scenes. Given: Take the important parts of the scene and add your own idea. The dart player becomes a dart player who fails... the strong man that lifts weights becomes a strong weight-lifting man who challenges the audience... and the old man with the walking stick becomes an old lady with a walking stick that asks for help and threatens aggressively with her walking stick ...

Soon you can see differences in the realisation and the quality of the ideas but every act receives applause and attention. The mood inside the group is productive and stamped with team spirit. Soon we recognise the great importance of fixed agreements and in keeping them. The group memorizes exactly how much space we leave for the fundamental idea of team playing: Do we really integrate the one in the wheelchair, do we cut short the one who has problems talking or do we give him space to find his words? This also includes organisational issues such as time accuracy and adhering to breaks as agreed.

Figure/story 3: The free play of the figures.
A new scene with a new object is presented on stage (however it is also possible to keep the old idea). After a short break the audience should step into the scene spontaneously and everyone should improvise all together. For the first time there should be a small interactive improvisation on stage. We are anxious to see how open and creative the actors will be in dealing with the situation. The exercise is a great success. It does not take long before everybody recognises the possibilities for a re-arrangement of the scenes in free play on the basis of collective decisions. The reason we enter into the action is to break down the hierarchy. As a result of our taking part we also facilitate the possibilities for improvising cooperatively. This part is also the pivotal point for the continuation of the story. The impulse to place the focus too much on the trainers' position in the moments of playful freedom must be suppressed. Taking up central sitting positions, too obvious a reaction to the scene on stage and attempts to involve the theatre workers could hinder free progression. Relaxation on a soft floor-mat: Being close to each other and the active participation which results in different parts of the process (e.g. clearing the space for the wheelchair or giving advice to another actor) is one of many notable qualities of the work with the group.

Day 2

Physical warm up, shaking out of "tired" limbs, preparing several parts of the room, stage and memory... The group prepares the room independently and the different areas are rebuilt without any help. Short warm-up exercises: Meetings on a foreign planet, several moods and rituals.

Figure/story 4: An imaginative journey.
Everybody lies on a soft floor-mat and closes his / her eyes. We meet the figures and all of them behave in a "characteristic" way. In this case it is a collective vacation.

Figure/story 5: In the colloquium single scenarios are formed out of the memories which are connected up. This should then become the starting point for the self-developed story.

Figure/story 6:
The scenarios, roughly cut, are replayed in a free and improvised way. After every scene there is a plenary discussion on which scenes should become part of the play. The scene about the cleaning ladies at the beach is soon established (Brigitte and Kerstin) and other ideas are arranged around this. The holiday-makers disturb the cleaning work. The "Killer" (Sebastian) wants to integrate his scene – the exchange of money ("with a suitcase full of money"). According to this money is exchanged at the beach when the cleaning ladies and the holiday-makers (Hartmut – the old man) have gone home.

A second scene is established: Heiko, who had chosen a scarf and a broom from the objects, developed the role of the witch. He wants to open her house as the second place of performance and Diane knows how to do it: She wants to play a cat which becomes enchanted by the witch. Heiko: "I will turn her into a fighting cat" The witch who is a little bit chaotic, uses the wrong spell and creates a mess during the enchantment. Her brother the wizard (Matthias) becomes flustered. Brother and sister have a big argument and as a result the witch decides to fly to the beach and to make holiday plans with her daughter (Anja). The wizard stays at home and in his black despair tries to employ some cleaning ladies. By mistake he calls a contract killer and has to pay an exorbitant price for "cleaning up". That night money should be exchanged at the beach but instead the killer and the wizard have an argument. The wizard beats the killer down, leaves the beach very scared and forgets to take the money with him; Imaginative journey on a soft floor-mat and / or exercises to relax.

Day 3 and Day 4

Short warm up: Meetings on a foreign planet – different moods and rituals – the figures are connected (e.g. "We are at the foreign planet of the old people every morning at 6 o'clock because old men and women get up early. On our first walk we meet them and say hello.)

Figure/story 7: The story, as it is now, is recapitulated. This shows differences in the actors' abilities to memorize. We find two "recorders" in our group who are able to reproduce the single passages better than any script. From now on they are important partners in questions like "How was it again?" The free improvisations based on the (invented) characters have a complex storyline. We do not want to hinder the process of improvisation through memory gaps and therefore we decide to summarise the significant stages of the scenes that are replayed in a short and unobtrusive text.

The story advances:

The next morning the cleaning ladies find the money and the dead body. They are afraid of loosing the money and hide everything as the holiday-makers arrive. But the witch's daughter finds the money which infuriates the cleaning ladies. The fighting-cat that had bothered the cleaning ladies for the entire morning suddenly catches the moneybag and does not want to give it back. Everybody starts hunting it.

From now on the storyline concentrates on the "big money" and we start to interview the figures. A journalist appears on stage and asks everybody "What would you do if you had one million euro?"

After this the play moves along. However there is a problem! All trials fail. The "cat" wants to keep the money and the group become more and more frustrated. For the first time the process of improvisation is stuck and we cannot go forwards or backwards.

Figure/story 8: Discussion of the problem:

What is discovered in the colloquium is that the "cat" and the person playing her – Diane, has built up her own idea about what to do with the money. This idea has mixed up reality with the play. The moneybag symbolises a lot of Diane's needs in her everyday life. Its contents symbolise potential realisation of these needs and losing it seems to correspond with losing her dreams. The "cat" even has self-destructive tendencies when she says: "I will probably go under, too". When we ask the "cat" for the conditions she needs to give the money back, she refuses in a calm but definite way. In addition to projecting onto the money, there are also group dynamic factors behind the "cat" / Diane's self-imposed isolation: her boyfriend Hartmut plays an "old man" who is sitting on the beach with his female "drinking crony" who is played by Kerstin. Diane is watching both keenly. Our assumption is that the "cat's" attitude is Diane's way of sabotaging the advancement of the playing process because she is jealous of the "drinking cronies".

A potential cancellation for a doctor-consultation on the last day of the project (the day of the presentation) involves replacing one of the "cleaning ladies". The "rivalry situation" is eased because Kerstin ("the drinking-crony") becomes the second "cleaning lady". In the following process we agree that the witch will try to re-enchant the cat. The destructive "fighting cat" should become a gentle house cat again. However during the improvisation the "cat" stands firm and there is only one option left: The witch turns the money into stones and helps everybody except the cat to go on a journey on a luxury cruise ship. The cat has to stay home because it was greedy. Diane looked upon this journey on the luxury cruise ship as the dream that she wanted to fulfil with the money. "A journey together with my lover on a luxury cruise ship and afterwards a marriage…" The cat is on the luxury cruise ship too but still does not want to give the stones back. One of the cleaning ladies who cannot swim is afraid that the ship might sink because of the heavy weight of the stones. Our last idea is that everybody has to pet the cat and finally it gives its prey back and we can celebrate it. We were all very surprised to have found the end of the story at last.

A title for the story: In the colloquium we collect all proposed titles and vote for this title: "The enchanted cat and the money".

Figure/story 9: Rehearsal:
We rehearse the play to consolidate the content and the scenes. We break only for small loosening-up exercises. After a vote we decide to record the play on our last day.

Day 5

We decided to record the film in accordance with the individual sequences of our play. The camera should follow the progression of the play as unobtrusively and intuitively as possible. For optimal effect there should be only one stage per scene. The technical requirements are realized with a digital camera (without any audio-equipment) operated by one of the trainers. There are only a few scenes that have to be replicated. At every rehearsal we discus every single scene with the group.

1. The tired cat is enchanted and becomes a fighting-cat.
2. The witch and the wizard have an argument over the untidiness
3. The wizard wants to employ a cleaning lady but calls a contract killer by mistake.
4. When the killer and the wizard want to exchange the money the former is killed during an argument. The money is forgotten about and left behind at the beach.
5. The cleaning ladies find the money but the holiday-makers want a part of it.

6. The enchanted cat catches the money and keeps it.
7. Everybody talks about several possibilities for getting the money back.
8. At last the witch conjures up a luxury cruise ship which everybody boards and the moneybag becomes a bag full of stones. As everybody starts to pet the cat it throws the stones into the water.

The group concentrates very hard during the recording and a productive spirit, resulting from the film production, intensifies the play even more. As it turns out the complex storyline is not to our advantage: easily produced through improvisation it became a kind of "stumbling block" in the reproduction. The film recording helped to solve those problems. The ability to reproduce as an essential part of theatre work with mentally handicapped people is questioned. Does the play really have to be same for each performance? How free can a play be when the actors are not allowed to change the end of each reproduction? The feedback at the end of the shoot was very positive. Above all, improvisation as an approach was favoured – resulting in freedom during the creative process – as was the experience of developing a product as part of a team. In accordance with the project's time frame and the desired accentuation of the scenic progression based on improvisation, the reduction of props and costumes was a positive development. As was demonstrated at the end, leeway with time was very important as regards the groups' unpredictable homogeneity in its "playing abilities". The time frame suitable for each actor to develop his / her character was formative in the playing process.

A productive basis for an independent and constructive elaboration of figures, roles and scenes can be reached using physical warm-ups and sensitive and interactive exercises that make the first improvisations with ordinary objects possible and which deliver playful scenes.

The danger with this enthusiasm for initial results is that the trainers may start to guide the process (albeit in a well meaning way). This problem is not always successfully dissolved with time. A team of two theatre workers may be able to stop each other but they could also create twice the problem. For this reason we had already planned, prior to commencing the project, how to respond to such a problem. Such a failure in the preliminary stages has to be discussed during the daily debriefing (at least). The film presentation – that which ended the project and took place two weeks after the end of the playing process – initiated a discussion on how a further continuation of the new theatre group would be possible. The next time the theatre group "The Lord of the Theatre" is adamant that it wants to appear in public and to present its play to an audience.

Exemplary Working Instructions

Theme
Developing little scenes with the help of trivial objects

Rough Target
At the end of this unit the participants should know that watching each other and a willingness to give time and attention to others leads to a play that is enjoyable and spontaneous; Striving for group formation and personal boosting.

Material and Media
Trivial objects, video camera

Progress of the Unit

	Arrangement of the Roles	Time Structure	Content	Yield	Explanatory Remarks	Refined Target
Introduction	Two theatre workers provide impulses. They guide and enter into the action in turn. Feedback after each presentation.	Three stages of stepping up the requirements (approx. 45 minutes per stage).	Developing short scenes with the help of trivial objects from the room.	First free stage presence. In this case, the space for experimentation is very important.	Developing a personal position in relation to the action that disengages from the classic role models.	Beginning to develop characters and playful competencies.
Development	Gradual withdrawal from the action – watching the weaker group members and supporting their free play.	Two stages: presentation, variation and re-presentation (45 minutes).	Changing the roles: The actors slip into the figures of other group members.	Watching one's own figure played by somebody else who plays it differently.	Through watching one's own figure played by somebody else and understanding the idea of a creative and free approach, situations arise.	Creative dealing with personal ideas in the acting-out of scenes.

Arrangement of the Roles	Time Structure	Content	Yield	Explanatory Remarks	Refined Target
The trainer is outside the action / recording of the rehearsal for a presentation in the colloquium.	Several stages that are distributed as impro-block during the course of the action. Always at the beginning of the scenes' progression..	The sequences are replayed several times with newly improvised characters.	Closing stage of the play's development. The video material helps in reviewing the contents.	The openness of the process prevents loss of interest as it is always changing. The use of the video camera supports this.	The process is understood as a working process that is always changing and being formed in an active way. The film documentation is also important in that it records the results.

(Arrangement label on left margin)

Target Groups: **Aims and Competencies**

The aforementioned competencies for the trainer should be taken up again as the learning objectives of the target group. Those should be used in the context of theatre work in social fields and should be embraced as qualities needed to negotiate everyday existence. With the help of theatre work, expanding the scope for action and reducing the "pressure of decolonisation" in the target group's reflected way of life ("Lebenswelt") is suggested. At this point it is only suitable to give tips or make suggestions as the process of prioritising and selecting learning targets has to be orientated towards the interests of the target group and the trainers' qualifications. The special everyday-skills that should be attained can be assigned to several fields of the learning objective.

Suggested Acquisition of Competencies

1 Competencies: Aesthetics

Sensibility, formation of taste, perceptual training and self-confident production.

2 Competencies: Ethics

Perception of others, developing patience, power of concentration, self-esteem, appreciating-behaviour, co-operative and interpersonal skills, communication, ability to articulate personal needs, dealing in a positive way with the sense of shame and sexuality, among others.

3 Competencies: Methods

Transfer, switching fields, improvisation, ability to express physically, ability to manage conflicts and to organize free time, testing attitudes.

4 Competencies: Field-Related Knowledge

Expanding the scope for space and time, Structuring a way of life for oneself that is focused on personal reflection ("Lebenswelt") against hospitalisation, arranging and persevering with public appearances, gaining awareness of the personal field, offensive presentation.

5 Competencies: Orientation

Ability to look "beyond the end of one's nose" and to respect the awareness of others and oneself.

6 Competencies: Interculturalism

Ability to notice, to bear and to resolve social and cultural differences and to adopt a position on ethnic differences.

7 Competencies: Gender

Ability to notice and differentiate gender roles qq.v ethical and intercultural competences

8 Competencies: Organisation

Concrete project-organisation; participation in tour planning and its realisation, group management; ability to manage stage props and technical equipment.

Structure of Institutions

The learning objectives have to be published in line with the concept of the institution and have to show the human and spatial resources. The institution has to have the juristically ensured type of enterprise that is specific to the individual country. The curriculum that is orientated towards the target group has to conform to the competencies that are formulated within the module. It can be understood as a specialisation within the (frame-) curriculum "Theatre Work in Social Fields". The training units that cannot be fulfilled by the institution can be provided by another institution that provides the same qualifications. At least 50% of the training (i.e. 300 hours of training) should be attained within the same institution for reasons of concentration and measurement of correct training.

Evaluation and Theoretical Reflection

Florian Vaßen

Theatrality

In our society the new media are becoming increasingly dominant, extending to the most remote areas of human life and has led to a growing theatricalisation of all areas of human beings' lives, whereby reality is staged both for the media and in the media. A never-ending chain of staged events, aesthetisization of power structures and theatricalisation of politics, the staging of the self for show, design and image as central categories of the public, refer to the problematic issues of a radically changed reality in an "event-" and "spectacle-society".

The term "theatrality" emerged mainly in the context of the theatre of the avant-garde in the sixties and seventies, theatre anthropology and the semiotics of theatre and also within the field of cultural studies which examines processes of socio-cultural and political communication, for which performance-related activities play a significant role. The term must, if it is not to be used to designate anything and everything, be specifically located in society. This is particularly productive if it happens through the conception of the theatrality structure, which determines the different areas of theatrality within a general social complex (Rudolph Münz: Theatralität und Theater. Zur Historiographie von Theatralitätsgefügen. Berlin 1998). Four culturally historical fields of theatrality become hereby apparent: Firstly, the theatre as an official art institution, secondly the theatricalisation of everyday life, thirdly non-theatre or rather the rejection of theatre (ban, censorship etc.) and fourthly anti-theatre as a counterworld. It manifests itself in irritating and common perceptions and modes of behaviour, confusing aesthetic / theatrical forms, whose imaginative potential circumvents social norms. As a rule one associates the so-called anti-theatre with trickster-figures like the harlequin, the fool, the buffoon and the clown with their subversive, supra-artificial and at the same time popular folk-like potential. Dario Fo, however, Artraud and the living theatre also belong in this category as well as current forms of experimental theatre.

The everyday theatrality of Münz' structure of theatrality does not only contain the staging of power and social norms, it also facilitates – on the level of the individual – a "playful development of the subject" as an aesthetic staging of the world we live in. Here too, a part of the world we live in is staged aesthetically but in a way that is different to commercialised, mediated theatricalisation; this staging of subject sketches creates "an aesthetic, unpressured constellation between art and everyday practice", whereby "the play always distances itself from the functional and thereby from mere preservation of life and moves towards formation of the self" (Jürgen Belgrad: Theatralität im Alltag. Spielerische Subjektentfaltung als ästhetische Inszenierung der Lebenswelt, in: Korrespondenzen. Zeitschrift für Theaterpädagogik 1996, H. 27 mit dem Schwerpunkt Theatralität, p. 34 - 43).

In summation one can say that theatrality makes possible an analysis of the way in which one views partnership, which is no longer formulated primarily in texts and monuments, but also and to some extent even principally in theatrical processes. The reality of non-artistic social reality is experienced with ever-increasing frequency as a staging and thereby moves closer to the reality of theatre. Experiencing reality in this new way can therefore be described with the help of this model of theatre; the genesis is, however, the reverse: "Everyday behaviour that relates to show" "generates forms of theatre", which in turn provide the model for everyday theatrality. Thus "theatrality constitutes society, society theatre", and now today everyday theatre / social life is often theatrality conveyed through media (Andreas Kotte: Zur Theorie der Historiographie. In Mimos. Zeitschrift der Schweizerischen

Gesellschaft für Theaterkultur 54 (2002) No. 1, p. 7 and 9). Without any doubt social theatrality has always been in existence, however its status and positioning within society, its structural relevance, has acquired a different quality for, in and accordingly through the new electronic media. Theatrality therefore becomes a socio-scientific or rather culturally scientific basic category.

In theatre work with people with special needs the concept of theatrality becomes very significant and can be applied to diverse aspects of the playing process. Firstly, the actors – like other amateur theatre groups – work with theatrical codes and attitudes, which are more or less unconsciously borrowed from the professional theatre of art. Aesthetic-theatrical forms thus constitute their play also. Secondly, as with other amateur actors, everyday theatrical constellations – that are often conveyed via audio-visual media – have an effect on the playing process: images, rituals, stereotypes, situations and roles are adopted from a staged reality. Thirdly, "self formation" takes the place of "purpose orientation", with the result that sketches of subjects are staged (to however limited an extent). Fourthly, a multi-layered potential for authenticity develops in the theatrical processes of people with special needs. What is experienced in everyday life and the postulate of immediacy are extended in the theatre work to an "instrumental" authenticity (following the ideas of John Dewey), which means to a mediated directness. That which is visible and which constitutes the as-if-principle as regards the theatre process could moreover make the increasingly invisible as-if-principle – that suggests reality of the new electronic media – perceptible as such, for "now more than ever before a simple 're-creation of reality' says less and less about reality... Actual reality has slipped into functional reality. ... It is therefore necessary to 'construct' something, something 'artificial', something 'posed' Art, therefore, is in fact what is required." (Bertolt Brecht, Werke: Der Dreigroschenprozeß. Ein soziologisches Experiment, in: B.B.: Große kommentierte Berliner und Frankfurter Ausgabe. Schriften 1, Werner Hecht (Ed.) Bd. 21, Berlin 1992, p. 496).

Only theatrical form and representation create the impression of authenticity. Role construction and the disposition of the actors, forms of language and the locus of the play make experiences of difference between people with special needs and their environment clear. Authenticity is consequently "not an absolute but a relative category" (Geesche Wartemann: Theater der Erfahrung.

Authentizität als Forderung und Darstellungsform, Hildesheim 1992, p. 155). To a certain extent it is impossible to tell whether the actors are themselves, whether they are playing themselves or whether they are playing a role (see the report by Bittner / Wellmann). The boundaries between reality, performance and theatre become extremely permeable, with the result that the playing process opens up in the most diverse directions.

Finally, this playing process, in spite of its closeness to everyday theatrality and despite (mostly inconsiderable) references to art, theatre can be a specific formation of anti-theatre, even in its closeness to daily theatrality and the mostly insignificant reference to the theatre of art. Strangeness is experienced and a different life other than the ordinary is perceptible. At the same time, being-different should not be covered and it should not disappear behind seeming "normality;" rather it should "disturb" and "spoil" this and be exhibited in its power and limitedness as a counterworld, producing with it an opposite standpoint, which contains some potential for subversiveness.

The theatre takes society to its limit. "The body and its conflict with ideas are thrown on stage" (Heiner Müller: Ich glaube an Konflikt. Sonst glaube ich an nichts. Ein Gespräch mit Sylvère Lothringer über Drama und Prosa, über "Philoktet" und über die Mauer zwischen Ost und West, in: H.M.: Gesammelte Irrtümer, Frankfurt 1986, p. 97). It is about formulating differences with the aim of interruption – of daily violence, marginalisation and selection that is also visible in daily pictures. This theatre playing of people with special needs is able to symbolise exceptions and deviations and therefore also heterotrophies. According to this, its social relevance is in turning against a politic that is reduced to pictures, signals and faces rather than in a direct political statement.

Annetta Meißner

Performativity

Performative methods seem to be very suitable for tackling the demands addressed by people with mental handicaps in theatre educational work. I reflected on this working approach with the help of my personal observations and practical experiences with the theatre group Confetti. I refer simply to some striking characteristics of the theatre work with mentally handicapped people and demonstrate the extent to which integration of these methods of performance-art can give time and attention to their needs.

In theatre educational work with mentally handicapped people it must be considered that the forms of expression of many of the actors are not as intentional as they would be with those actors who do not have a handicap. Working with a role – as actors without a handicap are able to manage – is often not possible for mentally handicapped people For many of them it is difficult to adopt the role and to maintain it permanently. Therefore the playing behaviour is often characterised by the interplay between fiction and non-fiction. The focus of the presentational work with mentally hndicapped people cannot be on the development of the roles and characters. Rather it is concerned more with the development of a common playing model that allows for improvisation and contains expressive forms and pictures that are comprehensible to the actors and correspond to the contents of the play.

For the theme of the presentation it is important to find figures and scenes using the method of improvisation which considers the actors' personal experiences. On the one hand it is necessary as many actors with a mental handicap find that playing a figure is not possible without the integration of personal experiences. On the other hand a communal development of the scenes offers a chance to see their view of the world and it is also incorporates the fun of playing.

The term "performance" as it is used in the context of art has its origins in visual art. After World War II a movement of artists, all using performative methods to express their art, was established. This movement had its beginning in New York's avant-garde and moved over to the art scene in Europe and

Japan. This term was first heard in German theatre studies in the seventies. Today it describes a special theatrical genre which was developed in the sixties and seventies (Fischer-Lichte 2001, p. 241). It was known initially as action-art. In the sixties two lines of performance, referred to as Happening and Fluxus, arose and attempted to abolish the bounds between art and the process of living. At the beginning of the seventies performance-art developed which intentionally set itself up against the informal character of the action-arts Fluxus and Happening. The work which refers to action and physical involvement is called performance-art by visual artists, dancers, musicians, composers and poets (Lange 2002, p. 29ff.).

The boundaries between performance, acting-theatre and dance-theatre have become fluid in contemporary theatre. In the last forty years theatre has begun more and more to use the qualities of performance for its own working methods. Today we call such a development the push of performativity that concerns all theatrical genres (Fischer-Lichte 2001, p. 247). In performance the acting person is not a fictitious figure. The actor is no longer separated into person and role because "the performer presents his concrete individual body with all his physical characteristics" (Fischer-Lichte 2001, p. 242).

In contrast to the acting-theatre whose referential function is the fictitious expression of figures, actions, relationships, situations etc. performative events have the effect of constituting reality. They do not portray the action but instead actually perform the genres (Fischer-Lichte 2001, p. 250). The fictional context of expression is abolished in the performance.

Performances can offer aesthetic experiences to the actors and to the audience also. Those can be realised in the perception of space, body, objects, sounds and physical and affective reaction genres (Fischer-Lichte 2001, p. 244). The audience is often involved in the art event and thus becomes part of it. Performance is an event where the person's actions take place in "real-time-space" (Lange 2002, p.23). Performance can comprise an intensive experience of time for the audience, because it only takes place in this moment and is unique. The action is not repeatable, because it only exists in the moment in which it appears. Its brief nature is also important so the character of the event is more important than the character of the work (Fischer-Lichte 2002, p. 242).

Performative methods always keep their processual improvising character which is integrated into a production. The actions are developed in the moment.

Factors like coincidence and uniqueness are intended and programmed for their effects.

Performative methods do not want to maintain fictions and roles. Instead the events are orientated towards the action which provides the appropriate setting for people with mental handicaps. Performative methods produce expressive pictures that reach the actor and the audience in the same way because there is a connection with the senses in the moment of acting. These sensorial experiences make possible a level of reflection which is not connected in any way to intellectual expression. The scenes are available at the level of the senses which is important for people with mental handicaps. With the help of performance-orientated methods people with mental handicaps can interact with the audience which for many of them is essential. Maintaining a fourth wall is not necessary here. Performative methods take place as an open process which provides people with mental handicaps with many possibilities for improvisation.

During practice the following must be reflected upon: what kind of risks can performative methods pose when working with mentally handicapped people, particularly in the presentation. Regarding the "normal" public, it is the theatre educators' responsibility to protect the actors from being exhibited. In my opinion the kinds of performances which do not take place in a protected frame or room do not seem to be suitable for working with people with a mental handicap. An integration of performative methods into the presentation context could, to my mind, offer such a protected frame.

Gerd Koch

Forms of Transfer

Everyday-qualifications may be acquired by assimilating daily experiences and processing them on stage. Being competent in distancing oneself from the role and in social-aesthetic recognition – both of which can be taught – can help when dealing with specific situations and in experiencing the surroundings in a different way. In addition, the fact that "something totally different" takes place has high everyday educational value. The following has to be remembered: "A ... danger ...would be a misdemeanour as regards the correct distance between reality and art so that they would be either too close together or too far apart. In order to prevent this, the reflection has to be similar to what is portrayed, but distinguishable at the same time. At this point the aesthetic theory of alienation has to begin. Furthermore the special medium of communication should not deny itself ("But that you are sitting in a theatre and not in front of a keyhole that is a reality, too! How can it be realistic to retouch it?" [Bertolt Brecht]) and lastly the art-district has to be filled in completely, so that on the one hand the discrepancy between teaching and learning and on the other hand between freedom and fun do not come to a standstill but interplay freely" (Günther Hartung: Die Autonomie der Kunst. Grundzüge der Brechtschen Ästhetik, in: Der Dichter Bertolt Brecht. Zwölf Studien. Leipzig 2004. p. 440)

While studying the relation between stage and the reflected world of living, one has to consider the problem and the differentiation as well as the structure of the transfer in a methodical way. It is necessary to differentiate, to support, to watch and to evaluate forms of transfer of members of the target group in a systematic way. Those forms are presented below (I have to thank Jens Schielmann for his advise on the importance of forms of transfer, like in the case of the use of media – not only by young people. He refers to the empirical examination of Tanja Witting and Heike Esser in 1996). Having knowledge of this and being able to work in this direction is part of the socio-aesthetical qualification of the trainer in theatre educational work with people with (and without) a mental handicap. It is becoming very important because the worlds of reflected living and of playing are often very different and the success of the transfer is the deciding learning target in theatre work which deals with the big theatre-term "theatrality" and that intervenes so skilfully in the social fields outside the group in a methodical way.

Problem-solving Transfer

If there are any problems while playing which cannot be solved after a long period of time and several attempts and if the process has been interrupted in its development, there is the possibility that the actors are thinking about the situation and the solution to the problem after the theatre project has been completed. A process of reflection such as this does not take the same amount of time. It is a different form of consciousness and does not necessarily become public, working along on a subcutaneous level. If the discrepancy has been very intense the impulse to handle it can be so strong that the thematic issue, the problem, the disturbance, the unconquered, what has not been solved etc. is introduced to the play-theatre-performance-process in a public way to the play. When the newly achieved and developed acting alternatives lead to success, a new scheme for handling this problem may arise, respectively the already existing schemes are brought into line with the playing situation (process of accommodation) or it may be possible that other people (from the world beyond the theatre group) are asked for advice.

Transfer that Refers to the Memory

When theatre work finishes successfully, specific aspects of the play may be memorised by the actor as well as the emotional reactions that were elicited by the play. One may notice that they remember emotional reactions spontaneously. This could be boredom, fun or frustration, which were elicited by the play but also shocking effects, astonishing effects and things that were said, noises and pictures.

Emotional Transfer

A playing process can awaken emotions like anger, fear, joy and pride that also last after the playing is complete. The duration and the effects of the lasting emotions will be different in length and intensity. So-called back-home-situations may distract from and cover the emotions during the playing process. Playing situations that are frequently repeated until they are mastered, are also kinds of production and transfer-situations for emotion(s) of different intensities and tensions that may be experienced as pleasant or unpleasant. Difficult emotions arise which also last beyond the completion of the play, so that it can be difficult to leave the play after it has finished and thus it continues to be played along. When those feelings are connected with self-affirmation (instead of burden), positive emotional transfer into other fields may be successfully achieved and an expansion of personality development can take place.

Instrumental Action-oriented Transfer

Action models can be tested in the real world or in the world of playing. They can be copied or used purposefully. If the action models of the play contradict the ethical principles that rule the reality too much, a transfer will be very difficult. However it is not only the models that are based on a special playing theme that are transferred: instrumental action models, for example, which train one to deal with others on the face of the play, with the set, the stage and backstage area, the lighting, technology in general and a computer for sound control. There can also be a gestural transfer of body language: Models that provide the play with reasons for action can be taken to other worlds and fields on a trial basis and can become habitual if they do not differ too strongly from the norms beyond the playing process. Flaunting taboos and so-called incorrectness, as can be required by the aesthetics of the play, can cause friction with the so-called real world, which can result in avoidance-behaviour and confusion at the reference-levels. This can feed back into the process of playing and rehearsals by stimulating conflict and creativity (see emotional transfer above). But it can also happen that something that was experienced, trained or designed in the so called real world (off-stage) is very similar to the processes of the playing area and thus can be managed better with the help of the methods that were learned through the theatre.

Ethical-moral Transfer

Ethical principles of the aesthetic world are often very different to those of the real world and they can even contradict one another. One should remember the debates about political correctness and freedom of the arts that are occurring and which belong to their way of production and their construction of the world: Confusion, deviation from the norm, which is a principle of artistic work. Ethics and morality in the theatralic and / or theatre educationally directed play and in its direction will not become a theme on a high abstract level, which will then be generalised, but it will be exemplified by situations and people: Exemplary teaching-learning-processes become connected with ethical-moral fantasies This has the advantage of direct, contextually-fixed sensual awareness but at the same time the disadvantage of the exemplary and the reduced, so that it might be better to have no ambition towards an ethical-moral discourse but one that focuses on attitudes as models of behaviour and which presents morals and ethics. Pictorial, situational and dynamic choice of role (role taking) will be distinctly before the aware transfer. People can refuse exercises and playing arrangements that offend their ethical-moral principles. For them the same standards of values – like those in the real world – are valid in the world of the theatre. Separating the two worlds' ideas of morals and values (being able to make abstractions and differentiations, knowing the frame) can be an aspect of the theatre educational setting as well as the influence of one world on the other.

Associative Transfer

When stimulating impressions of the real world by considering pictures, noises, situations, speaking models and gestures of the theatre-play-world, an associative transfer has taken place. This is especially true when the awareness of both worlds is very similar (as in performative happenings on stage and off stage) or where the degree of reality is particularly high. In such cases one has to presume that an associative transfer is favoured, which means that associative transfers are eased up or intensified by playing arrangements that are similar in their point of view to the real world.

Transfer that Refers to the Fantasy

Artistic work is acting in the field of fantasy. Because of the difficulty involved in exploring the transfer that refers to fantasy the following phenomena should be referred to: development of dreams, wishes, irritations, projections, madness, (the general possibility for eccentricity of the people who were diagnosed by the anthropologist Hellmuth Plessner), surrealism, imagination and utopia. For example a dream could take place in landscapes and/or group situations that are derived from a phase of the theatre play, or the actor could meet people from the play in his dreams. This would also be a transfer.

Experiencing Time Transfer

The way in which time is structured within a play is often different to the real world. What is hectic, stressful and also ritualistic (as set by somebody else) can be transferred to the playing worlds and can offer in the first instance some security. They can be removed by a tempo that has been developed and newly designed by the playing group itself. The playing time can be some kind of "time out" or "personal time" or can become a new "real time": The experience of different periods, the experience of differences in the experience of time –

living time versus dead time, heteronomous time – an analogy to the living working(time) to the dead working(time).

Informational-reality-structuring Transfer

This form of transfer can be separated into reality-structuring and informational transfer. The first one takes place when experiences of a play are applied to estimations and evaluations of the real world. The second one takes place when information from the theatre play which could be useful in the real world is transferred – examples include: strategies of the play or information that is "pulled out" and could be useful for knowledge of reality outside of the group and which are partly managed by becoming aware of the effects through trial and error: The problems one has to struggle with during the play can sometimes be very similar to those in the world outside of the theatre play. Thus one's ability to react may be boosted (see problem solving transfer, instrumental action-orientated transfer, associative transfer).

Matthias Bittner

A Micro View inside the Project II "The Lord of the Theatre"

View 1

When Matthias gets on stage with his wheelchair he is playing the role of the wizard who is on the way to his conspiratorial date with the killer. The wizard is alone on the beach and so he turns his wheelchair towards the audience and waits. Nervously he looks at his watch, talks to himself, mumbles and falls silent. Out of the background the killer comes nearer, puts his arm on the wizard's shoulder and says "Here I am" The wizard turns around and opens his mouth. He is afraid and winces like the audience on the bench in front of the stage.

Thesis 1: The play with people with special needs is not occupational therapy and is not allowed to develop "charitable" tendencies

View 2

Round of introductions. The group's temper is good. Before we started the project we met each other in the empty dinning hall of the sheltered workshop. After a short period of time we decide to talk in an unconventional way as is common in the field of theatre. Those who are working at the sheltered workshop are on "time off" and as a result are in a positive mood in advance of the week of playing to follow. The actors do not have any "staging-pressure" because the group can decide on the second last day if they want to present their play. Our focus is on playfully improvising the development of small self-devised stories and sequences that become a complete storyline during the co-operative work. Our guideline is the process and not the target and we are primarily interested in a preferably high-level of freedom in the work. The expectations for the following week include statements like: "We will see", "I do not know", "That is much to learn" and "I want to have pop music".

View 3

I am sitting in the theatre hall and I am thinking about a festival for handicapped and non-handicapped teenagers. The cooperation classes of the primary school, the special classes and the life-supporting organisations have trained their theatre groups for the three day-festival: Shadow plays, theatre with a "narrator" etc. Soon the different disabilities are out of sight and are touched up with the help of stage ideas and group dynamic transformation mechanisms. The highlight is a comment by one of the trainers during the following conversation on the success of the cooperation: It was fantastic to see how the non-handicapped took care of the handicapped people, how they took their hands, how they supported them in the play ... that was really fantastic.

Thesis 2: The possibilities of theatre for people with handicaps disappear when it is primarily used to improve the social competences of the surrounding world.

View 4

The sporting equipment of a gymnastic hall very often directs one to "sporty" objects that are connected with sporting actions. Through this "non-dramatic" process, access to playful improvising becomes easier because there is nothing more in the way of "making up" a story than the big initial idea. Matthias, the wheelchair user with the spastic tetra paresis and the big speech disorder, drives to a home-training bicycle and with enormous exertion heaves himself out of the wheelchair and stands for a moment. After this he sits down again, turns to the audience and lifts his arms cheering. Heiko chooses a roll of paper: He lies down on stage, gets off and appears again while he blows a fanfare to himself. He needs much power to even lift the roll and in the style of an artist he lifts it over his head. Then he lets it fall down and shouts with joy. For sure Matthias demonstrates his own abilities that are really well connected with the development of independence. He could also demonstrate it to his physical therapist who would compliment him on his advance. As he spreads his arms in a demanding way our applause starts with a little bit of irritation. But Heiko performed as a weight lifter inside a circus marquee and the applause belongs to the "strong man" and is spontaneous.

These two scenes have the exercise of power as their focal point. One of them makes us interpret a level of self-presentation while the other one presents a level relating to role in our eyes. What arrogance! How can one decide this just because the performance of weight lifting seems more enormous than standing upright at a bicycle? The watcher is interpreting the daily activity without distance and in a non-aesthetic way. The embarrassing moment for the spectators' rules of self-perception is during the piece of acting which follows: The poor handicapped boy is doing something remarkable in his eyes. He does not even recognise that he is not playing a role as he should be, but now he wants applause for it. Of course everybody claps their hands because nobody wants to hurt the boy's feelings. But is this assumption really true? Who presumes to decide it and why does this even happen? Those two questions should not be answered at this point.

Back to the reflection of the "valence of the developed scene": What does happen when both scenes are considered? What happens in the space between? It is some kind of parable on our own point of view and our efficiency-orientated world. The action of "getting up" is a real attraction for a wheelchair user and in the same way it is a performance of weight lifting for the very strong

Heiko. Matthias demands his applause for standing upright at the bicycle in the same way that Heiko received it for the sensational performance with the "paper weight". A new play starts on a new level. Reflecting on both scenes leads to a relativistic view on achievement and standardisation. About-turn and challenge of these. If Heiko does not get some applause in his role as the weightlifter, it could happen that he reacts inside of his role and may start to "threaten" the audience. This is different in the case of Matthias: Absence of applause would mean personal mortification. According to this the first question has to be: Who asserts this? And after it: Why should the performance not get a chance to be accepted as a part of the role, also as it is similar to the real person. Of course this decision makes it necessary to ask the group for ideas for change and extension. It would only be a real mortification if the trainer would not do this.

In further progress on the little scenes Matthias plays somebody who is lying on the ground and does a couple of exercises with two chairs. Spontaneously a group mate gets to him and starts to correct Matthias' role: "No that is wrong...do it like this...oh no, that's wrong too, you have to..." After a short period of trying and failing, Matthias stops this scene by playing getting angry and throwing the chairs away. The "trainer" became powerless because Matthias has "demonised" the "instrument of reprimand". Progressing further Matthias creates the role of the angry wizard that is unable to handle the untidiness of his sister, the witch. This causes big trouble and he engages a contract killer by mistake.

Thesis 3: It is unimportant to know the following: Where does the play start and where the production of self (Me not me)?

Thesis 4: The trainers' task is to create space for the actors' underestimated potential. (Drill instructor)

Bibliography

Belgrad, J.: Theatralität im Alltag. Spielerische Subjektentfaltung als ästhetische Inszenierung der Lebenswelt, in: Korrespondenzen. Zeitschrift für Theaterpädagogik 1996, vol. 27, p. 34 - 43.

Bertrand, A./Stratmann, E.: Basales Theater im Unterricht. Dortmund 2002.

Bielenberg, I.: Im Mittelpunkt steht der Mensch. In: Bundesvereinigung Kulturelle Jugendbildung (Ed.) EigenSinn & EigenArt. Kulturarbeit von und mit Menschen mit Behinderung. Remscheid 1999, p. 13 - 19.

BKJ – Bundesvereinigung kulturelle Jugendbildung (Ed.): EigenSinn & EigenArt. Kulturarbeit von und mit Menschen mit Behinderung. Remscheid 1999.

Brecht, B.: Der Dreigroschenprozeß. Ein soziologisches Experiment. In: B. B.: Werke. Große kommentierte Berliner und Frankfurter Ausgabe. Schriften 1, Werner Hecht (Ed.), Bd. 21, Berlin 1992, p. 448 - 514.

Dekker; K: Es geht um das Theatermachen. In: Ruping (Ed.): Theater Trotz & Therapie. Lingen/Ems 1999, p. 182 - 210.

Domma, W.: Theaterpädagogische Grundlagen. In: Theunissen, G. (Ed.): Schüler machen Theater. Frankfurt a. M. 1984.

Fischer-Lichte, E./Roselt, J.: Attraktionen des Augenblicks – Aufführung, Performance, performativ und Performativität als theaterwissenschaftliche Begriffe. In: Paragrana. Internationale Zeitschrift für Historische Anthropologie, 2001, p. 237 - 253.

Göhmann, L.: Der Weg ist das Ziel. In: Bundesvereinigung Kulturelle Jugendbildung (Ed.): EigenSinn & EigenArt. Kulturarbeit von und mit Menschen mit Behinderung. Remscheid 1999, p. 63 - 73.

Göhmann, L.: Kunst oder Marmelade? Ästhetik und Ethik in der Theaterarbeit mit Behinderten. In: Ruping 1999, p. 138 - 144.

Hartung; G:. Der Dichter Bertolt Brecht. Leipzig 2004.

Hentschel, U.: Theaterspielen als ästhetische Bildung. Über einen Beitrag produktiven künstlerischen Gestaltens zur Selbstbildung. Weinheim 1996.

Himstedt, S.: Moments of being. In: Müller, A./Schubert, J. (Ed.): Weltsichten. Beiträge zur Kunst behinderter Menschen. Hamburg 2001, p. 188 - 193.

Höhne, G.: Theater trotz Therapie. In: Theunissen, G. (Ed.): Kunst, ästhetische Praxis und geistige Behinderung. Bad Heilbrunn 1997a, p. 234 - 251.

Höhne, G.: Theater trotz Therapie. In: Ruping, B. (Ed.): Theater trotz Therapie. Lingen 1999, p. 75-96.

Kleve, H./Koch, G./Müller, M. (Ed.): Differenz und Soziale Arbeit. Sensibilität im Umgang mit dem Unterschiedlichen. Berlin, Milow 2003.

Kotte, A.: Zur Theorie der Historiographie. In: Mimus. Zeitschrift der Schweizerischen Gesellschaft für Theaterkultur 54 (2002) No. 1, p. 7 - 9.

Lange, M.-L.: Grenzüberschreitungen. Wege zur Performance. Königstein/Ts. 2002.

Meißner, A.: Kunst kennt keine Behinderung, Prozess- und produktorientierte theaterpädagogische Arbeit mit Menschen mit geistiger Behinderung am Beispiel der Theatergruppe Confetti. Unpublished Master Thesis at Institut für Theaterpädagogik. UdK Berlin.

Müller, A. / Schubert, J. (Ed.): Weltsichten. Beiträge zur Kunst behinderter Menschen. Hamburg 2001.

Müller, H.: Ich glaube an Konflikt. Sonst glaube ich an nichts. Ein Gespräch mit Silvère Lothringer über Drama und Poesie. In: H.M.: Gesammelte Irrtümer, Frankfurt a. M. 1986, p. 69 - 106.

Münz, R. Theatralität und Theater. Zur Historiographie von Theatralitätsgefügen. Berlin 1998.

Ruping, B.: Ihr Anderssein ist unser Ausgangspunkt. In: Bundesvereinigung Kulturelle Jugendbildung (Ed.): EigenSinn & EigenArt. Kulturarbeit von und mit Menschen mit Behinderung. Remscheid 1999a, p. 75- 86.

Ruping, B. (Ed.): Theater trotz Therapie. Lingen 1999.

Schoeppe, A. / Schellpepper, K.: Spiel- und Theaterpädagogik mit geistig behinderten Menschen. In: Theunissen, G. (Eds.): Kunst, ästhetische Praxis und geistige Behinderung. Bad Heilbrunn 1997, p. 120 - 143.

Theunissen, G.: Kunst, ästhetische Praxis und geistige Behinderung. Bad Heilbrunn 1997.

Theunissen, G.: Empowerment und Integration geistigbehinderter Menschen. In: Bundesvereinigung Kulturelle Bildung (Eds.): EigenSinn & EigenArt. Kulturarbeit von und mit Menschen mit Behinderung. Remscheid 1999, p. 39 - 51.

Wartemann, G.: Selbstdarstellung und Rollenspiel geistig behinderter Akteure. In: Müller, A. / Schubert, J. (Ed.): Weltsichten. Beiträge zur Kunst behinderter Menschen. Hamburg 2001, p. 199 - 222.

Wartemann, G.: Theater der Erfahrung. Authentizität als Forderung und als Darstellungsform. Hildesheim 2002.

Vester, M. et. al.: Soziale Milieus im gesellschaftlichen Strukturwandel. Köln 1993.

Roberto Mazzini, Michael Wrentschur, Martin Vieregg, Armin Ruckerbauer

Transforming Desire into Law –
Legislative Theatre as a Tool for Transitive Democracy with Migrants and Homeless People

Roberto Mazzini and Michael Wrentschur

Preface

The following text is based on two different Legislative Theatre projects. One was carried out with migrants in Italy led by GIOLLI; the other one was part of the project "wohnungs / los / theatern" carried out by Inter*ACT* and Culture Unlimited in Graz, Austria. Because both projects used more or less the same methodology, the first chapter is written together, before focusing on the two module projects.

Legislative Theatre was tried out first in Rio de Janeiro from 1993-1997 when its founder Augusto Boal (cf 2002) was elected Vereador. The main questions were how to activate and support an increase in civil participation by using theatre tools and how to transform social desires into law.

With the help of the "jokers," many communities – black students, handicapped people, workers, inhabitants of favelas, etc. – created forum theatre pieces about their specific problems, oppressions and desires which were performed in an interactive way in public spaces, schools, community centres and other institutions. All the ideas coming from the "spect-actors" were documented and analysed in the sense of a common desire or idea to solve the problem identified. In the case of the desire or the main idea of the people, it has to be found out if it is necessary to abolish a law, to modify an existing law or to create a new law. The result of this step is the starting point for a legal initiative in the parliament. By using all the methods of the theatre of the oppressed, a dialogue was created between the people acquainted with special problems and those who make political decisions. This experiment has created what Boal calls an attempt of "transitive democracy"; Legislative Theatre has become a tool for democratic and civil participation, where people become experts in their own lives.

There are some variations of Legislative Theatre, but even though it is the youngest form of the theatre of the oppressed it has spread to different countries like Canada, Great Britain, Germany, Austria, Italy, and the Netherlands. The situation in Rio was very specific, but in other parts of the world, Legislative Theatre has been adapted and developed.

The main phases of the Legislative Theatre process are:

1. Sharing the idea with a group of people who aim to increase the civil participation and creating an initiator group that can start the process.
2. The group should contain some theatre practitioners, some experts in juridical language and some politicians or members from a political association. Contacting a politician who is interested in this process is helpful for the next steps.
3. Selecting target groups where the process can be implemented (finding groups for collaboration, addressing specific oppressions in your society).
4. Intervening in a specific community, collecting problems by interviews, focus groups and discussions. Every kind of psychosocial tool can be useful. If the theatre of the oppressed is used, image theatre is excellent for telling stories.
5. Creating a forum model concerned with the most important issues collected. Forum plays are shown to the entire community in order to find solutions. Forum theatre is the best technique in this case because it allows people to express their ideas for solutions without judgement and makes a great impact, both emotional and intellectual; moreover, it is a ritual that strengthens the community as a whole.
6. Working out of solutions, which emerged from the process of forums in one or more communities in order to make formal proposals of laws, or other legal decisions, to be presented to the suitable institution. Sometimes the law already exists and the community demands that it be respected; sometimes it is matter not really of a law but of a negotiated rule (e.g. at school). Legislative Theatre can affect any institutional level, but it is important to choose the right level.
7. What happens in the institution is later given back to community by theatre so that they can know the results of their action. In this step every kind of theatre of the oppressed techniques, but also theatre itself can be useful, such as invisible theatre, image theatre and newspaper theatre.
8. The population can assert different forms of pressure on institutions in order to be heard: demonstrations, participation in the local council session, collecting signatures, etc.
9. The movement is circular, so it can happen that a new proposal is made by the group, or that it succeeds, or that new ways to manage the conflict are taken. The important thing is to follow the real process, not the schema.

Besides these steps, special events can be added and invented to strengthen the main process, for example, invisible actions to make established laws respected in the chamber in the square, where to collect ideas from the population about how to vote in a specific session of the local council. The process itself is a form of democracy where dialogue is used to build laws from the bottom up in a circuit between institutions and civil society.

A Legislative Theatre process also needs a certain context:

1. **Cultural elements:** a culture where institutions and citizens are not considered to be too far removed from one another, where a citizen is aware of having power and not only the power to vote; a concept of policy as a democratic tool for participation and a concept of leadership that facilitates the participation and not the manipulation of people are useful cultural frames for a legislative theatre experiment. These cultural elements can also be developed through an intensive use of the theatre of the oppressed and by the Legislative Theatre process itself in a circular pathway.

2. **Political points:** the presence of organisations concerned with civil participation, some friendly politicians, who appreciate honestly the general idea of increasing the people's participation and some political institutions open to the citizens facilitate all these conditions and help to create a greater impact from Legislative Theatre.

3. **Social elements:** the community approach and network approach to social problems are a framework that help to build up the Legislative Theatre process. Also the presence of active social movements and a large number of associations, non-profit organisations, etc. greatly support Legislative Theatre. If the society is too fragmented into individuals, if it lacks a sense of community, it is more difficult to gather the general desires.

All this does not mean that you cannot try to implement this process without some of the elements; you can always start, being careful about what you need and what should be strengthened, discovered, sought after. This brings us to the main question of the following section: Which competencies do facilitators / group-leaders need to go through a Legislative Theatre process? How can these competencies be taught and learned?

Michael Wrentschur and Roberto Mazzini

Structure of the Module
Legislative Theatre with Migrants and/or Homeless People

Qualification on Completion of the Module:
Legislative Theatre Facilitator ('Joker')

Format and Minimum Timeframe

Modules 1, 5 and 6 of the Pilot Curriculum "Theatre Work in Social Fields"[1]	150 hours
Theory input	150 hours
Practical input and training sessions	500 hours
Training, planning and realizing a legislative theatre project	200 hours
Reflection, documentation and evaluation	100 hours
Total:	1.100 hours

The course consists of:

- Introduction to the Theatre of the Oppressed method and techniques (30 days – 6 hours a day)
- Further training where participants lead their colleagues using the learned techniques (30 days – 6 hours a day)
- Training for the Legislative Theatre process: each couple of participants project and lead a project with migrants and/or homeless people in different towns under the teachers' supervision:
- 100 hours of projecting and organisation and 100 hours of leading
- During the entire course, a specific module such as meta-theory, reflection on practice (12 days – 6 hours a day)
- Evaluation and monitoring (12 days – 6 hours a day)
- Other courses and units with learning contents described

Evaluation Criteria

Preparation, planning, realization, facilitating, managing, documentation and evaluation of a legislative theatre project with migrant and / or homeless people.
The candidate should already be able to plan an intervention with theatre in the generic social field and to concretely lead a group with an artistic work of high quality.

Admission Requirements

The application should consist of different levels:
- An application form
- A colloquy with each interested person, led by a three-person team that evaluates the candidates based on the criteria of motivation, experience in the field of immigration or the homeless, some basic experience in theatre
- A practical proof consisting of games and group exercises, where the team observes the behaviour in a group: the criteria for selecting concerns, the capacity to stay in the group and to be in touch with others.

The facilitators should have some practice in leading groups with a theatre method and professional experience in the relevant social field. It is useful to have knowledge of a foreign language to help them in the contact phase with migrant groups.

Recommendations for Sequencing Courses

Before using the legislative process, it is better to train the facilitators in the general methods of the Theatre of the Oppressed and in the main techniques of forum theatre and image theatre because the latter is a process that uses all the previous techniques. Additional courses could be included on action research, concepts of community work, urban district and socio-cultural work, and devised theatre.

Roberto Mazzini and Michael Wrentschur

Competencies and Learning Objectives of the Facilitators

1 Competencies: Aesthetics

Although legislative theatre is a very complex form and process of theatre, it is mostly concerned with theatre. Everybody working in this field has to understand and to use the whole range and possibilities of theatrical elements and aspects such as body, movement, space, rhythm, relations and ensemble work in keeping with the pilot curriculum "Theatre Work in Social Fields" (Koch et.al. 2004, p. 259f). In this sense aesthetic competence has much to do with the activation of creative processes.

Aesthetic competence means dealing with the specific needs and resources of the participants and activating their creative potential, sensual awareness and ability to express themselves and articulate their desires and interests. Facilitators must be able to feel the rhythm and impact of a theatre scene and help the group to work in the direction of improving the aesthetic side of this work; in this sense it is important to pay attention to the development of the product. It can help to know about dramaturgy and other theatre forms and styles. In principal, the aesthetic, the ethical and the social processes belong together.

2 Competencies: Ethics

Such competencies are closely linked to the concept of the theatre of the oppressed in defining and analyzing oppressive situations, socio-political conflicts and problems. Social and political processes can be activated by aesthetic processes; people can become aware and conscious of their political and moral attitudes and strategies. The work itself requires a profound respect for the target groups. The facilitators should be aware that an institution, which calls you to intervene, has its own objectives just as any group has. They should be able to negotiate in order not to collide with either the institution or the target group. Manipulating target groups in order to achieve the institutional aims is a permanent risk in our work, as is manipulating target groups to achieve your own political objectives.

3 Competencies: Methods and Application

Applying this method requires a deep ability to be maieutic and to listen intensely to the target groups you are going to work with. Besides a solid background [wichtig, dass ‚background' nicht als bak-kground im Buch erscheint, im Englischen muss das als ‚back-ground am Ende einer Zeile erscheinen.] in theatrical methods and tools, sensitivity to and awareness of group and communication processes and the development of the individual participants and the group are important. Flexibility in using the methods and actions is needed as well as clear decisions about why they are used. They refer to the process and its requirements on the one hand and on the structure of the project and its aims on the other hand. Dealing with legislative theatre processes also means using not just theatre methods and actions but also research others such as methods, awareness of special strategies for public and media work, the needs, abilities and skills of the participants and knowledge about the flexible use of methods.

4 Competencies: Orientation and Field-Related Knowledge

Facilitators should possess a general knowledge about the field of immigration and a specific knowledge of the territory (groups, conflicts. alliances, resources, limitations). The same applies to the field of homelessness. It is necessary to get into contact with homeless institutions and projects, professionals and politicians who are working in this field in order to be informed about the social framework and network. Besides that, it is important to know about the lifestyles, everyday life and the specific socio-economic and socio-cultural conditions of the target groups and of the language. Competencies relating to orientation and the field also have to do with the knowledge of other theatre concepts, groups and projects working in this field.

5 Competencies: Research and Communication

People working with theatre in social fields also need the ability to speak and to write about their work and to participate in the relevant discourse. This is important for communicating, planning, developing and presenting projects in public, having relationships with other professionals working in social fields and taking part in conferences and congresses, special courses and the study of relevant literature. Competencies relating to literature have to do with the knowledge of relevant texts about Legislative Theatre and with literature about the relevant social fields, e.g. the study of immigration or of homeless people.

6 Competencies: Interculturalism

Due to the fact that the theatre of the oppressed is often linked to issues and conflicts of racism, intercultural competencies are important for reflecting, perceiving and being aware of prejudices, projections and cultural differences, which need not necessarily mean differences between migrants and non-migrants. There are a lot of different lifestyles, contexts, values, and classes within an existing society. To work with a group of immigrants, it is necessary to know the specific culture you want to address; it is also important to be able to displace even your own point of view into an intercultural perspective. It is important to know some foreign languages in order to be able to communicate with the specific target group (this is a requirement for admission).

In the field of homelessness, it is important to negotiate a whole range of prejudices coming from the 'competition' among socially marginalized people. On the other hand, they themselves are considered 'different' and 'poor' in combination with a whole range of stereotypes. In a broader sense, facilitators have to reflect on and analyse intercultural and socio-cultural conflicts and problems on a micro, macro and group level. Theatre events can create a space for new intercultural experiences and communication.

7 Competencies: Gender

The Theatre of the Oppressed and Legislative Theatre are often linked to projects against domestic violence and sexism, social inequality and the imbalance of gender and to the question of how to change these situations on a personal, social and political level. In the context of gender mainstreaming, it is important that the facilitators learn that gender issues are related to each migrant group and can affect the participation in the project, depending on the specific male-female relationship in that particular culture. Gender mainstreaming means the analysis on both a macro and micro level as well as the situation in the theatre group itself and the work situation between men and women. It is important for facilitators to reflect on their own experiences, projections and constructions of gender.

8 Competencies: Project Management

Project management competencies in the sense of developing, conceiving, managing and implementing a Legislative Theatre are very important because the different layers – the process of the group, the context of the participating institutions, the contact to politicians, lawyers and the media, the networking and the financing of the project – need a clear and strong structure and process. To manage a project also implies developing a project after having studied the specific situation and needs which come from the territory and context you are working in. It means really entering into a dialogue with the interests, desires and perspectives of the people and their realities. Ways of balancing the aims, plans and processes must be found. In addition, a system of reporting, documentation, reflection and evaluation is required.

Outline of Learning Content

Due to these competencies, the following learning contents can be part of the module course:

- General conception of the Theatre of the Oppressed as a tool for personal, social and political change and empowerment
- History of the Theatre of the Oppressed, specifically about the Legislative Theatre experience in Rio de Janeiro and other countries; worldwide propagation of the Theatre of the Oppressed
- Basic principles and concepts of this theatre, which are different from others
- Basic theatre training similar to the published Graz curriculum (Module 1 of the Graz curriculum, Koch et al 2004, p. 260)
- Techniques such as Image Theatre, Forum Theatre, games and exercises of the five categories, social mask and character games, rehearsal techniques, relaxation and trust exercises
- Steps to building up a forum play
- Work phases leading a group
- The Joker's role and the maieutic approach
- Project management (Module 6 of the Graz curriculum, ibid., p. 269)
- Social competencies and group leadership skills (Module 5 of the Graz curriculum, ibid., p. 268)
- Methods of field studies and (action) research
- Concepts of community work, urban district and socio-cultural work
- Theoretical concepts of social, gender, intercultural, economic and political imbalance, inequality and power relations.

Roberto Mazzini

Module Project:
"Legislative Theatre with Migrants"

How the Project Progressed

The experience of the Legislative Theatre with immigrants in Italy took place in three towns, Vicenza, Rovigo, Livorno from 2003-2005.

The Italian context was, and still is, characterised by these main aspects:
- Immigration and safety issues are at the top of the agenda of the two opposing political sides;
- Many immigrants do not have legal status and work illegally ("under the table");
- The Italian Social Forum has criticised and boycotted CPTs (centres for temporary detention) but ...
- New and severe legislation (the so-called Bossi-Fini law) was approved, forcing many to try to legalise their immigration status which led to ...
- A significant increase in the number of requests for assistance.

In this scenario we thought it would be interesting to focus on the immigration issue and attempt to implement a Legislative Theatre process. Another aim was to use theatre to counteract the mass media's manipulation of information regarding immigration. In fact many researchers pointed out the "constructive" influence of mass-media in creating stereotypes and prejudices by selecting news that filtered reality, to show only a part of the phenomenon. The entire theatre process took time to implement. Listed below are the main phases that we have been able to document in retrospect.

We have joined the two main experiences (Rovigo and Livorno) and, where necessary, have underlined the obvious differences between the two.

Process and Phases

Pre-phase

The first small Legislative Theatre experience was held in Vicenza in 2002-2003, and was about social spaces for youth; associations and political representatives from the left wing political parties – the opposition – were involved; these parties lost the election in June 2003.
- In Rovigo, in 2003, Arci, a left wing cultural association, applied to the Region for a new project regarding immigrants and mass-media.
- In Livorno, in 2003, Giolli applied for a project entitled "Facce Bianche Facce Nere Facciamo Informazione" ("Black Faces, White Faces – Lets get informed) that had a Legislative Theatre component.
- Giolli also contacted the Municipio XI, a sub-Local Council of the city of Rome that was experimenting with a "participatory budget" programme.
  A Media Research Centre in Modena was also contacted for data about stereotypes conveyed by the mass-media.
- Contacts with journalists, associations of, and for immigrants, political representatives, public administrators, were made at the beginning of 2004.

Organisation and Early Research

Once two of the three projects were approved, we started to get in touch with as many bodies as possible in Rovigo and Livorno, both from the public and non-profit sectors.
- We created a promoter group with journalists, volunteers, members of field organisations. (The response and participation in Livorno was less encouraging than in Rovigo).
- Contacts with immigrant organisations were reinforced to disseminate information on the project, because we wanted to have a mixed group of workshop participants.

We launched a publicity campaign to advertise for participants. Many people wanted to participate (especially in Livorno) so we held a selection based on motivation. Unfortunately in Rovigo immigrants participated only initially and the final group consisted for most of the time only of Italians. We conducted research on two local newspapers, to understand how they reported articles on immigration-related events. An analysis of the stereotypes emerging from the news and a study of the positive news from a magazine published by immigrants was also conducted. We tried to network with people, organisations and mass media as much as possible.

Start-up Workshop

We started a typical Theatre of the Oppressed workshop, with all the typical phases (warm ups, de-mechanisation, search for knots, creation of nuclei, cleaning the nuclei, rehearsing, transforming). In Rovigo we held regular 2-day intensive workshops; in Livorno we held 2 weekly courses in accordance with participants' needs. The content of the courses included techniques like Image Theatre, Forum Theatre, Newspaper Theatre and issues raised by participants.

Formation of the Theatre Group

The group grew into a theatre group in few months, in line with local and group conditions. Taking into account the specific group dynamics was helpful during this crucial phase. When a group is united it is possible to explore oppressive issues in a safe setting.

Open Rehearsal

Each group prepared skits taken from both the news and from daily life and presented them as Image Theatre, Forum Theatre, Newspaper Theatre, to groups of immigrants and Italians invited to an open rehearsal. In this way the audience acts as consultants on a specific topic.

The issues in Rovigo were:
- Young immigrants at school and their integration
- Queues of immigrants at the police station applying for temporary permission to stay in Italy
- Conflict in a Muslim family due to the father's tradition and daughter's new culture
- Clothes sold illegally by immigrants (an Italian shop was also discovered selling such clothes): different rights and responsibilities

The issues were different in Livorno:
- Police violence against foreigners in a local cafe and the indifference of the Italian witnesses

- The "chador" issue at school: the manipulation by mass media of the news
- Working illegally (under the table) and how to prevent accidents in such conditions

More so than in Rovigo, these stories came from immigrants' daily lives.

Interactive Performance

The theatre group met with a variety of audiences (Italians, Senegalese, Northern Africans, Eastern Europeans) to perform the work they had prepared.
- We used Image Theatre: an image of reality is presented and discussed through body language.
- We used a Forum-play: a conflictive story is presented and spect-actors intervene to try to solve it, and act out as alternative.
- We used Newspaper-Theatre: a true new story from mass media is presented and is revealed/contrasted through improvisation.

On the 6th March 2004, we held a large event where the three Forum plays prepared in Livorno were shown.

Chamber in the Street

We organised two Chambers: in Rovigo about "care givers" from Eastern Europe, and in Livorno about "illegal work".
- We invited specialists, associations, politicians, trade unions, political parties, public administrators and citizens.
- The issue was presented by a Forum play, then a workgroup divided the audience into groups to explore solutions that could be proposed to politicians.
- A legal assistant helped us translate the proposals into formal language.

We ritually held voting sessions for several proposals and wrote a list of recommendations, which were sent to those concerned at the City Hall.

On the 1st March 2004, a session of Chamber in the Street was organised in downtown Rovigo, with some counsellors assisting to explore the following issues:
- Economic exploitation of "badanti" (carers for elderly people, mainly from Eastern Europe)
- Conformist adaptation versus integration
- Contradiction: Italians demand that foreigners act within the law, while Italians themselves show how laws can be broken

141

- Lack of social policy
- Racism: some families don't want to employ black workers
- Mafia: "badanti" are organised by mafia-type organizations from their own cultures

The audience made three main proposals to send to the Local Council:
- Training sessions for "badanti" conducted in Communal Centres;
- To encourage networking between public and private bodies working in this area;
- Financial assistance to families who legalized the immigration status of "badanti".

Evaluation and Documentation

In June 2004, we held a seminar in Livorno to reflect on how to evaluate the Forum plays' impact. In collaboration with a specialised organisation, we drew up a questionnaire to use as a pre- and post-test, that would be given to audiences during the Forum Theatre sessions. These were distributed and collected and a team screened them for relevant outputs. A brochure and a video were planned and prepared to publicise the experience in other towns and cities; the entire process was documented and this gave added value to the daily work. In March 2005 we also prepared a seminar with Peter Mayo, University of Malta, and invited some local organisations, to reflect on citizenship, Legislative Theatre and participation within the framework of Paulo Freire's ideas.

Perspectives

In Livorno the 3 groups were more stable and united, so it was decided to continue with the Theatre of the Oppressed, to explore other problems such as drugs and violence.
- It was planned for several shows to be performed to a variety of audiences and a new project regarding immigration was planned in Livorno and presented to the Provincial Administration.

In Rovigo a second Chamber in the Street further explored the "badanti" issue, and a roundtable with local journalists was planned to discuss the influence of mass media on stereotypes.

Exemplary Working Instructions

1) Theme: developing an experience of Legislative Theatre with immigrants

2) Overall Objective: forming groups of immigrants to organize this process. At the end of this unit the participants should have the experience to form a process of Legislative Theatre with immigrants.

3) Material and Media: flipchart, paper, markers, digital camera, video camera, CD player, newspapers, props and various objects for improvisation, stage design, lighting.

4) Conducting the Unit:
The following theme requires an introduction:

Every time we try to reduce reality, or experience according to a plan we are, according to Watzlawick, creating a map, and as he says "a map is not the territory!".

- Therefore, what we are writing now is a selection of ideas, viewed from our relative and particular point of view.
- Moreover, the tendency to have recipes to solve any problem is almost culturally instilled into us, and the technological culture in which we are now immersed convinces us that human behaviour is predictable to a large extent – if one simply uses the right technology.
  This epistemological vision is criticised by Edgar Morin, and by the "approach of complexity": from this point of view, human life has an inherent amount of unpredictability, connected to the essential subjectivity of humans.
- Nor is human behaviour predictable under a stimulus-response connection as some psychological approaches claim.

What do these reflections mean for our project?

1) The main thing from our perspective is to be aware that when working with people, a lot of attention must be given to what is actually happening; a lot of intuition and creativity is required in order to have a direction and an

objective, but it is also necessary to have the ability to change direction if necessary.
2) Interpretation-free observation, as much as possible, is another important tool that we use in our projects; in this way we can learn from reality and share our observations with the work team, not to make judgements, but rather to further understand and explore more deeply.
3) By valuing the so-called "mistake, error, unexpected reaction" we can keep our actions closely linked to reality and create a better resonance in the group. Sometimes what we propose brings forth unexpected reactions and this can either be seen as a mistake or as a resource.
4) It is also important to remain objective and calm if we do not achieve our goals, knowing that something interesting, or a new discovery is taking place.

Therefore the following indicators serve to orient our actions and practices, but do not claim to be always valid; there are too many factors at play in human beings, too much complexity and subjectivity, which makes human behaviour unpredictable despite supposedly infallible technology.

Particularly Successful Segments

A really good moment during the project was in Rovigo, where we were able to analyse all the articles about immigration from two main local newspapers, which had been collected by a journalist over a period of three months. The emotional impact was significant when we divided the articles into two categories: positive news and negative news; not surprisingly we saw that the positive articles were few, but some of these were really surprising, like being proud that immigrants were not learning Italian but rather our "Veneto" dialect, and so this tradition is being kept alive thanks to them. Reading negative articles led us immediately into the realm of stereotypes: it was so obvious, and we laughed a lot reading an article about a crime story that was made more dramatic as each day passed. I think the group were very quickly made aware of just how much the mass media can manipulate information.

An important and emotionally touching moment in Livorno happened when the group of actors, mainly foreigners, were acting out a scene concerning an

	Role Allocation (amongst facilitators)	Time Structure	Content	Background and reasons	Final Objective
Open rehearsal	One observes and writes what emerges from the interaction, one to video the proceedings, one leads the interaction as Joker	3 hours: 0,5 h. warming up 0,5 h. presentation of one scene 1,5 h. debate 0,5 h. closing	In this case the scene was about the "badanti" articulated in three different situations. Technique: ▮ Warming-up: simple game like «good evening», «circle and cross» ▮ Presentation + Debate: constructive Forum and then debate ▮ Closing : ritual game like «The sentence repeated».	The audience is asked to act as consultants, for a variety of reasons: to clarify the scene, to involve them further, to increase information for actors. Reasons for exercises, step by step: ▮ to create atmosphere and a connection between the audience and actors; ▮ to collect ideas from the audience in an active way; ▮ to strengthen the relationship.	To have a clear story for public performance
Chamber in the street	One as Joker, one documents	6 hours: 0,5 warming up and introduction 2 hrs. Forum play 2 hrs. work-group 1 h. plenary session for proposals 0,5 h. closing	In Livorno the issue was illegal work and safety. Technique: ▮ warming-up exercises like "people to people" ▮ Forum Theatre ▮ brainstorming ▮ simulation of a voting in a City Hall	The Chamber is a place where we express our citizenship, starting from a analysis of the problem, the audience makes proposals to be sent to the City Hall. Reasons for exercises, step by step: ▮ to prepare people to enter the process, creating a mutual knowledge ▮ to collect solutions and proposals ▮ to add more ideas ▮ to prepare a real event and motivate.	To approve some proposal so that migrant working conditions are improved.

accident at work, and all the bad consequences for a worker working illegally. The audience were strongly affected by this scene, and I guess they realised immediately how difficult such situations can be for immigrants, as they made the shift from intellectual knowledge to "sympathy" to express it in Boal's terms.

Target Groups: Aims and Competencies

Competencies of the Target Group

1 Competencies: Aesthetics

The project itself can result in an increased use of theatrical expressive elements (movement, gesture, voice, rhythm, imagination, creativity, expression, etc.), which can be transferred into the daily lives of participants. As Boal says, "being human is theatre", and that became increasingly clear the more we all worked together. Every skill underwent great or small improvements and people reclaimed forgotten elements of their lives. Exploring creativity in its general sense as a result of immersion in theatre is useful, especially in these current times where people are often required to adapt themselves to immediate and significant changes.

2 Competencies: Ethics

The experience can create a deeper awareness of the oppressive situations in which some live, increases the sense of solidarity for victims and a higher sensitivity to power relationships within daily life. The solidarity between participants in the Livorno project definitely increased.

3 Competencies: Action

People often become more active in everyday relationships both at a micro and macro level. Also, certain knowledge about theatre is a possible outcome for participants. Personal development (self-esteem, affirmation, enrichment of social life, enrichment of emotional life, attention to individuals and / or the group, empowerment of the individual and / or the group) of the participants, can improve the quality of their lives (new challenges, new tasks, new social contacts, new jobs, new skills and knowledge). In this sense the project works towards social inclusion and against racism and discrimination.

4 Competencies: Orientation and Field-Related Knowledge

After the project both the people participating, and the audiences, will be more aware of specific topics (migration, homelessness or others). Hopefully the network developed with institutions and organisations during the project will be useful for participants for future contacts and requirements. In general, the project should create a deeper knowledge of the issue the group has dealt with, as well as the groups and territory affected by the project.

5 Competencies: Interculturalism

The workshops and the extended project, which include the Forum, field research, meetings, etc. give the participants a chance to develop intercultural sensitivity. The work within the workshop tends to de-construct stereotypes by encouraging people to work together, to live a common experience, to have a common goal or "super objective". The Forum, which shows a section of life from the migrants' point of view, also gives participants and the audience a deeper consciousness.

6 Competencies: Gender

Where it is possible, the experience of men and women working together leads to a different perception of the opposite gender. When gender issues are explored on stage both the actors and the audience develop a deeper awareness during the process.

Goals of Participating Institutions

We had four levels:

Local Administration

In Rovigo, the City Hall was indifferent to the project, whereas the Province supported it. The target was the social inclusion of "badanti" into the local area so as to avoid their exploitation and conflict between Italians and Eastern Europeans. In Livorno the Province limited itself to approving the project so as to comply with European Union requirements.

Non-profit-oriented Associations

In both cities their objectives were social inclusion and action against racism. They participated in workshops and resulting activities, facilitating contact with the wider population.

Migrant Associations

They were in general more interested in their members' practical needs and were weary of being invited to work with others; amazingly the prejudice that one community can hold towards another is often so strong that it is extremely difficult to overcome.

The Mass-media

Some individuals were involved and wanted to help disseminate the correct information, but generally speaking the local mass-media continued portraying the picture of migration which is mostly based on criminal events and fear.

Evaluation and Reflection

In short, what is Legislative Theatre?
- A process where one tries to connect civil society and Public Administration, in order to produce new laws
- A virtuous circle of continuous communication between citizens and institutions to increase participation and control from the bottom up
- A hypothesis of "transitive democracy", not direct, not delegated, where people use their own power every day and not just for elections

Based on these ideas, we started to experiment with what happens when one tries to apply this to reality.

Our provisional results, outputs and reflections are as follows:

1. A Legislative Theatre experience can be adapted with less conditions than Boal's if one has a strong organisation, plenty of time, connection with the territory, and a network of collaborators. Boal was simultaneously a politician and a theatre practitioner in Rio de Janeiro for 4 years; it was a unique situation, but it doesn't prevent theatre being performed under different circumstances.
2. It is difficult to involve immigrants because they are pressured by the need to job search, by legal issues, distrust, lack of free time, etc.
3. A Body or a Movement that supports the process is important so that people are not deluded about the results.
4. It is necessary to plan a strategy to overcome the competition, suspicion and distrust between organisations and institutions, and to understand how to use the mass media positively, and what issues are critical in the given territory.
5. The theatre ritual and atmosphere can help the people's participation because the experts' power of speech is removed, and speech and expression is democratized.
6. It is important to think about how to give continuity to the process so that it is possible to see some results and in doing so, strengthen the process.

But this experience can be accompanied by risks and doubts that at the moment are taken from different experiences of Legislative Theatre, or hypothetical situations that we can imagine could happen:
Right-wing popular movements such as "Lega Nord" in Italy can benefit from this approach, but by expressing regressive proposals instead of progressive. Society is not good, when institutions are *bad*! One should be careful when a strong, racist popular movement exists, so that they do not adopt and manipulate the Legislative Theatre process.

The risk arises of confusing theatre space with the real world:

- The hypothesis of "metaxis" – Boal opposes Aristotelian "catharsis" to "metaxis", which simultaneously belongs to two worlds, theatre and reality – persuades people to transform themselves and the world, starting by transforming in the theatre context; metaxis works if there is enough distance between the two realities, "aesthetic space" and "daily life". What happens when this space is reduced because Legislative Theatre is closer to politics and Institutions? Is theatre, a marginalized art, powerful enough to compete with such a strong power? What are the conditions that make it possible to bring the two worlds closer? Political culture is stronger than theatre. Is it useful to manipulate theatre towards politics and institutional levels?

We must be careful to keep the power of theatre at the centre. There is a risk that the process might shift into politics and lose its theatrical dimension.

How do we involve marginalized groups such as immigrants in the process when they have important basic needs to contend with?

External conditions influence the group (e.g. finding a job can reduce the motivation to be involved).

- The English Cardboard Citizens group pay actors in order to keep up their motivation despite economic factors; this choice can be useful for the homeless, but in our experience it is not enough for immigrants, because they are looking for well paid work; consequently their presence at the workshops is intermittent. We have to study how to facilitate people's participation, and question whether the typical workshop session is the right one for our target group; in Austria, for instance, a meeting with more informal time and a communal lunch break were added to the process and it worked.

Besides these issues we must consider the effect of creating an illusion; people are invited to participate in theatre, or perhaps a tour, and then the project finishes and the people involved go back to reality; the lights are turned off but every person remains with his / her hopes, desires, dreams. How do we help them find the strength to face that?

Which structure-framework is needed for legislative theatre?

One possible pattern is:

- A permanent weekly workshop: this offers people a place to meet each other, creates confidence and trust, allows them to get a taste of the work without too much involvement, offers a regular reference point in their daily life, and the chance to get to know new people, etc. To have an open space with no strict rules seems to be important for homeless people and also fits in well with African cultures.

Depending on the case in hand, it could be important to vary the classic workshop, for instance adding some usual activity like sharing a meal together. This informal moment helps to create a pleasant group atmosphere and does not separate theatre practitioners from the participants.

- Once a year a Power Play, that is an intensive week where burning issues are worked on by the group, using interviews with people not participating in the workshop. This idea comes from David Diamond and it is a moment where the community gathers to focus attention on what is to be changed; the task is to collect ideas about problems within the community, in a soft theatrical way, so that even people, who may be afraid of theatre, can contribute.

This phase can also be useful to involve the entire community in the play construction, so that every possible individual has the chance to give his / her contribution. It is important not to focus only on the small workshop group, because they participants probably do not fully represent the worlds of the homeless or immigrants or other disadvantaged groups.

- Selection of a group of actors that want to perform; not all people want to act, even if they enjoy acting in workshop groups or the Power Play. Some are afraid or simply not interested. Other people like to improvise, act, and make a show. So we decide together who will be playing, taking into account specific talents (music, dance, singing, painting…); but how are they selected and with what criteria?

How to connect with other groups, bodies, institutions?

We do not work in an empty social space; other groups and Institutions are working with us; it is crucial to get in touch with as many organisations as possible, for many reasons:
- to avoid competition and a waste of time and energy;
- to benefit from information, connections, alliances, resources and opportunities;
- to signal the importance of the project;
- to create a network to sustain the process.

How do we deal with the competition between organisations?

It is often the case that people involved in different organisations are not used to working together, and worse, they accuse each other of not doing good work, or they are competing for resources, or they have different approaches to the same problem. With the Italian experience it was clear that contacting associations of immigrants was difficult because of this competition. Also, within the same ethnic community it may be that people are divided by religious or political affiliations or they may just be following a "guru". So it is important make sure that all sides are contacted, even if it happens that later on the two sides are not able to work together. It is easier with groups without formal structures as is often the case with the homeless, but, on the other hand, if they are organised, it can facilitate the contact and trust.

If there is not a sympathetic politician available how should the legislative theatre be managed?

What are the conditions of the process that may deceive people into thinking that they are being listened to or that they have power?
- The lack of an involved politician can block the process, because there is no one from within to present the proposals to the Local Council. We suppose that this is not a "sine qua non" requirement but to have someone from inside the target institution is of course always a powerful card.

On the other hand, we believe that it is possible to get the attention of politicians step by step; sometimes just starting the process by involving the mass-media, receives political attention for the process. In Austria they started without political support but succeeded in performing at the City Hall, and gained a lot of mass media attention.

How do we target organized civil bodies or individuals?

We have yet to solve this dilemma.
- In Boal's work organised groups like black students, landless peasants, homosexuals, and so on were targeted.
- This choice reflects the idea that a homogeneous group is better able to express their own needs, making the work less complex. On the other hand,

what about individuals that are not members of a group, like most of our western citizens?

Our identity is not related to a unique social role but constructed from a variety of social environments.

- We think it is better to start with groups if they already exist, but at the same time analysing the social networks that we are going to work with and the stability and relevance of groups we choose to involve.

Another aspect is how to choose the target groups? Do we have to select them for their political ideology, or their social relevance, or the mutual pleasure of working together, or do we use other criteria?

- We pre-suppose that there is not an answer for every situation, so we should just carefully consider the possible choices.
- Moreover, we must address the question concerning the presence of popular conservative movements. They may be popular, but should we involve them in the process or not? How do we prevent them from manipulating the process? To date we have not experienced this problem but if we were to work in some areas where the "Lega Nord" (a racist movement that wants to separate the North of Italy from the South) has a strong following. How would we handle possible requests for repressive, conservative or racist laws?

We believe that our role as Giolli and as theatre leaders in general is governed by values, that is, we are not politically or ethically neutral; we all have values and points of view, even if we do not declare them or are aware of them.

- Therefore, we should strongly stick to our values and refuse to be manipulated as soon as we feel that there is that risk, no matter from which side that pressure originates.

This analysis should be further explored for the entire context we are working within, the so-called "theatre work in social fields".

Psychosocial and theatrical competencies are required

Social workers are often naive; they deal with the consequences of political decisions but they don't want to be political!

- To implement a process like Legislative Theatre requires not only theatrical competencies. This doesn't mean that one should feel omnipotent, but it suggests that a team of people specialised in different fields and conscious of this complexity is required.

- This is useful when it comes to negotiating with groups, planning social action, dealing with politicians and being aware of which institutions one should be addressing, etc.

With the Legislative Theatre it is of special importance to have a legal expert who is able to translate popular proposals into legalese, is familiar with existing legislation and regulations in the area which needs intervention, and who understands just how far a proposal can be taken.

The importance of documenting the intervention

Documentation of the work is useful in many ways: one reason is the ability to produce materials at a later date in support of the project, or being able to stimulate people who are marginally involved by organising for example, a photo exhibition or a video presentation, or giving CD-ROM to associations that can hold debates on the issues presented.

Moreover, the play that represents the key problem can be modified step by step if one has records of what happened during the public Forum session; in this way the theatre scene becomes more and more relevant to the discussion of the problem at hand.

The key role of mass media

If your work can attract political attention it is also due to the management of mass media. This point is often underestimated by theatre practitioners, but if one succeeds in getting media attention, the project will have greater impact, mainly because it will stimulate attention to the requests at a political level. In Italy we tried to involve journalists in Rovigo through a research on "immigration and media" and a final roundtable to evaluate the project's impact. Furthermore, we asked for their collaboration in the future, to give more rich, deep and detailed information to citizens.

The attention of journalists does not come free of any agenda: a lot of interest and a debt to the so-called "public opinion trends" can interfere significantly with the image they will portray of your work. Therefore, to capture the attention in the correct way is one of the fundamental challenges for an effective project. The sector is too large and varies from country to

country, from big cities to small ones, etc. so it is impossible to offer further suggestions here.
- In our experience it was helpful talking to a journalist friend who explained how one should move in this complicated and delicate sector.

The **evaluation** was planned at different levels in order to cross-reference the results and assess both the outcomes and the process.
- We include four aspects that we evaluated:

The Participants' Perspective

During workshops with participants, we regularly evaluated the process using active exercises where people are asked to express their level of satisfaction with activities, about whether their lives had been enriched, about their integration into the group, new social contact with other participants and about their sense of empowerment. Moreover we crosschecked these affirmations with observations during the process, by apprentices and other workshop leaders. More or less every 1-2 months participants were interviewed by an external person about their level of satisfaction with the project and the critical points generated by previous observations and reports from workshop leaders. We also verified whether the working conditions were favourable or not: the room, the schedule, attention to special needs, safety, overall organisation; evaluation was done at the end of every session by active techniques encouraging speech and action.
- The results were generally positive, except with regard to the schedule and accommodation for some people coming from outside of the city.

The Perspective of External Institutions

We had two meetings with the institutions and associations supporting the project, with volunteers, associations of immigrants, a Peace Education Centre, some journalists, and some interested individuals.
- We discussed the outcomes and changes resulting from the project in the middle and end of the process.

Generally speaking there was a lack of participation from immigrants associations in both towns, which was more significant in Rovigo. Journalists,

volunteers and some associations from Rovigo gathered together and showed their appreciation of the project, even if only the journalists saw a benefit form this project in terms of clarifying their responsibility towards constructing a social perception of immigration.
- Some representatives from Institutions said the work had favoured social inclusion thanks to the positive relationships created within the groups, which in three out of four cases were ethnically mixed.

The performances in Rovigo and Livorno were well attended which was seen as an inclusive action, and a move towards opening up discussions about sensative issues, usually not discussed publicly.

General External Perspective

In each case the audiences appreciated the performances of the Forum-play and the Chamber in the Street.
- Observations from third parties during the performance, and a double questionnaire (given to the spectators at the beginning and the end of the performances) show evidence of this point of view.

In Rovigo the local press paid attention to what was going on and portrayed a positive, if slightly superficial image of the project.
- In Livorno, on the contrary, there was more indifference and we didn't succeed in engaging the press.
- Experts in the field appreciated the accuracy of the performance about illegal work, which was shown in Livorno.

For the next project, that we are applying for, we would like to have more feedback about the quality of the artistic performances, and the quality of the inclusion process.

Project Leaders' Perspective

By observing and asking participants and workshop leaders, the project director verified that there was an improvement in the emotional lives, integration of the group, as well as individual empowerment. The final discussions also confirmed that new contacts had been made between colleagues.
- There is no doubt that participants were satisfied, except for some of the first group in Livorno but only during the initial phases of the process. The

opportunity for people to get to know others and express themselves in a "theatre setting" both internally and in front of the public, were the most appreciated aspects of the project.

The artistic quality of the work was not so good, especially in Livorno due to sporadic participation, mainly by immigrants; as a result some actors had to be replaced by colleagues just before the public performance.

- The process was socially inclusive, thanks to the ethnically mixed groups. This generated mutual exchanges and increased awareness of others. Italians, especially, became more aware of immigrant living conditions.

The final product was inclusive in that audiences were put in touch with immigrants, their specific problems and points of view.

- The working conditions were generally good, except for some noise outside the Livorno work room; the scheduling in one case in four was not considered good: the time available for work was too compressed.

Foreigners with language difficulties may have felt excluded and not sufficiently supported by mediators or volunteers resulting in a lack of willingness to attend. The project as a whole was too complex to be fully understood even if parts of it were clear enough; as a result we cannot say that everybody fully understood what we were doing step by step.

The tools applied were:
- Active theatre techniques (that make the group's intentions immediately visible);
- Interviews (by telephone, face to face, and in groups);
- Group discussions;
- Questionnaires (at the end of the process to participants and during the Forum-play to the audience);
- Observations (made by workshop leaders, third parties and apprentices).

During the project we held bi-monthly meetings to evaluate the involvement of immigrant associations, the planning timetable, and to monitor the process within the group and the territory. This component was crucial to keeping the project linked to reality; the effort of regular attendance at these meetings showed in the results, and the opportunity to change the direction of the process at any time.

The effects of the project varied at different levels:
- Participants showed a general satisfaction with the group, the experience, the Forum, and the new relationships; on a personal level many of them felt

they had improved self-esteem, confidence, expression and communication skills; new relationships were established among Italians and immigrants.

- Aesthetical, ethical and action-related competencies were strengthened, improved and stimulated. Some felt that their quality of life had changed and improved. At the group level, a sense of teamwork was experienced, especially in Livorno. The group felt they were more aware of their rights, and felt more empowered both as individuals and as a group.

- Associations: scarce collaboration from immigrant associations; this was true for both Livorno and Rovigo, due to the competition between several associations in Livorno, community leadership resistance to the project, and, in Rovigo, a lack of organisations willing to be contacted.

- Political context: there was a general lack of interest from politicians; this was experienced in both cities; although they were repeatedly invited, they didn't attend.

- Civil participation: attention was given to the issues of immigration, illegal work and stereotypes; working for rights was increased by the project and gave people the strength and clarity to reclaim these rights. Empowerment and participation were strengthened and could be a basis for further interventions.

- Institutional level: there was little involvement, in Livorno even though it is locally governed by the left, and in Rovigo because they were politically against this project. The Provinces were in favour, but in essence this was only true of Rovigo.

- Journalists and media: in Rovigo there were some journalists who entered into the process, but generally the impact on the mass-media was inconsiderable.

- Territory: the audiences appreciated the plays and enthusiastically debated the issues; new ideas emerged together with increased awareness of the problems. We don't know exactly what the outcomes were after the play. According to Boal we should expect some changes to their daily actions.

Michael Wrentschur assisted by Armin Ruckerbauer and Martin Vieregg

Module Project: "Legislative Theatre with Homeless People"

The legislative theatre project with homeless people in Graz took place between May 2002 and April 2004 within the framework of the socio-cultural theatre project wohnungs / los / theatern, which has already been reported on elsewhere (Ruckerbauer / Wrentschur 2004). The following should ideally be achieved by means of the theatre work: the improvement of the situation of homeless people and the creation of new living spaces in personal as well as in public / political areas, i.e. through the process of theatre work to encourage joint creativity, an increase in self-worth, a broadening of social competencies, the ability to cope with problems and the capacity to act, and, with the help of Forum Theatre, to strengthen the voices of the homeless and of socially marginalized groups and to heighten the perception of the needs and interests of the homeless both in the population and in those who are politically responsible.

As described elsewhere (Ruckerbauer /Wrentschur 2004, p. 200), everyday culture and life experiences are regarded as fundamental to the artistic process in the project wohnungs/los/theatern. Existential experiences of the human being and of everyday culture are transformed with the help of the art of the theatre and take effect socially. The theatre work is based on the one hand on methods of motion and improvisation theatre and on the other hand on principles and methods of the Theatre of the Oppressed (Mazzini / Wrentschur 2004). The connection between aesthetic and social demands is important; the theatre work is understood to a high degree as an artistic and social process of investigation on the part of the participants and those affected and thereby ensures to a high degree the involvement and the cooperation of the participants.

Important principles and positions for theatre work arise out of the circumstance that the directors view themselves as creators of possibilities for play. They offer theatrical means and "tools", which the members of the group employ creatively to give expression and theatrical form to essential themes and matters of concern. This requires that participation is of a voluntary nature and is based on a readiness to bring one's own practical knowledge and experience to the project. Nevertheless, in order to guarantee the continuity, an employment contract stipulated the amount of payment for rehearsals and performances for those participating.

In accordance with legislative theatre, the project moved through many stages (see preface) and ended in a performance in the Graz City Hall with the proclamation and handover of matters of concern, demands, and suggestions from the homeless to the politicians responsible for the city of Graz.

In the following we give a detailed outline of the background, the basic conditions, the individual stages, and the methods of working.

How the Project Progressed

Background and Basic Conditions

Legislative theatre is a complex form of artistic intervention as it occurs not only in social but also in political contexts. In order to succeed, a range of basic conditions are necessary: for the purposes of project management competence and field competence, it is essential to adapt oneself to the relevant social and political structures, not only as regards the situation of the homeless in Graz but also in relation to networking with relevant institutions and the composition of the group.

Homelessness in Graz

In Graz, a city with a little less than 250.000 inhabitants, 1000 - 2000 people on average are homeless each month. The majority of them are accommodated in homes for refugees or facilities for homeless people. The number is also rising because of increasing unemployment. 700 beds are available in 23 institutions. It is a declared goal of the city of Graz that no one should involuntarily have to sleep on the street, yet the facilities are always overcrowded and / or the personnel resources are limited. Moreover, there are too few places for the mentally ill and, particularly, aggressive people. Furthermore, reintegration into society seems difficult; along with the strained situation on the housing market, the stigmatization of being homeless brings with it a series of barriers to accessing agencies and the housing and labour market (Ohnmacht et al. 2004, p. 6 - 11).

Cooperating with Partners and Networking

Co-operations exist with the City of Graz Men's Hostel (Männerwohnheim der Stadt Graz), the City of Graz Women's Hostel (Frauenwohnheim der Stadt Graz), Caritas (Ressidorf, Team on, Arche 38), Vinzidorf, the Federal Association for Aid for the Homeless of Austria (Bundesarbeitsgemeinschaft für Wohnungslosenhilfe Österreich, BAWO), the ETC – European Training Centre for Human Rights and the University of Graz Institute for Educational Science. These cooperating partners were very important in the course of the project. Institutions made it easier to establish contacts and took over in part certain responsibilities: the central demands and suggestions were worked on with the BAWO; the ETC was available for all legal questions; the university worked on a thesis with the accompanying research.

Composition of the Group

The group consisted originally of men and women, who had become homeless for very different reasons. They were all between 20 and 60 years old and from Austria. They came to the project from relevant facilities. In the meantime, a large number of the cast have moved back into homes of their own. The highest number of participants at any given time was 16; after the first performance, the group number diminished until a core group of 6 - 8 people remained.

As we have described elsewhere (Ruckerbauer / Wrentschur 2004, p. 202ff), despite the variability in reasons for homelessness, several similarities in the respective psychosocial situations as well as in practical experiences with governmental agencies, institutions, family, friends, and society became apparent during the course of the project. The "slipping down" on the social scale connected with stigmatization, prejudice, isolation, and social exclusion causes feelings of shame and failure as well as a high degree of sensitivity and vulnerability. Crisis situations can crop up abruptly, which make it difficult or impossible to participate in the process of the theatre work. All this "is again and again a heavy burden for the group work which demands much flexibility, tact and sensitivity ... It is helpful on the one hand to accept the fragility and on the other hand to take advantage of the help from the people providing support from the respective facilities, to network and consult with them" (see p. 204).

Processes and Steps of Legislative Theatre Work

The legislative theatre developed by Boal in Rio de Janeiro was characterized by the fact that those responsible politically were a part of this process. The sequence of the process developed there (Boal 1999, p. 37ff.) served as a model for the Graz project, which had to be adapted to local conditions. Unlike in Rio de Janeiro, we had to establish contact from the outside with the politically responsible and convince them of our project. The essential steps and stages are summarized briefly below in order to give an overview of the almost two-year-long process, accompanied by brief assessments, aphorisms and personal testimonies.

Preliminary Phase: Workshop and Public Exhibition

Preliminary and conceptual work for the project had already begun at the end of 1999 and in late autumn 2000 led to "Theatern I", a three-day-long theatre workshop with homeless people from the men's hostel in Graz. Trust, sensitivity, movement and expression exercises, improvised everyday scenes and communal meals constituted the content. With the agreement of the participants, the workshop was documented in photographs. A photography exhibition entitled "Eh schon wissen" was held in April 2001 in the Graz City Hall Gallery on the basis of photos created in the course of this first workshop. An interested audience could perceive the expressiveness of the actors and the particular authenticity and originality of the people, which was conveyed through the images. This led to an effort by the politically responsible who were present to make resources available for the project.

Result

Two important outcomes of this preliminary phase consisted of the unexpectedly great desire to act and the creative involvement of the participants as well as the important decision in this early stage to integrate the public through the artistic medium of photography. Both prepared the ground for the continuation of this project.

Establishing Contact with Institutions and the Kick-off Workshop

After the pledge of aid in summer of 2002, contacts were renewed with facilities for the homeless at the level of management and with the people looking after the homeless, and direct contact was made with those affected. The project and theatre work were thus introduced and the kick-off workshop, which took place soon after, was promoted. It began with a meeting for everyone (the people affected plus the people looking after them) in a cafe, a renewed presentation of the idea and of the rules of the game for theatre work, explanations regarding the project and a visit to the rehearsal space. Group games, exercises for rhythm and expression, sensitivity-building exercises, the creation of sculptures and images and scenes and a "Miniforumtheater" on the theme of "What outrages you?" formed the content of the workshop, which ended with a feedback session and a preview. It became clear at this point which of the participants wanted to continue and what the schedule for how to proceed should be.

Result

In this phase it was completely essential to create an appropriate framework with good care and provision, whereby the participants felt they were in good hands and could make contact with us and with the work. In addition, a gender-specific approach proved helpful: due to the initial low involvement of women, we held another kick-off workshop in the City of Graz Women's Hostel, which caused the group to grow. Furthermore, it was interesting that during this workshop images and scenes, which would occur again and again emerged from the question "What outrages you?".

Formation of the Theatre Group with Regular Theatre Work and the First Public Appearance

In the ensuing period the group worked once a week for 2 - 3 hours. For a time it was run as an open group with consequent fluctuations. This stimulated the group but then increasingly made the group process more difficult: for those who attended regularly, the theatre work became more and more natural, whereas the newcomers were difficult to integrate because they had more trouble finding themselves in the process. Furthermore, it turned out that many participants were overtaxed by their physical or psychological problems.

Eventually the group was "closed" to include only those who could make a binding commitment. They signed contracts and received an expenses allowance from then on for sustained participation.

After the group had existed for two months, they prepared for the first presentation in a renowned "Off Theater", which took place the week before Christmas. It was based on voluntary participation. The concept involved exercises known to the group such as different kinds of walking, status and encounter exercises as well as improvised tableaux. Two short scenes - "Booted out of the family" and "Flat-hunting" - were presented, in which the audience participation was possible.

Result

The presentation led to an active interest on the part of those affected and institutions; however, the group divided in half as a result. Those who acted were strengthened by the presentation; they wanted to continue. For others, it became clear that they didn't want to express or position themselves publicly.

Intensification of the Theatre Work and the Development of Performance Pieces

In the next phase, the theatre training intensified for the remaining group members with an emphasis on expression, body and ensemble work, to which exercises and techniques from Ruth Zaporah's "Action Theatre" (2005) in particular were applied. Stage presence, the continuity of the play and ensemble acting were thus intended to be developed and strengthened.

Research was carried out parallel to this: questionnaire interviews with homeless people concerning problems and possible solutions to homelessness in Graz were conducted by members of the group. On the basis of the results of this research and the experiences of the members of the group, the most important themes and problematic areas (for example, "being given the run-around," administrative procedures, problems with the job centre, discrimination, no reasonably priced flats, etc.) were determined; images and scenes were consequently improvised around these topics.

From the material for scenes developed during improvisation, a sequence of events was jointly developed; the group autonomously established the order of the scenes, which portray the "downward spiral" that homeless people can fall into. Intensive work on the roles and rehearsals followed the development of the sequence of the scenes.

Work was carried out on the formulation of a declaration of rights for homeless people and an improvement of their situation, which was consequently directed toward politicians in Graz. The declaration was a result both of research among the homeless and of the group process in which they shared problems, experiences of oppression, and wishes and ideas concerning change.

Result

The sustained theatre work in the remaining group paid off. Besides developing theatrical abilities, confidence and the ability to give expression to difficult themes and problems gradually grew. The research conducted by the participants and its results were always a valuable help for the development of scenes and images. The connection to the people affected and to their concerns was strengthened by this.

Performance Concept

The performance concept for "Nobody is perfect" reflected the social and aesthetic process of the group. A dramaturgy was developed which promoted the possibilities for audience participation.

In the first part, the focus is on the group itself. When the lights come up, they are standing in a line at a "safe distance" from the audience. A space is opened for reciprocal projections: who are the people on stage / in the auditorium? I know that the actors are homeless. What does that mean for me? After the group turn their backs to the audience, the actors gradually turn around one by one, introduce themselves and make a short statement. Then they begin to move and encounter each other in positions of varying status. They begin with improvised tableaux and, by means of movement, voice, and language, make statements about the "inequality" between people, about privileges, reasons for homelessness, their feelings, the experience of falling and "being completely at the bottom", giving rise to emotional images tinged with (self-)irony and a generous helping of sarcasm.

In the second part, short everyday scenes are shown: what do homeless people experience in Graz? The sequence of scenes begins with someone being thrown out of an apartment, a night outdoors, and the subsequent search for help from family, friends, government agencies and institutions. This becomes difficult: it is connected to the experience of meeting with disapproval, bureaucratic barriers, stigmatization and discrimination, above all in relation to the attempt to reintegrate into the housing and labour market. The sequence of scenes has the character of a vicious circle, a spiral, which seems to lead down into poverty, exclusion, and eventually the compulsion to accept precarious and unacceptable job opportunities.

In the third phase, the audience is invited to take part in the play according to the rules of forum theatre and to try out changes. The role of the homeless can be transfromed in connection to the question of how it is possible to opt out of this cycle. Where do individual possibilities for action exist and / or where are structural changes necessary?

In conclusion, suggestions about how to improve the situation of homeless people in Graz are proclaimed by the actors and distributed to the audience to be signed. One of the songs composed by the group goes like this:
> A Überdosis Lose
> It's a hard way
> It's our way
> Feel free...!!

Result

The exciting thing about the development of the concept of performance was that it consisted almost exclusively of material regarding the content and the scenes which the group had developed up to that point by itself, and that had been put together dramaturgically by the facilitators. An extremely high degree not only of authenticity but also of participation was thereby created, both forming a basis for close identification with that which was portrayed.

Interactive Performances

The interactive performances were an essential component of the Legislative Theatre process. Between December 2002 and March 2004, "Nobody is perfect" was shown in a theatre of the Off-Scene (uniT-Container), in institutions for homeless people, and for members of Forum Wohnen. The audience was invited to participate and to engage in a discussion.

The concept for the performance was developed on an on-going basis, improved upon, and shaped in accordance with the responses to the performances and the discussions in the group. In part, new sequences and scenes were created; others were discarded. Essential to this stage was the continuous documentation of audience participation, suggested solutions, and contributions to the discussion at each performance.

Result

At all performances, the mixed audience participated with commitment, which led to a greater readiness for dialogue about the living situation of homeless people. The performances revealed very soon which structural and political changes are necessary and where individual scope for action is possible. In addition, they enormously strengthened the self-confidence of the actors, who themselves were partly surprised at the power and emotion of their work and who were very pleased about the involvement of the audience.

Reflection and Formulation of Policy Suggestions

At the end of the series of performances, all audience participation, the ideas for solutions and suggestions of the audience were examined. The most important results were summarized and discussed in the group. "Can general 'desires' be found in the suggestions? Which ideas can be helpful in 'real' life?" From these, a range of suggestions and demands for the improvement of the situation of homeless people were discussed, formulated, and internally ranked according to their importance.

At the same time, contact was established with the people carrying out a study commissioned by the city of Graz on homelessness and help for the homeless (Ohnmacht et.al 2004). In a joint workshop, the results of the study and the Legislative Theatre process as well as the demands and matters of concern regarding policies were presented, compared and discussed by the authors of the study, the members of the group and members of Forum Wohnen. Contacts with politicians were also cultivated, as well as exchanges and discussions with jurists from the European Training Centre for Human Rights at the University of Graz, who screened the proposals for their legal content and references and highlighted accordingly the relevant legal material and political fora.

Result

Those affected had in the course of the theatre process become experts. The aesthetic process led to a political one and enabled the participants to articulate their matters for concern and demands clearly and comprehensibly. They became active participants in a process whereby those affected, those providing care, researchers, and the political agents developed suggestions for improving help for the homeless.

Performance in the Graz City Hall

At the end of March 2004, the results, demands, and suggestions emerging from the study and the Legislative Theatre process were finally all presented together in the Graz City Hall. The play was also performed interactively for the relevant city and local council members and representatives from government agencies and NGOs.
The suggestions and demands were very symbolically read out loud from the seat of the city government; the signed declarations were handed over to the relevant city politicians and were then discussed in the chamber.

Result

As a result of the Legislative Theatre process, a dialogue was established between those affected and those who make the decisions. The members of the group represented themselves and their matters for concern impressively and were taken seriously as partners in dialogue.

And afterwards...?

After this almost two-year-long process, the responsibility for the way to go forward lay with the politicians responsible; for a long time, there were no replies. About six months after the performances in the City Hall, the politicians were requested in writing to give information about what had been implemented so far from the proposed matters for concern and demands. The replies were a long time in coming and were then unsatisfactory, for they took very scant notice of the formulated demands and everyone moved his or her contribution into the foreground. In the interim, the city of Graz had nevertheless created an advice centre for the safeguarding of housing with the intention of preventing eviction, in the framework of which people can be protected from the imminent loss of a flat, and the acutely homeless can be advised. This centre – just recently opened – is supposed to be better connected to the existing institutions than any previous initiative. Some low threshold employment projects have also been realized, plus several new community housing projects.

Result

It goes to show that a Legislative Theatre process is more difficult as regards political implementation if it isn't supported by political institutions but is brought to them from the outside. The internal political decision process is no longer comprehensible and cannot be influenced. Moreover, it would probably have been better to concentrate on one or at the most two demands. Where a large number of proposals are made, even though they may be well thought out, it clearly allows politics to act very selectively and simply to ignore many of them.

Exemplary Working Instructions

In theatre work with homeless people, it is fundamentally important on the one hand to invest much time and space in confidence building and the ability to cooperate and, on the other hand, to encourage a desire to play - joie de vivre - and creativity through body, movement, and improvisation exercises. Only when all of these elements are present is there a working basis, which makes it possible to articulate unpleasant and difficult themes and express them through both images and scenes. To this end, a highly respectful atmosphere and attitude, which allows those participating to feel that here they are accepted as they are and are important. The perception of one participant who works in an institution for the homeless is as follows:

> This group, where you are simply accepted one hundred per cent, that is to the credit of both of the group leaders because they are so open and you can be who you are with them. I often admired this in secret. I don't know at all if both of them are conscious of this, but they seem to me to be relatively healthy people psychologically and because of that, they can be this way. And everyone is who he is and everyone is accepted. Not like in school, where you have to do this and that, you can't do that, you have to be like this, you have to dress this way; it was absolute freedom! Except for what concerned the performance, then it was like, now we have to perform and now we have to rehearse, yes, but as a human being, everyone was accepted as he or she was, each one of us. And for me, that was a very important experience, that this is actually possible. And that was surely good for the others as well. I don't know if they thought about it as much, but that is an extremely important experience" (Vieregg 2005, p. 47).

Great emphasis is placed on dealing with one another as respectfully as possible. Neither verbal nor physical violence is acceptable, nor is appearing at rehearsal in a drunken state. That is why it is important to develop a way of dealing with each other and with conflicts in the group and to create spaces outside of theatre work in which these pressurized situations can be addressed, worked through, and resolved. Small rituals at the beginning and end of a rehearsal, like the "How's it going?" round, are examples of these. In addition, it is necessary to check up on and clarify again and again what the group wants to share responsibility for thematically and show publicly.

With this in mind, the units, which lasted three hours as a rule, were structured according to a specific basic structure:

- The "How's it going?" round
- Warm-up games and sensitization exercises (body, space, group)
- Exercises for expression, rhythm, and getting into the play
- The arranging of images, development of small scenes or improvisations with and without thematic reference to being homeless

	Role Allocation	Time Content	Content	Reason	Specific Target
Lead-in	Both of the facilitators take it in turns to instruct and are involved in all of the exercises	18.00-18.10 18.10-18.20 18.20-18.30 18.30–18.45	**How's it going?** - asked in a round **Exchanging a clap:** An impulse to clap is passed on with great speed and intensity in a circle, the direction can change... **French telephone:** A mirroring exercise in which each person mirrors another person in the circle, who is mirrored in turn by another person. **walking, standing, running** **Complete the Image** – An improvised arrangement of and reaction to images (without speaking): in pairs, in groups of four, the whole group...	· To create the transition from daily life with its problems into the play and the realm of the theatre · A a starting ritual which is returned to again and again · To move directly from the starting circle into playful interaction with the group... · To move once again in the circle, in the body... · A a movement improvisation in the group with a focus on space, nearness, and distance. · As a transition to thematic work	· To experience the group that is present in the circle · To develop a sensitivity to another person's condition as a basis for further work · To strengthen attention, presence, concentration, cooperation, sense of rhythm · To focus awareness on the person opposite and to strengthen one's ability to imitate them · To flow into a stream of movement and expression · To develop a feeling for acting and moving in the space · To give expression to constellations of relationships by reacting in space · To develop a joint composition with minimum material. · To use the body as a means of expression · To react spontaneously and to improvise
	The facilitators provide the impetus from the outside; all members of the group improvise simultaneously; one of the facilitators documents				

Development	The facilitators provide the impetus from the outside; all members of the group simultaneously improvise; one of the facilitators documents		**Development of image material for scenes** The most important scenes are put in order after voting on the question, what absolutely must be in the play? Images are then arranged collectively under various key words and made dynamic in different ways through movement, voice, language . . .	· To approach a theme through play and to eagerly dive deep into the problem	· Creative contact with one's own ideas · Realization of scenes and images out of the concerns and themes in the ensemble
Crea-tion	The facilitators are part of the final round	20.50 – 21.00	**Layout of images / scenes:** Variants are tried out and rehearsal techniques are used on some of the images and scenes that have been developed, thus organizing them more clearly for the actors and enabling one to discover the levels underneath them and to bring out the characters **How's it going?** - asked in a round	· To produce theatrical material which is suitable for a public performance · To create jointly an exit point from the theatre work	· To find out about the effect, dynamic and rhythm of the images and scenes; to plumb the depths of the possibilities of different interpretations · To give feedback in a circle; to exchange with each other about emotional states and the development of the practice session

■ The "How's it going?" round

One unit, which took place in Phase IV, is outlined below as an example. It is to be noted that plans of this kind played a role in our work only in so far as they reframe a fundamental concept and an idea for the sequence of events, which was altered again and again because of the situation and the process in the group.

1) **Theme:** to arise out of issues of concern and themes to scene outlines / sketches.
2) **Rough goal:** By the end of this unit, the participants should have learned that they are able to improvise and act out collectively images and material for scenes regarding the themes and concerns, which are important to them.
3) **Materials and media:** A4 paper with thematic suggestions; digital camera for documentation.

Particularly Successful Segments

Example 1

Although before the beginning of the very first workshop we had been very sceptical whether it would take place at all, whether enough people would come, and whether they would want to get involved at all, something completely different happened: the participants were commited, creative, expressive, and enthusiastic. In the final feedback round, we the facilitators were emphatically asked and encouraged to go on and continue with the project.

Example 2

In the middle of the development of a scene about a family conflict, which should end with a "booting out," two actors fight with each other: B. (who should play the role of a mother, who is furious with her children because they don't help around the house) accuses A. (the actor playing one of the children) of only thinking of himself when working on the scenes, of being egoistic, and of not being aware of her at all. The situation escalates; B. drops out of the play, packs her things and is in the process of leaving the rehearsal. A director speaks to her: "B., I see that you are very angry right now. Can you imagine entering into the scene once again with this energy from your rage and, in the role of the mother, seriously telling your son in the scene your opinion?" B. is surprised by the question and has to laugh a little and, cheering up after a little, tries this out right away and is very satisfied with the result of the "outraged mother" and should continue to be so.

Example 3

After a significant body of material for scenes has been gathered and the work in the group has intensified, it's time for a decisive step: in a serious, sometimes loud and heated conversation, the group struggles in the truest sense of the word over the order of the scenes, over that which anyone who has become homeless might go through. A very candid conversation develops that a few weeks earlier would have been unimaginable but now, after the social and aesthetic experiences and investigations, has become possible.

The directors have difficulty at first in following it. They spread out papers with scene titles and key words on the floor, which are moved around until the sequence suits everyone – the group has developed the basic structure and the order of scenes autonomously.

Example 4

One week before the performance in the City Hall, a rehearsal takes place in the meeting room there. The inhibition in this "venerable" room can be felt at first; with the first of the warm-up exercises, which use the whole space, it begins to disappear little by little. When the group reads the demands while walking and then from different places – such as from the mayor's chair – and communicates the sentences from the declaration to the entire room, the inhibition changes into a self-confident, strong expression. The group gains control of the space and fills it with its own concerns!

Example 5

The performance and discussion in the City Hall are actually over. The moderator ends the event when a member of the group loudly indicates again that she would like to say something – in front of the full local council hall she makes the closing remarks, which were taped:

> To conclude I would just like to say something, something that is very important which I am very concerned about! I am happy that you all have come and that some of you have even taken part. We have worked very hard, worked out everything ourselves, and put it together for you. In the name of the group, I would like to express our thanks that there are people who are interested in how we are doing!

Michael Wrentschur in cooperation with Martin Vieregg

Target Groups: Aims and Competencies

The specific problems and difficulties of the group have already been pointed out elsewhere (Ruckerbauer / Wrentschur 2004). The goal of the project was formulated so as on the one hand to lead to joint creativity, an increase in self-esteem, an expansion of social competencies and to improve the problem-management skills and the ability to act, and, on the other hand, to strengthen the voices of homeless people and those on the margins of society in order to increase the awareness of the needs and interests of homeless people in the general population and those responsible politically.

Weintz (1998) has already pointed out that aesthetic and social competencies occur imperceptibly in play-acting and that it follows the character of informal learning processes. In this respect, Legislative Theatre work with the homeless does not follow any instrumental Learning Targets or specifically intended changes in behaviour. Through theatre work, rather, a possible space for educational processes and the acquisition of different competencies is created. From this arises the question:
Which competencies can be fostered, activated, and supported through a project of this kind in participants affected by homelessness?

The description of competencies, which can be acquired through the Legislative Theatre project, correspond for the most part to the competencies for facilitators described above. Their conceptual delimitations are in part not so absolute. The accompanying academic research and evaluation of the projects served as a basis for this outline of competencies:

1 Competencies: Aesthetics

Theatre work trains sensory perception and the ability to improvise; it fosters cooperation and the ensemble, extends physical and linguistic powers of expression and develops a feeling for rhythm and space. The basic traits of theatre are freedom, fun, imagination, spontaneity and liveliness and can offer an alternative world to the seriousness and the rules and structures of everyday life.

A spect-actor said the following about the aesthetic competencies of the theatre group:

> What I really liked was that sometimes there were such funny things. For example, an actor was waiting at the labour office and then said, "Now I'll let them wait, too." That brightened things up in between, because then you have to think about serious things again. I liked the fact that you could also laugh [...] I was truly surprised at how they improvised – that really wasn't bad. We also had improvised once in an improvisation theatre seminar, and that was very difficult – this was quite clever. I was very surprised (Vieregg 2005, p. 188).

2 Competencies: Ethics and Social Skills

In the context of Legislative Theatre, the development of moral and political power of judgement, the question of what injustice and oppression represent is at first a fundamental ethical and social competence. The theatre process constitutes a case of the dawning of consciousness about one's own social position in the structure of social inequality as well as about the possibilities of exerting influence, of the articulation of needs and interests. In the context of the group and community we are concerned with the development of a feeling of self-worth, of a perception of the self and the other; with the ability to cooperate and to make contact by means of respectful and dignified behaviour. It is necessary to develop patience and have a change of perspective time and again, articulate needs and to test contacts with various people inside and outside of the context of the group.

An actor about himself:

> I have simply become more self-confident in acting. I don't mind giving my opinion in front of several people as much as I used to – I used to only say certain things in private to another person, now I do it in front of several people – it doesn't make any difference (see p. 191).

Another example: during one rehearsal, a homeless man who had just been kicked out of a shelter came to watch. The group received him benevolently, took time to engage with his problem, gave tips and information about possible accommodation but were not sparing in their criticism of his behaviour, which had led to being kicked out of a shelter.

3   Competencies: Action

The development of action competencies is closely connected to ethical and social competencies. The testing of new behaviours and actions is one of these. Legislative Theatre work with homeless people is concerned with the opening up of possibilities for action, also in situations of powerlessness, discrimination and conflict resolution; part of this is the assessment of social situations and dealing with differences in status. The creation of tension in theatre work can equal the everyday competence of enduring and knowing how to handle tension in difficult, conflict-laden situations.

H. told the group at a regular group meeting that he practices a theatre exercise again and again in his daily life. If there is a situation in the facility that makes him furious, he starts to curse loudly with numbers, like in the exercise "abstract emotions" (Boal 2002, p. 222), in order to cool down again. The opponent is for the most part amazed; the situation does not escalate further.

R. told us after the end of the project that now he doesn't let them get rid of him so easily when he wants to know something or needs something from a government agency, office or advice centre.

4   Competencies: Field-Related Knowledge

This refers to both the area of the theatre work and the field of help for the homeless. Diverse insights into the world of the theatre widen the horizons; parallel to this, knowledge and information increases about the situation of the homeless, institutions, aid and discourse surrounding this problem. The dawning of consciousness regarding the field is what is important in this regard. The conscious and prepared intervention in the field through public appearances and presentations is also one of the field-related competencies.

An actress:
> I had to portray a rather dynamic AMS advisor in one scene. It really is true that relatively often you are actually branded. Thus everyone who is unemployed and hasn't got anything for a long time is seen to be simply too lazy to work. […] I think it should be that the official is also civil to someone who is homeless – that he treats him like he's a human being and not some number (Vieregg 2005 p. 169).

5 Competencies: Orientation

These are competencies, which go beyond the actual field of theatre work and help / policies regarding the homeless and which support the ability to find new approaches and points of orientation in daily life.

An actor about one of his fellow actors:

> That he found the will to live – how is this possible? And now more than ever before and he got support in every way from every corner, even when he had said "I don't want to go on anymore." Well, you hang on a little longer, and a little longer, and there's a push, and he did more and more and more. You saw how he got better in time, better and better. And today, the way he took the catering course and the computer course and everything else, finished his last exam, it's fascinating. The way such a group can help, what only a group like that can start, surely something different for everyone, but the group alone started an awful lot (Vieregg 2005 p. 194).

We learn from one carer from a social institution that R. shows no nervousness before an interview, and answers the question how he can be so "cool": "It's just like the theatre."

6 Competencies: Interculturalism

As socially disadvantaged groups often stay together in competition rather than in solidarity, the development of intercultural competence constitutes a great challenge. Thus "domestic" homeless people feel they are worse off than "foreign" homeless people. Even if this subjective view is not empirically tenable, it refers not only to the battle over the distribution of resources, which are in short supply on the margins of society but also to widen the focus of intercultural competencies. It refers to the perception of ways of life, which are socio-culturally and socio-economically other and the dealings with them, i.e. the readiness to be able to perceive, tolerate, and act out socio-cultural and socio-economic differences.

7 Competencies: Gender

While the homeless are normally segregated according to their sex (when provided for, sheltered and looked after), a particular opportunity as well as a challenge lies in the mixed composition of the group. The co-operation of men and women in a theatre group can lead to a high degree of sensitivity in how they deal with one another: it can support the perception and differentiation of gender roles – also through a conscious change in roles – as well as the scope for action in stressful situations.

Martin Vieregg

Evaluation

Structure of the Accompanying Academic Research

The thesis "'We are here... and have something to say!' Emancipatory – participative aspects of education from 'wohnungs/los/theatern' – a socio-cultural theatre project with homeless and former homeless people in Graz" can be seen as a kind of social and educational accompanying research for the project. This research primarily takes a look at the question of which educational processes have taken place within the framework of this theatre project. To answer this question, attention is focused on the socio-economic and psychosocial situation of homeless people in the first part of the thesis. The most varied aspects of homelessness become clear in the theoretical and empirical analysis of sociologists like Pierre Bourdieu (1987, 1999), relevant studies, and the play "Nobody is perfect II." The analysis demonstrates what work is necessary in the field of education - education supports the autonomy of individual people and creates possibilities for social participation. The second part of the thesis is concerned with different educational traditions, predominantly with concepts of an emancipatory participative educational model, such as the shaping of political ideas according to Paulo Freire (1973), socio-analysis according to Bourdieu and biography. It emerged that despite overlap with professionally-oriented educational traditions and those traditions which impart values, these traditions come closest to meeting the requirements drawn up beforehand as well as the concept of the theatre project. The third part forms the core of the thesis, which features of the Theatre of the Oppressed according to Augusto Boal (1998, 2002) and Simone Neuroth (1994). General features of theatre according to Ulrike Hentschel (2000) are also described. In connection with educational aspects, nine theses are outlined, which are finally contextualised within the problems and needs of homeless people. In the last part, the educational processes are examined on the basis of the performances and qualitative interviews to see which can be detected within the framework of the project.

Relevant Research Findings

Analysis of the Play

Examined according to the method of sequence analysis, the play showed that what was portrayed can be generalized to the greatest possible extent and thus can be seen as a successful product of scene research. Homelessness is a phenomenon with many causes and mainly comes at the end of a long struggle for survival. People who are in danger of becoming homeless or who are acutely homeless often feel great shame and have a sense of guilt over their situation. The fear of social stigmatization (hobo, tramp, etc.) leads the person only too late to find professional help. It becomes clear from the play that another central problem is how to deal with crises and the art of coping. More often than not constructive solutions cannot be found; in place of these there are illnesses (addiction, depression, etc.), the lack of a voice and the ability to act. Power over one's own life gets increasingly lost. The result of this is low self-esteem, which in daily life leads to many failures, the collapse of social networks and isolation. In the area of help for the homeless there are deficits and problems in relation to government agencies (access barriers, lack of counselling services); in the area of politics, there is a lack of ideas for reintegrating the homeless. The sociological analysis has shown that homelessness cannot only be seen as a personal or even a private problem. Not only the play but also sociologists, such as Beck and above all Bourdieu, criticize the increasing influence of neoliberal ideas in economics and politics. An increasing orientation toward competition and profits, rationalization, and privatization increase the demands made on individuals and aggravate the already difficult situation of a labour market shaped by globalization. Thus poverty and homelessness affect above all those who are already at a disadvantage in their job, such as people with little cultural capital, young people, women, older and foreign employees. In a time of the individualization of society and its problems, the reference to social inequality and the societal and political responsibility for it seems exceptionally important.

Evaluation of the Forum Phases

Altogether seven of the thirteen performances, audience participations and discussions were documented and evaluated on a structural and individual level. The structural level became noticeable above all in the working out of suggestions for improvement. Some ideas from the performances – for example, the establishment of an information office / headquarters / exchange or the demand for schooling for AMS advisors – found direct expression in this paper, which was handed over to the politicians in the performance in the City Hall. Other themes and aspects (for example, the demand for sufficient housing possibilities for families who have become homeless or the drawing up of a leaflet where all homeless institutions and their data are written down) have been thought about in the performances and have been put into a concrete form and developed further by the group. In the course of the theatre process, further demands develop, such as the participation of those affected in counselling situations for help for the homeless or in the working out of laws and projects which are not directly connected to audience participation. All in all, an extensive catalogue of demands which could be introduced into the discourse regarding a specific subject emerges, the political effectiveness of which is difficult, however, to estimate. Through the participation of the theatre group in strategic meetings of the platform "Forum Wohnen", the interests of those affected could be represented directly to the experts. Furthermore, through the joint presentation of the study of "Homeless in Graz" and the forum theatre performance, the problem of homelessness made an impression on the politicians in attendance. The city councillor responsible for social policies, who insisted on replacing an employee in the social security office, adds:

> It was exciting, I was nervous, yes, it happened, just what was supposed to happen in this play, I slipped into the role and noticed how difficult it actually is, because it suddenly came to me, naturally I am bound to the regulations and now I am in a dilemma. What do I decide to do now? It was completely clear to me – to help quickly. I could understand that very well (Vieregg 2005, p. 162).

In general she thought:
> I couldn't imagine this meeting without the play because as a politician, I can speak for an hour or two, but I couldn't convey what was expressed in the play, namely this sadness, this empathy [...] (see p. 162).

It can be said in principle that the political engagement of the theatre group was taken seriously and that its contribution had a supporting effect on demands for improving the situation of homeless people in Graz.

A look at the personal level revealed that there isn't any one particular or right position that makes a difference between success and failure. In each situation, various actions are possible and the situations also call for various actions. Generalizing, it can be said that the communication of an emotional state or of a bad situation can be a relief and can introduce solutions. Furthermore, a self-confident performance and the ability to (re)-act with various emotions and strategies are ideal for being successful in the different fields. In a discussion with the audience it was discussed whether in reality there are scopes of action for those affected at all. In addition, it was asked whether the ideas about the participation of the spect-actors made any sense for the actors. This question was spontaneously answered in the affirmative by one actor and can also be answered objectively in the affirmative in view of the results received to date. The question of how far the audience participation and / or the whole theatre work have produced emancipatory–participative educational processes is now the focal point.

Educational Processes

The evaluation of data revealed that the project facilitated an enormous range of educational experiences for its participants. It was possible for each person to get what he or she needed at a particular point in time to enlarge his or her respective scope for action. The same was true for the woman who was not homeless. Despite her double role, she could fit in well with the group and have valuable experiences. Social competencies such as the ability to cooperate and the ability to deal with conflict were fostered by the theatre work, whereby the construction of social networks and the solidarity within the group particularly stood out. Furthermore, the actors gained some distance from their current situation by playing roles, through which on the one hand the circumstances could be more easily realized and on the other hand it was also easier to acknowledge existing emotions such as rage. In this way, positive energies, which could be used constructively inside and outside the theatre, could be made use of. The interview partners felt that the rehearsals and above all the performances were tremendously enjoyable. The resonance and the contact between the audience and the actors were regarded as a great gain, which can be confirmed equally by the evaluation of different voices from the audience. The sense of belonging and the activities within the theatre group positively influenced the subjective feelings concerning social status of several of those taking part. The actors also got good reviews from the homeless community, where their courage to publicly portray the problem of homelessness was admired. Experts and the actors themselves are convinced that creativity, the ability to express oneself and self-confidence were strengthened through participation in the project. In general, one got the impression that the will to live and their joie de vivre had increased. All actors, with one exception, have freed themselves from homelessness and have entered working life again. This development cannot be explained by the theatre project alone. However, it can be assumed that in the course of the project, there were valuable impulses for the fostering of individual independence.

Footnote

1 Pilot course 2002 - 2004 at the Karl-Franzens-University of Graz, Austria

Bibliography

Boal, Augusto: Legislative Theatre. Using Performance to make Politics. London/New York 1998.

Boal Augusto: Games for Actors and Non-Actors. Second Edition. London/New York 2002.

Bourdieu, Pierre: Die feinen Unterschiede. Kritik der gesellschaftlichen Urteilskraft, Frankfurt am Main 1999 (1982).

Bourdieu Pierre: Sozialer Sinn. Kritik der theoretischen Vernunft, Frankfurt am Main 1987.

Freire, Paolo. Pädagogik der Unterdrückten, Reinbek bei Hamburg 1991 (1973).

Hentschel, Urike: Theaterspielen als ästhetische Bildung. Über einen Beitrag produktiven künstlerischen Gestaltens zur Selbstbildung. 2. Auflage, Weinheim 2000.

Koch, Gerd/Roth Sieglinde, Vaßen, Florian & Wrentschur Michael (Eds.): Theaterarbeit in sozialen Feldern/Theatre Work in Social Fields. Frankfurt am Main, 2004.

Mazzini, Roberto & Wrentschur, Michael: Theatre of the Oppressed in Social Fields / Theater der Unterdrückten in sozialen Feldern. In: Koch, Gerd/Roth Sieglinde/Vaßen, Florian/Wrentschur, Michael (Eds.): Theaterarbeit in sozialen Feldern/Theatre Work in Social Fields. Frankfurt am Main, 2004, p. 174 - 186.

Neuroth, Simone: Augusto Boals "Theater der Unterdrückten" in der pädagogischen Praxis. Weinheim 1994.

Ohmacht, Stefan et. al.: Wohnungslos in Graz. Sozialwissenschaftliche Dokumentation der Sozialarbeit für wohnungslose Menschen in Graz, Analyse der Betreuungsangebote sowie Strategiekonzept Wohnungslosenhilfe Graz. Studie im Auftrag des Landes Steiermark und der Stadt Graz. Kurzfassung. Stadt Graz, Sozialamt 2004.

Ruckerbauer, Armin & Wrentschur, Michael (2004): Theaterarbeit mit wohnungslosen Menschen am Beispiel von "wohnungs/LOS/theatern"/ Theatre Work with Homeless People, e.g. "wohnungs/LOS/theatern". In: Koch, Gerd/Roth Sieglinde/Vaßen, Florian/Wrentschur, Michael (Eds.): Theaterarbeit in sozialen Feldern/Theatre Work in Social Fields. Frankfurt am Main 2004, p. 199 - 205.

Vieregg, Martin: " Wir sind da ... und haben etwas zu sagen!" Emanzipatorisch – partizipative Bildungsaspekte von "wohnungs/LOS/theatern" – einem soziokulturellen Theaterprojekt mit wohnungslosen und ehemals wohnungslosen Menschen in Graz. Diplomarbeit am Institut für Erziehungswissenschaft der Universität Graz, Graz 2005.

Weintz, Jürgen: Theaterpädagogik und Schauspielkunst. Ästhetische und psychosoziale Erfahrung durch Rollenarbeit, Butzbach-Griedel 1998.

Zaporah, Ruth: Action Theatre. The Improvisation of Presence, Berkely/California 1995.

Jennie Hayes, Henrietta Ireland, Roger Sell

No Fear Theatre for Wicked Kids – Theatre Work with Young Offenders

Structure of the Module:
Theatre Work with Young Offenders –
Using Devised Theatre Methology and Aspects of Dramatherapy Process in Working within the Youth Justice System

Qualification on completion of the module.
Theatre Practitioner in Applied Devised Theatre Techniques

Format and Minimum Timeframe

400 hours   student contact time
100 hours   research and documentation
100 hours   taught practice
200 hours   project development

Short Module Descriptor
Initial phase of context research and development of material; Initial contact with agency and client group; Development of project strategy; Development of documentation strategy; Collaboration process and development of the project; Evaluation and dissemination.

Elements of Assessment
Continuous appraisal of research strategies; compositional strategies; collaborative strategies; applied devising techniques.
Portfolio documenting and evaluating the process and the product.

Module Objectives

To enable you to extend your existing strategies for devising theatre and apply them to a specific social context.

Learning Outcomes

By the end of this module you should be able to:

- demonstrate abilities to collaborate and negotiate within a social context;
- effectively integrate devising methodologies within public collaborative performance;
- apply a range of compositional in relation to specific set of social and cultural parameters;
- have a detailed understanding of the work of influential practitioners in the field and the theoretical models through which theatre practice in social fields can be evaluated ;
- articulate the wider cultural context in which these practices operate;
- access techniques and methods that may be drawn on productively to extend your own practice;
- apply certain dramatherapy processes to specific situations;
- understand the implications of the Youth Justice System and to respond sensitively and productively with the contexts of the client group.

Admission Requirements

- At least two years practical experience of devising theatre methodologies;
- Previous Higher Education achievement in articulating in a variety of ways the process and product of theatre making;
- An interest in Theatre within a social, political and cultural field, and an ability to evaluate the relationship between social context and behaviour.

Henrietta Ireland

Competencies and Learning Objectives of the Facilitators

1 Competencies: Aesthetics

The module aims to explore the affects of cultural, social and family beliefs and perspectives on engaging with theatre activities.

Our common practice criteria are to:
- prevent antisocial behaviour
- prevent offending behaviour
- encourage inclusion
- promote positive social and communication skills through the use of theatre

Learning Objectives

1. To collaborate with a project initiated by the Youth Justice board for preventing anti-social behaviour and offending in young people from the ages of 8 to 12.
2. To heighten awareness concerning the needs and abilities of young offenders and to reflect on the contexts that these young people confront. There is also a reflection on the wider regional and national implications through the evaluation process.

2 Competencies: Ethics

The aim is to engage children whose anti-social behaviour has come to light by two or more agencies, to improve integration, social skills, self-esteem and communication in order to encourage the expression of feelings and emotions and to develop ideas of thought and narrative through the use of theatre and drama techniques, culminating in a collaborative performance.

Learning Objectives

The objective is to create a piece of theatre that embraces all of the above and channels each individual's emotional energy and creativity into a positive outcome.

3 Competencies: Methods and Application

The student practitioners had a number of individual and personal aims. Firstly they wanted to continue their theatrical vocation within a social context and affirm their learning and skills. They wanted to increase their knowledge of group dynamics, particularly around issues of challenging and offending behaviour. They wanted to increase their skills to enable them to work with children.

The aim of the Youth Offending Team was clear, they wanted to run a drama group for some of the younger children referred to the agency. However, it was recognised that for the purposes of managing challenging behaviour, a high ratio of adults to children was necessary to make the project a success; it was also recognised that facilitators with theatre experience would be preferable.

The social worker present within the group of facilitators added clarity around issues of confidentiality associated with the client group, and helped with managing challenging behaviour. She gave us an extra understanding and insight into some of the social hardships that this group of children may have experienced.

The postgraduate had a specific, personal interest in the causes of offending behaviour and their treatment. A male group facilitator was vitally important for the children in the group as he provided an essential male role model for the children, many of whom did not have any positive experience of a male role model in their lives.

The drama therapist provided essential experience of working with this type of client group combined with a contextual knowledge of the Youth Offending team.

Set design and props were designed and made during sessions with the support from the YOT art practitioner. For some of the sessions we had a group mentor represented by a young person aged 16 with an interest in dance and theatre, who had volunteered to work on the project.

4 Competencies: Field-Related Knowledge

Context

Two specific geographical areas were identified as being areas of social deprivation. The young people engaged in this project were residents of these areas.

The Children

Six children were selected to participate in the project, which allowed the facilitators to work on an adult child ratio of between two to one and one to one. There were two female children and four male, the children were aged between 8 and 12. The children were identified as being at risk of social exclusion by two or more agencies/services e.g. Child and Adolescent Mental Health Service and Education or social Services and the Police or any combination of the above. All the children had behavioural disorders consistent with poor or disrupted attachments and had poor social and communication skills. Some of the children knew each other but did not previously have close relationships with one another.

Outline of Learning Content

The Youth Offending Team (YOT) aims to prevent re-offending (the committing and re-committing of crimes) in children aged between 10 and 18, who are on a Court Order. The project objective is to identify the needs of the child and the risk factors that are causing – or may cause – the child to offend and then to work with the child through the identified problems.

5 Competencies: Orientation

The Crime and Disorder Act recognises the importance of early intervention with children and young people to prevent offending. Developing an identity is an integral part of child and adolescent development, which is influenced by a number of factors.
Social roles are influenced by a number of factors including:
- Early childhood experiences
- Position in the family

- Ethnicity and cultural background
- Gender
- Sexuality
- Responsibilities
- Financial and material wealth
- Educational abilities and attainment

Vennard and Hedderman (1988) identified six principles of effective practice such as making the length of the intervention proportionate to the offence; targeting crimonogenic needs, eg. targeting the factors that contribute directly to offending behaviour.

Learning Objectives

The project should aim to reach as many of the core indicators for as successful an intervention as possible and therefore take into account as many of the parts of the afore-mentioned principles as possible.

Theatre, drama and art are suggested as effective modes of intervention. Chapman and Hough (1998) suggest that activity-based programmes, which are carefully designed and delivered, can address a range of criminogenic needs including:

- Antisocial attitudes, beliefs and values
- Antisocial associates
- Lack of pro-social models
- Cognitive interpersonal skills
- Dependence on drug and alcohol
- A sense of achievement and community integration
- Employment
- Social isolation
- Mental health

These should also be taken into account when designing a project.

Outline of Learning Content

Many of the stages of this project can be identified in Renee Emunah's "Integrative five Phase Model of Drama" (Emunah 1994). Of all the models ours reflected most of the elements and therapy processes, which include:
1. Dramatic play
2. Scene work
3. Role play
4. Culminating enactment
5. Dramatic ritual.

We actually identified these themes at the end of the project in a retrospective manner rather than deliberately setting out to achieve them.

6 Literature Competencies: Research and Communication

There are many texts and books that refer to the power of drama and theatre in providing an emotional outlet and safe space for social 'practice'. In her book "Acting for Real" (1994) Renee Emunah describes drama as a vehicle not only for experiencing and integrating new aspects of ourselves but also for expressing the suppressed 'shadow' aspects of ourselves. Phil Jones (Drama as Therapy, 1999) writes "clients may create roles where they encounter actual feeling states, they cry, feel anger and hope, these are not experienced as fictional; real tears are wept, real anger is felt, yet at the same time it is within a fictional construct."

> Children use drama as therapy spontaneously, with no outside direction or pre-imposed structure. Dramatic play is the child's method of symbolically expressing and resolving internal conflict, assimilating reality, achieving a sense of mastery and control, releasing pent-up emotions and learning to control potentially destructive impulses through fantasy. Expressing unacceptable parts of the self, exploring problems and discovering solutions, practising for real life events, expressing hopes and wishes, experimenting with new roles and situations and developing a sense of identity (Courtney, R. 1968).

Drama and theatre have always dealt with the interface between reality and fantasy, Mast has said that the "actor participates simultaneously on everyday and dramatic levels of reality" (Mast 1986).

Learning Objectives

The project provided an excellent social context in which practitioners could practice and develop their theatre and collaborative skills. There were seven facilitators taking part in the project:

1 drama therapist
1 art therapist
1 social worker
3 student theatre practitioners
1 evaluator and research practitioner

An Adolescent Mental Health Nurse Specialist gave clinical supervision to the project team.

7 Competencies: Interculturalism

Culture may be identified through different social groups. In this study a location of deprivation was identified, which differed significantly from other areas in the city.

Exeter is a Cathedral city in the South West region of England in the county of Devon with a population of 112.000. Devon is a mostly rural and agricultural area but the economy is dependent on tourism and burgeoning small businesses. Exeter is for the most part a vibrant and thriving City with businesses choosing to locate their premises within this popular area. However, there are also pockets of extreme social deprivation and poverty. For example, Wonford, an area within the city, is identified as being within the bottom 2% of Britain regions as regards low income and high unemployment, with few young people moving into further education. This stark contrast between Wonford and adjacent areas is clearly illustrated through the statistical league tables for education. In the case of two areas located only one mile apart, one is found to be in the top 200 best performing schools nationally and the other is in the bottom 200 worst performing schools. It is precisely because of the contrasting levels of wealth that these deprived areas have been recognised as areas for regeneration and the government has given money to aid these areas and improve the quality of education, housing, community provision and special policing to reduce the incidence of crime.

Learning Objectives

The Valley Regeneration Scheme, as it is called, specifically promotes constructive and positive ways of engaging families and young people. It is largely from these areas that our children were referred.

Outline of Learning Content

The aim was to give each child a focus and a personal responsibility to the project, to themselves and to their fellow-participants. Each child would invite their family and/or friends. Their performance would give them the chance to succeed in front of people, who were important to them. For each child attending a project of this nature, this presents a significant experience. Each child would also be responsible and in control of the 'ending'. For children who have suffered severe chaos in their lives, often with inappropriate and traumatic endings to relationships, this would provide another challenging experience.

8 Competencies: Gender

It is a recognised fact that most adolescent males find self-expression particularly hard and that their verbal communication and social skills are often poor. In Ron Huxleys paper, "Big Boys do Cry: Helping our sons Increase their Emotional IQ" (2005) he tackles this issue comprehensively and looks at the social causes and their effects on the male child/adult. William Pollock, PhD, in his book "Real Boys: Rescuing our Sons from the Myths of Boyhood" (1998) states that the consequence of this confusion for males includes higher rates of depression, anxiety, aggression and substance abuse.

Learning Objectives

In order to respond to this need, the project module utilised a theatre programme as a means of engagement. Our specific objective was to engage specially identified children in a theatre project in order to improve social and communication skills thereby decreasing one of the risk factors associated with the risk of offending and anti-social behaviour.

Project Group

The group consisted of 4 boys and 2 girls aged between 8 and 12 with complex emotional and behavioural problems.

9 Competencies: Project Management

Student practitioners should be responsible for designing and structuring the sessions. The dramatherapist / coordinator should provide an outside perspective and help with identifying the specific aims and objectives of each session. During the sessions the student practitioners led the sessions and activities while the social worker and the dramatherapist maintained the boundaries and provided specific support and engagement for those children who were finding the sessions particularly challenging.

Learning Objectives

It is essential to note that these roles need to be interchangeable, in order to respond directly to the needs of the children, while maintaining the structure and continuity of the sessions. Some children may attach to and work better with one specific facilitator whereas other children might not express any preferences. However, it is vitally important to maintain the structure of the sessions and clarify boundaries and rules. It is furthermore of crucial importance that these two tasks are carried out by separate individuals.

Outline of Learning Content

The overall management and occasional re-structuring of the facilitative roles of the team on a sessional basis was the responsibility of the coordinator/drama therapist.

Overall this reflects a reflexive approach to managing a group and requires high levels of trust, transparency, commitment, energy and collaboration between facilitators.

Module Project:
No Fear Theatre for Wicked Kids

How the Project Progressed

Given the extent of the mental health needs identified within the group it seemed important to consider a psychological approach and this would be consistent with the approach of any other related project. Of the three major forces in psychology, humanistic psychology contributes most closely to the fundamental practice of drama therapy. "Humanistic psychology emerged in the late 1950's as an alternative to psychoanalysis and behaviourism, which were the two dominant schools at the time. Humanistic Psychology aims to address the fullness of the human potential, the capacity of humans for creativity, art, spirituality and self realization and transformation. Humanistic psychology contains no absolutes or definitive answers." (Jones, P. 1999), Maslow (1968, 1971), Rogers (1951, 1961), Buhler 1962, and May (1961, 1975) and other humanistic psychologists base their work on models of health rather than pathology and they view human nature as intrinsically good.

All the children took part voluntarily in the project and their parent(s) or guardian(s) gave their consent for them to attend.

Evaluation of Referral Process

Children were referred if they fitted into the most of the elements listed below:
- Children with poor social and communication skills
- Children with a history of failure to function in groups (excluded)
- Children with low levels of self-esteem and self-confidence
- Low achievers with a self fulfilling prophecy of failure
- Children with poor attachments and relationships with adults
- Children who had experienced unsafe relationships with adults

Structure of the Sessions

There were fourteen sessions and each session lasted for one and a half hours. The first six sessions took place in June and July and then there was a break for six weeks during the summer holiday. A further eight sessions took place from mid September until November; six were developmental sessions, one was a re-introduction and evaluation session and one was the performance session.

The first six sessions were focused on setting boundaries, creating a group agreement with the children and building on relationships, trust and communication between children and facilitators. The group learnt about each other through telling and acting out stories of journeys and exploration, fear, fantasy and reality. The aim of some of the exercises was that the narratives might reflect the real internal world of the child. The second part of the project aimed to develop one story with a view to producing a performance for an audience.

Location

The location for the work needs to be accessible to all the participants. It should be non-stigmatising, neutral, child-friendly and tolerant of noisy children, a theatre space that is large, bright and safe for children.

Basic Session Plan

Each session was planned in advance and all previous sessions were evaluated rigorously prior to the next session. The facilitators allowed at least two hours for this process before collecting the children for the group.

We collected every child from home in a mini bus after school. The journey gave the children a chance to re-integrate with one another and re-engage with the facilitators, and formed a strategic part of the group process. The first twenty minutes of each session were spent re-engaging the children using activities and exercises, establishing boundaries and explaining the aims and objectives of the session to the children. This was often a difficult and chaotic time for both facilitators and children as the behaviour could often be wild and unpredictable as well as challenging and confrontational. It was vitally important that all the group members felt safe and this depended on a close working relationship between the facilitators. The next forty minutes focused on a specific task such as creating narratives, learning drama skills, practising role play or character development using a variety of techniques.

The break: There was a ten-minute break for refreshments.
The cooling-off Period: The last twenty minutes were time to reform as a group, de-role and take part in some focused, low-energy activity.
We then took them all home on the bus.

Evaluation of Plan

Some parts of the practice were excellent: The bus provided a reliable and trustworthy means of getting children to sessions; there is no possible way that these children would have managed to attend if we had not done this as many came from chaotic and unreliable families. The bus also provided a vital space and time for integration and engagement. However, we often lost control of the children on the journey from the bus to the performance space. The energy levels were high at this time and boundaries were not clearly set from the very beginning of the project. We tried some strategies for improving behaviour by extending the drama to the bus and telling the children that they all had to be 'secret agents' and therefore very quiet. This worked sometimes; at other times they made very bad 'secret agents'!!

The first twenty minutes became easier as the facilitators began to get to know each other but the first few weeks were difficult and some times confusing. The refreshment break was a good idea and the children enjoyed the ritual, however it often broke the concentration and focus of the group and the children would often revert to their more familiar chaotic and uncontrollable behaviour, which sometimes meant that we would have to cut short the session and take the children home early.

The cooling-off period was meant for de-roling and calming down but with such an anxious and highly stimulated group this was sometimes not achieved and, as mentioned above, did not happen. On reflection, I am still not sure how to overcome this problem. Maybe the session time should have been shorter, lasting perhaps just an hour, and then the children could have calmed down and had a drink on the bus on the way home.

Exemplary Working Instructions

Session One

This session focused around 'getting to know each other' and establishing a group agreement which was written onto a piece of A3 sized paper. The children came up with suggestions that incidentally matched those of the adults:

- No fighting
- No swearing
- No mobile telephones
- No one to leave the room unaccompanied
- No bullying
- Everyone to come every week
- No kissing

Every member of the group agreed the contract. Interestingly, at some time during the project every group member broke the very rule that he/she had suggested. Does this indicate that for a group of traumatised children, where the adults in the world they inhabit appear to break every rule, rules and agreements have little or no value? Perhaps with such a group 'agreements' are a waste of time.

Session Two

The aim of the session was to get the children to begin to act out a story and the objectives were that each child would start to use his/her imagination and express ideas through drama. We started to explore some themes around making journeys. The group members were encouraged to first find different ways of travelling across the space. They then acted out a story of a journey that was read to them and finally they devised their own journey stories.

Conclusion

It was interesting that the children chose to focus on materialistically focused narratives about finding money, treasure or winning the lottery and the stories were about one person.

Session Three

This session was led by the art specialist. The aim of the session was to stimulate the children's imagination. The objective was that every child would illustrate his/her journey to the session; there were no rules and the journey could be made as realistic or fantastical as each individual chose.

The second part of the exercise was for each child to illustrate a journey to the place they would most like to visit, again the destination could be based on reality or fantasy. They would then share their journey with the whole group via a narrative story. In a simple sense this would be a very basic individual presentation (performance) which if necessary could be supported by a facilitator.

Conclusion

The children focused well on the task and produced some wonderful artwork full of colour and imagination; the imaginative possibilities were far greater than had been evident in the previous week. Some children were unable to give the presentation themselves but were happy to allow a facilitator to give a directed narration of their story.

Most children were elated by the experience and had a great sense of achievement; some were disappointed by their inability to finish the task. Energy levels and tension escalated at the end of the task so that it was decided that we would end the session early.

Session Four and Five

The aim was to devise and perform a short story based around a journey. The objective was that each child would devise and negotiate his/her own roles and responsibilities. The group split into three sub-groups with one of two facilitators in each group. Each group devised and worked on a journey story, which was movement-based with a little dialogue.

Conclusion

Some very positive working relationships were formed during the two weeks between the children and the facilitators. The model was always child-centred but the children began to learn to listen and reflect more in the smaller groups and some children began to show higher levels of self-confidence.

Session Six

A small audience of three people were invited to watch the Journey Stories. All the children managed to make a contribution to the performance and they were all delighted by their achievement. Each child was given a certificate for completing the first six weeks and each child was given a specially chosen card with a personalised message from the facilitators, such as "We love having you in the group because you make us smile". One child chose not to take her award but when she arrived at her home she asked for it and ran into the house to show it to her mother.

Overview of the First Six Weeks

The Video Camera

Most sessions were documented using the video camera. This was essential for recording the progress of the group and for reflecting on the group dynamic. However, it proved to be useful in another way that none of us could have predicted. If a child refused to engage with a task or activity and then began to disrupt the rest of the group, we would often suggest that he/she took the video footage. The camera was plugged into the wall rather than using the battery, which meant the child had limited space in which to roam and it allowed the child to view and take part in the activity in progress as an observer. This allowed the child to 'find his/her own space' while remaining connected to the rest of the group, and when the child felt ready, he/she could easily join in with the task. Behind the camera lens was a safe place and this proved to be a constructive method of reintegration on many occasions.

Facing the Challenge

The first six weeks were very challenging for the facilitators. It was necessary for them to form a close collaborative relationship with each other as well as with the children. The most difficult obstacle to overcome was how to respond to challenging behaviour. We used several different tactics:

- The first was to try to engage the child in a positive activity.
- The second was to ignore the behaviour.
- The third was to challenge the poor behaviour and restrain or hold the child.

Children can be experts at creating a sense of total chaos. At these times it is essential for the facilitators to support each other and to work very closely together in order to contain the behaviour. Supervision helped the facilitators to understand challenging behaviour. It is also essential at this time for making sense of the behaviour and the dynamic that goes on in the drama space. It helps the facilitators to keep their relationship and dynamic transparent and provides a safe time and space for challenging relationships.

The theatre process provided some really golden moments when the children came up with some fantastic ideas, thoughts, reflections and actions. It is rewarding for the facilitators to be part of a process, which allows each child to feel that they have value and are able to put something back into the world in which they live. These feelings are unique for children with this kind of life history and it is encouraging to feel that one may be able to give them the opportunity to experience what many children take for granted.

Session Seven

The facilitators felt that the middle point of the project would be a good time to introduce some new group members. During session seven the children were informed of the intentions for the following sessions. The children seemed to be happy with the proposal. A hot seat for interviews was set up so that the children could ask us and each other questions about the project and about the other children that would be joining the group. The interview technique gave the facilitators the opportunity to explain to the children about TWISFER and for them to ask the facilitators why they were engaged in the project. This session was used to do some evaluation of the previous six weeks and the children were asked what they enjoyed doing and why they came. One little boy was clear about the fact that the project was where he met his friends.

Session Eight

The new children attended the group. Despite the best session plan and extra adults, the session was extremely challenging. The newly referred children were not invited back.

Conclusion

On reflection, the experience identified how much the original group had achieved in the first six weeks and having the comparison clearly indicated the progress that the children had made both socially and expressively.

Session Nine

In this session we focused on improvisation. The aim was to positively reinforce the actions that the children chose to make, thus increasing their self confidence and a belief that they could perform. The objective was that each child would have the opportunity to move freely in and out of different roles in response to a character or scene that was set by a facilitator. The scenes were facilitator led because the children didn't have enough self-confidence to start an action.

Conclusion

The children really enjoyed participating, both as members of an audience and as performers. They quickly established roles and moved freely into dialogue and narrative. As the exercise was developed so effectively the facilitators decided to move into some simple exercises, which looked at changing the outcome of the story. The children had spontaneously chosen to create a scene where an old lady was robbed of her bag; the children then acted out the consequences of this action, in which the old lady became ill and suffered a heart attack. The children were asked if they could think of creating a different ending. This was hard for two of the children who didn't appear to want to change the outcome. It was not until the end of the session and the scenario that the two girls acted out the return of the bag to the old lady. It was felt that this was a clear example of how difficult these children find it to change their behaviour and alter outcomes, but the drama and the theatre space offered the children an opportunity to 'act' differently.

Session Ten

In this session our aim was to create a narrative out of which we hoped to devise the performance. The objective was that each child would choose an item out of the 'secret bag' and tell the group a story about the item. We then combined the individual narratives to form one story. The 'Story Bag' worked very well and there were some very interesting and imaginative narratives that were developed from the items within the bag.

Session Eleven

Each child remained responsible for their narrative and chose a central character to go with it. The aim was that each child would take responsibility for his/her section of the narrative. The objective was to develop the character and strengthen the narrative and also to think what might be their central prop for the scene. The children worked hard and focused well on the task; again they made close working pairs with specific facilitators.

Session Twelve

With the assistance of the art teacher the children were able to create their specific props. Some of the children worked very hard and then set about destroying their work, which was a little depressing but it seemed to be linked to feelings of inadequacy and an impulse to fulfil the prophecy of their own failure. The children then chose a space in the room that represented their performance space. They also chose some material from the dressing-up bag. Then they practiced their characters and worked on their narratives. The project group found it a very difficult balance to provide enough practice so that the children felt confident enough to perform but not so much practice that the children lost interest and disengaged.

Session Thirteen

A rehearsal session: The children seemed to be very anxious and unsettled at first but with the help of one of our visiting European TWISFER partners, the session was a great success, with most of the children feeling confident enough to show their scenarios. In an age where most entertainment provides instant gratification, depends only on visual stimulus, where most games are solitary, eg. the child and the computer; it was a joy to witness these children laughing, participating, enjoying, being with, and watching each other play. An invitation was given to all the children to give to their parents or carers in order to invite them to the performance.

Session Fourteen: The Performance

The performance took place in the same building as the sessions but it was located in a different space. This was to give the children a feeling of 'occasion'. We set up lights and located their props in their own individual performance areas.

The story was devised by the children, but the thread that wove the stories together was put together in a repetitive form of announcing. In effect it was like a chorus and enabled the children to easily recall the cues and prompts for their own personal monologues. This worked very well and prevented arguments between the children. There were five scenarios and all of them were linked in the same way but each piece was contained and the children were clear about what they were responsible for.

The story was about an enchanted forest. A wicked biker (a person who rides a motor bike) comes into the forest and steals the unicorn's horn. Unless the horn is returned, Winter will last forever. (This is the chorus.) In our first scene we see the 'keeper of the forest': she has a money tree in the garden and the money is used to give to children when they lose a tooth. She leaves her forest dwelling in order to deliver some money when she comes across the unicorn crying piteously. "What has happened to you?" she asks. The unicorn tells her story using a dance to enhance the narrative. (The child in this scene loved to dance). "Oh no", says the forest keeper, "we must go to tell the bear." We find the bear eating nuts and honey and talking about food. When he sees the couple he asks, "what has happened?" "The Wicked Biker came into the enchanted forest and stole the unicorn's horn. Unless the horn is returned, winter will last forever." They chant, "Oh no", says the bear, "we must go and tell the pixie." They find the pixie cutting logs and loading them into a wheelbarrow, "What has happened?" he asks. (Chorus) "We must go to see the wizard," suggests the pixie. Off they go to find the wizard. "What has happened?" the wizard enquires. (Chorus) The wizard suggests that he will make a magic wall using a magic paintbrush. He will put the wall around the forest to prevent the biker from returning. BUT, with that, the biker returns and crashes into the wall and is thrown to the floor. "Please can I return to the forest", he begs, "only if you return the unicorn's horn", the wizard replies, "because, if the horn is not returned winter will last forever." The biker returns the horn. "May I come into the forest now"? he asks. "Well," says the wizard, "you may return but only if you keep to the forest laws and only ride on the paths for bikes." "All right," says the biker, "I am sorry for what I have done and promise always to ride on the bike paths, (most of the time!)" The biker is allowed to return and all live happily ever after...

This simple story is very interesting on a number of different levels. Each child chose a subject that had a special relevance or meaning to them. The theme of money only comes into one scene and at this time the money is intended for others. The fascinating part of the story is that it revolves around a crime, a theft, and the children chose a very interesting way to resolve the problem and find a solution. The thief must take responsibility for his actions, he is made to understand the consequences of his actions and how it has effected others and he must then apologise to all those who have suffered, particularly the victim of the crime. Because of his actions he himself is hurt and in a way becomes the victim of his own irresponsible behaviour. He is not allowed to return to the community until he promises to abide by the laws set by the community. He agrees and all live happily ever after.

This constructive model of restoring justice is recognised by the Youth Justice Board in England as being a highly effective way of changing criminal behaviour, with the four main elements being key elements being:
1. Accepting responsibility
2. Understanding the consequences as told by the victim and all those who have been directly of indirectly affected by the crime
3. Making an apology
4. Finding a way to 'pay back the community, to right the wrong'.

The Restorative Justice Model has been widely recognised as an effective way of managing criminal behaviour and reducing re-offending. It is more effective than punitive methods of managing offending behaviour and many of our local community policemen have been trained to adopt this approach when working in the community. Every member of the Youth Offending Team has been trained to use this model.

This model was born out of four existing models: the 'Victim Offender Reconciliation Programme' (VORP), which was developed in Canada in 1974, 'Victim-offender mediation in Austria' (1989), 'Family Group Conferencing' in New Zealand (1989), and the publication of the academic theory of 're-integrative shaming' (1989), which was John Braithwait's criminological theory. In brief, Braithwait's theory successfully integrated several established theories of criminology into one explanatory model that could successfully account for the known truism of offending. Finally, the 'Wagga Conferencing Model,' which was developed by the New South Wales Police Force in New Zealand. None of the children who took part in the theatre project had ever taken part in a Restorative Justice Panel and yet they came up with it as a natural solution. The other clear development was that they were able to devise a fantasy that depicted a reality and were thereby evidencing their ability to think metaphorically, where previously their thinking had been concrete, linear and unimaginative.

The performance night was difficult to manage as the children's anxiety was played out in a number of different and for them familiar ways. Most of the children in the group would have had bad experiences of 'endings' in their lives: the end of relationships, the end of school, the end of the day. Many of them seemed determined to play out this pattern of self-fulfilling destruction and there were a number of attempts to sabotage the performance. The thing that drew all the members together and provided them with the comfort and security that they needed was each other. When they eventually decided to collaborate as a group, the power of the group was far greater than the power of each individual and it was seen that the power of the individual within the group to nurture each other was profound. The group enabled the individuals to locate their self-confidence and their ability to nurture.

The Audience

With a drama therapy model the enactment, or the scenes are witnessed by the rest of the group. This allows the individual to feel acknowledged and valued within the group. In drama therapy much consideration is given to the dramatic work that occurs for those involved in the enactment, but much less is given to the notion of audience. Key theoretical texts such as Schattner and Courtney's "Drama in therapy" in both volume 1 and volume 2 (1981) or Robert Landy's "Dramatherapy" (1986) or Renee Emunah's "Acting for Real" (1994) have no index entry under 'audience'. Brook sees the audience as giving theatre its fundamental meaning (1988, 234). In the 'heat' of the encounter between audience and performer, the 'peak' experience is achieved. He describes the encounter as 'a meeting, a dynamic relationship' between the prepared performer/s and the unprepared audience, (1988, 236). One of the fundamental criticisms that he had of groups such as drama therapy groups was the lack of an audience. Through creating a piece of theatre the project group were clear about bringing the audience to a designated space and had rehearsed a story that they wanted to show.

The invited audience for the project group were family and friends. The performance provided an opportunity for these children to show a little of themselves to their parents and to people that they felt were important in their lives. They were acknowledged, listened to, respected and admired. This was a unique experience for these children and probably a unique experience for the families. It is a fact that in the past, these families would have had more reason to feel ashamed of their children than proud, but on the performance night, for this night, they were proud and the children were proud and felt a sense of achievement and we the facilitators were privileged and fortunate to be able to share this experience.

It was the purposeful inclusion of the family into the children's world, which made this project different, which took it beyond the drama-therapeutic model. The experience was cathartic because of the sharing. The audience was an intrinsic part of the process. It was felt that the project demonstrated that a drama therapy model could co-exist along side a theatre model with very positive outcomes for the participants. The performance provided a thread through the dramatic process and it was understood by the children that the aim was to make a performance. This helped to focus the children and gave the project a sense of purpose. It was also the "End": the group did not meet again after the performance. However, they were sent certificates with a photograph of themselves and the Words 'You're a Star' written in the corner.

The project continues in that the group are hoping to reform with a new facilitator and it is part of the long term objective of the YOT and the project to continue to use drama and theatre in this constructive way. Two of the children are now successfully integrated into other theatre groups and one has taken up drumming.

Jennie Hayes, Roger Sell

Target Groups: **Aims and Competencies**

Competencies of the Target Group

It should be noted that whilst many of the competencies, as outlined below, were met by individual participants within this Module, some were only likely to be achieved through sustained contact over a longer period of time than was available. In addition, with a different group of participants, attainment of these competencies would vary greatly depending on the starting point of individuals within the group, their background and previous experience, external support structures and the skills and intentions of the project facilitators.

1 Competencies: Aesthetics

Ability to develop and build on creative ideas from session to session; to engage with a sense of narrative; to consider the dramatic possibilities from that narrative; to find enjoyment in the creative process; to perform in front of family and friends.

2 Competencies: Ethics

Ability to develop trust between adults and young people and between the young people themselves; to recognise individual and group achievements in the group process; to accept the role of artist/theatre worker as group leader/contributor.

3 Competencies: Methods

Ability to channel emotional and creative energy into a positive outcome; to understand creative interdependence in a group context; to develop a role; to understand the preparation necessary for performance.

4 Competencies: Field-Related Knowledge

Ability to express feelings and emotion through theatre; to demonstrate increased self-esteem; to develop confidence in themselves and in their interaction with others; to develop confidence in performing; to develop sustained concentration for tasks; to develop an ability to collaborate towards performance.

5 Competencies: Orientation

Ability to develop one's role within a group context; to provide support for each other; to listen and watch as well as perform and lead; to develop awareness of other's needs; to focus concentration towards performance; to make appropriate use of an unfamiliar arts space; to understand and attain a common group aim.

6 Competencies: Interculturalism

To develop acceptance and tolerance of all individuals within the group; to resist patterns of destructive behaviour; to contribute to the resolution of conflict.

7 Competencies: Gender

Ability to develop sexually appropriate behaviour with adults and peers; to work successfully in a mixed gender group; to practice cooperation and non-aggressive behaviour.

8 Competencies: Organisation

To contribute to creating and respecting group-devised guidelines for sessions; to be consistently available for sessions; to operate video equipment.

Goals of Participating Institutions

The module was researched and prepared over the period March – June 2004, delivered between June and November 2004 and documented between January and April 2005. The working title of the module in the beginning was "Theatre work with Young Offenders". The eventual title of the project, which was suggested by the young people taking part was "The No Fear Theatre for Wicked Kids". It began as a collaboration between two agencies, Dartington College of Arts, including Centre for Creative Enterprise & Participation

(CCEP) and Exeter Youth Offending Team (YOT) working in collaboration with 'The Valley Regeneration Scheme' (preventing anti-social behaviour).

Dartington College of Arts (www.dartington.ac.uk) is one of the few specialist arts colleges in the UK – a university sector Higher Education Institution offering a range of opportunities for BA, MA, MPhil, and PhD qualifications. All its energies are devoted to the study and performance of contemporary arts and to the development of the artist's role in society.

Centre for Creative Enterprise & Participation (CCEP). Within the strategic aim of developing regional partnerships, Dartington College of Arts established the Centre for Creative Enterprise & Participation (CCEP) in September 2002, a development from the College's World of Work Unit, which was set up two years earlier. CCEP is a team of 13 specialist staff leading on the College's Widening Participation and Reach out to Business and the Community Strategies. The work of the Centre ranges from school and community projects, through student employability and graduate networking to our Creative Enterprise Development programme supporting the creative industries in the South West. This programme comprises:
- Specialist business support (surgeries and seminars)
- Continuing professional development (CPD) and workforce development
- Innovation services (research and consultancy)

As part of the Twisfer project we have worked with Jennie Hayes, from the CCEP team, who has presented the role of evaluation facilitator. Jennie's role as researcher within CCEP provides the potential for a working dynamic linking teaching, research and the development of innovative projects within the cultural sector. Within her research programme, exploring community based arts practices, she has been able to work with a number of initiatives in the region including working with the emerging network for participatory artists in the South-West to jointly organise a seminar series and co-ordinate successful fundraising to establish the network on a formal basis.

Exeter Youth Offending Team (YOT) is a multi-agency team consisting of social workers, police officers, mental health specialists, family support workers, specialists in education and a youth worker. This multi-agency team aims to prevent re-offending (the committing and re-committing of crimes) in children aged between 10 and 18 who are on a Court Order.

The personnel directly involved in the module were: Staff from Dartington

College of Arts with particular experience of contextual theatre practice within a regional, national and international context, recently graduated Theatre (BA Hons.) students from Dartington College of Arts and professional staff from the two Government funded organisations based in Exeter. The development of the module was seen in the light of the draft Strategic Plan of the College under the heading Partnership and Collaboration.

Impact of TWISFER module

The module provides the opportunity for further research into regional issues of contextual practice. The students working on the module experience a range of contextual theatre practice. This module enabled them to be firmly embedded in the demands of the project without the frames of institutional curriculum and assessment dictating the rhythm of work. They were expected to deal with issues of personal location, employment and travel and to work to the rhythms created by the distinctive nature of working within a professional organisation and in collaboration with professional workers in the field of Youth Justice.

Jennie Hayes

Evaluation

It is a key issue for theatre practitioners working within the Criminal Justice System to find ways to evidence the impact of their work in ways which are both sensitive to the work itself, and the people involved, and meets all stakeholders' needs.

With the development of UK government social inclusion policies since 1997, there are high expectations for arts projects to deliver demonstrable social outcomes, often leading to an over-simplification of the effects of the work. There can be a feeling that there is a need to 'tick the boxes' within government strategy to 'prove' the work has value and, in the longer term, to secure funding to continue it. There is also an issue of the complexity of agreeing potential outcomes with a varying number of partners with potentially different agendas. Over the longer term, there is also the problem of establishing causality, particularly where there are a number of different interventions.

On the Module project for TWISFER, we were aware of all these issues whilst attempting to evaluate the success of the project for those involved[1].

The project successfully targeted a group considered to be socially excluded in relation to a number of factors such as: having a parent involved in crime, drug misuse, mental health issues, evidence of self-harm, truancy, police contact, low self-esteem etc. The children were selected from an Anti-Social Behaviour Project (ASBP) as those who might benefit from engagement with this project. The ASBP itself works with children who are vulnerable due to a number of 'risk factors' as outlined above. The project successfully engaged children whose anti-social behaviour had come to light by two or more agencies.

The sessions were devised with the individual participants in mind, and included theatre techniques for enabling participants to feel comfortable in a space, for group cohesion and to draw on the development of group and individual strengths.

There were a number of parties actively involved within the project each of which contributed to the evaluation:
- The children who participated in the workshops (names omitted for confidentiality reasons)
- Members from the youth offending team (YOT): project leader Henrietta Ireland and Sandra Toogood who were involved in the sessions; Jim Wood, Youth Offending Team Leader
- Dartington College of Arts students who planned and ran the sessions jointly with Youth Offending Team members: Natalie Coombes, Laura Pace and Brian Guntrip
- The Anti-Social Behaviour Project (referral agency) and Intervention Worker, Sallie Horner
- Dartington College of Arts academic staff: project leader (Roger Sell) and evaluation facilitator (Jennie Hayes)

The evaluation mechanisms we used were as follows:
- Weekly review and planning discussions attended by students and YOT members and (less frequently) by Dartington College of Arts academic staff and the Intervention Worker

- Mid-way review meeting, led by evaluation facilitator, attended by students and YOT
- Observation by evaluation facilitator, YOT leader and intervention worker
- Analysis of video documentation
- Mid-way peer interviews during workshop, led by students and YOT
- Interview with intervention worker, Sallie Horner, by evaluation facilitator

Impact on the Participants as Expressed by Participants Themselves

The children were aged between eight and twelve. Indicators of their understanding of the benefits were:
- Participants expressed satisfaction and enjoyment in their involvement in the project through one-to-one discussions with the intervention worker. Six out of seven of the group verbally expressed their feelings of enjoyment of coming along to the group. In comments after the performance, participants expressed happiness and pride in their achievements in performance. Participants vocalised the part of the project they enjoyed most (in peer interviews).
- Attendance was high and consistent for this group (attendance was not compulsory) indicating a high level of satisfaction. There were particular instances of children who had not successfully participated in a group context prior to this project.
- Most participants were interested in undertaking further activity indicating a high level of interest. One participant expressed a desire to continue theatre work in an ongoing drama group.
- One participant who has never successfully been involved in a group called the group his 'drama friends', indicating a new sense of 'being part of something'.
- One participant enjoyed telling his family about his activities in the group.
- All participants showed an increased willingness to take part and concentrate as the sessions developed. Participants demonstrated increased focus and attention towards performance.

Impact on the Participants as Expressed by Other Agencies (YOT, DCA, Intervention Worker)

A number of factors were observed by other agencies both within the workshop /performance setting and outside the group.
Within the workshop sessions there were:
- Higher levels of concentration by participants at later sessions than at earlier sessions and lower levels of disruption at later sessions
- Greater cooperation between individuals in the group at later sessions
- Increased willingness to perform as the sessions progressed
- Increased capacity for imaginative and creative developments (particularly in relation to the development of the interplay between the real and the fictitious)
- Increased ability to resist patterns of sabotage and destruction and transform behaviour
- Increased confidence in use of the arts space and in developing ideas

It was observed that the children had formed an unusual (for them) sense of belonging and identity (indicated in, for example, the consensus on the development of the theatre group name and one child's calling the group 'my drama friends' and the difficulty of introducing new children to the group at a later stage). The YOT welcomed the opportunity to see children have this level of engagement. There was a real sense of pride coming from the children in performance. The YOT felt that integration, social skills, self-esteem and communication were improved in all participants in the group.

The above-mentioned behavioural changes indicated some level of transformation for the children, related particularly to group integration, confidence and communication skills. Some children had the opportunity to behave differently within the theatre workshops than they would, for example in a school environment, where the expectations of their behaviour were different, thereby allowing them a safe space. Beyond the workshop sessions there were benefits identified by the behaviour of individuals from the group whilst participating in other settings, e.g. at school. There were indications of:

- Increased self-confidence
- Decreased levels of disruption in school (one child)

Whilst we had hoped to encourage the expression of feelings and emotion within the group, it was felt that the timescale of the project did not allow the opportunity for this to develop in the way it might with a longer-term project.

Impact on the Students as Expressed by Students Themselves

The project involved a number of Dartington BA Theatre Students, three of whom actively participated in the majority of the twelve-week project, and took part in evaluation and planning sessions. They identified for themselves that they had:

- Gained knowledge of engaging a community from scratch
- Increased their potential job opportunities
- Widened their perspective of the notion of theatre
- Received help with the transition from performance student to professional
- Developed workshop skills
- Had the opportunity to learn through experience
- Learnt how to deal with disruptive behaviour

Impact on the Agencies Involved as Expressed by Those Agencies

The institution (Youth Offending Team) saw benefits in the project through enabling children to express themselves in ways that would otherwise not be possible. One member of the Youth Offending Team (YOT) gained knowledge of theatre techniques (Sandra). The YOT valued the opportunity to actively engage children in a creative project. The Intervention worker felt the programme of work contributed to her aims of the Anti-Social Behaviour Project.

Artistic Outcomes

It should be noted that the performance was seen as a sharing mechanism for friends and family, rather than a 'polished' performance. As such an evaluation of the performance as an artistic product was not undertaken.

Each participant developed their capacity for engaging in creative activity in new ways. Whilst initially their storytelling and ability to engage with theatre was rooted directly in their own experience, they all grew in an ability to develop imaginative thought in areas beyond their own experience. In addition, the content of their creative imaginings evolved to include emotions and feelings rather than simply actions. In addition, when asked to perform, each displayed willingness and interest in doing so. Each adapted to the idea of producing a piece of theatre, a remarkable achievement for children from difficult backgrounds. The participants developed ideas of thought and narrative through the use of theatre and drama techniques and this culminated in a collaborative performance.

The project successfully created a piece of theatre that channelled each individual's emotional energy and creativity into a positive outcome. There were significant moments of wholehearted engagement in the creative process by children who hadn't demonstrated this to that extent previously. Audience members enjoyed seeing their sons and daughters achieve in a way that had previously not been possible. Theatre techniques were used to engage the children in creative ways and overcome their difficulties in group-situations.

Working Conditions

The venue (Phoenix Arts Centre) was a positive place to meet as it was 'neutral ground' and gave participants the opportunity to enter an arts space for the first time and to 'take ownership' of it. Participants (and later their families) were able to use an arts space otherwise generally not used by them. However, the room used was noisy and didn't give enough opportunity for small group work (due to the size of the room). Although this was recognised at an early stage, it was not possible, for practical reasons, to change the room. The small group size was positive as it allowed for one-to-one interaction and development.

There have been many difficulties along the way, including beginning the project in a different town (Bradninch) and having to change the location. However, this in itself strengthened the team relationship and led to a positive approach to problem solving. The context of the team as a 'learning unit' has been crucial to the ethos of the project. It was noted that this has helped to address commonalities with the children in the group, as everyone has a learning role.

The commitment to meetings / time / sessions / preparation was better than expected. The level of responsibility for the project leaders was high and came from a number of directions - to produce what is necessary for TWISFER, to the children involved, to provide enough support for inexperienced student-artists, to deliver a successful project for the Youth Offending Team as well as ensure that each session was well planned in the context of a wider workload. Concerns were expressed about the level of expertise of Dartington students to manage the process and product with this group of children who had disruptive tendencies and behavioural issues. This was resolved by Henrietta Ireland taking increased responsibility for session leading.

The way in which children were targeted (through the Anti Social Behaviour Project) meant that we were able to ensure we were working with children at risk, and enabled us to follow up progress through their intervention worker. The children were collected and returned home by minibus to ensure they were able to attend. Without this, many would have not been able to find the parental support to attend. The timing of the sessions was chosen to facilitate attendance.

Post Script

After the project ended, we were concerned to ensure that there was some continuity for the group for those who wished it. The group took part in a series of five sessions led by drama students from Exeter University. However, this involved the participants joining in with an existing group and there were problems with integration. Although there were some positive outcomes from this, it didn't meet the needs of the group as hoped. One participant, however, took on responsibility for lighting and sound effects for a performance, which was very successful.

Outside this initiative, two of the participants are now regularly attending weekly 'stage school' sessions, paid for by the Anti Social Behaviour Project. For one of these children, there has been a marked increase in self-esteem and she has made new friends. It is unlikely she would have felt able to do this without the work she did in the TWISFER project. The other child has an outgoing personality and although would probably have managed stage school attendance prior to the TWISFER project, the project helped him to know what to expect when entering this new environment on his own. One participant is now taking drumming lessons and the Intervention Worker believes the project helped this participant with confidence issues, particularly when 'performing' in front of people. Since the project she has taken part in a school assembly, which had not happened beforehand. Two of the participants are having horse riding lessons. One participant has expressed the fact that he misses the drama group, and a difficult home situation has prevented his full involvement in other kinds of activities.

Generally the Intervention Worker believes the TWISFER project has helped raise the confidence of the participants to enable them to undertake other activity.

Some Questions

The evaluation of the TWISFER project raised a number of questions that we are only beginning to address with this group. In a further project we might include more in-depth evaluation mechanisms, particularly those that effectively integrate participatory evaluation into the project. The questions for further exploration include:

- How can we effectively integrate participatory evaluation into a short-term project without disrupting the artistic programme?
- How do we encourage children who have difficulty in expressing themselves to articulate how they feel about the theatre project?
- Is it possible to assess longer-term impact on the same children in, say, 6 months or 5 years?
- How does having an observer as part of the group affect the participants and the working team?
- How can we explore the impact of the work outside the immediate workshop sessions when many of the children's parents have communication and parenting issues?

Footnotes

[1] The evaluation reflects the major part of the project delivered in Exeter during late 2004. Earlier in the year an attempt to develop a project in the town of Bradninch was aborted due to difficulties in engaging with the community involved. Because we therefore were unable to sustain work with the target group for any significant period of time we have not included the outcomes of that part of the project in this evaluation.

Bibliography

Anderson, Benedict: Imagined Communities. Verso 1991.

Barry, Peter: Beginning Theory: An Introduction to Literary and Cultural Theory. Manchester University Press 1995.

Brook, Peter: The Shifting Point. Methuen 1988.

Burke, Peter: Popular Culture in Early Modern Europe. Temple Smith 1978.

Chapman and Hough: A Guide to Effective practice. Evidence based Practice, HM Inspectorate of Probation 1998.

Crang, Mike and Thrift, Nigel: Thinking Space. Routledge 2000.

Diamond, Elin: Performance and Cultural Politics. Routledge 1996.

DCMS (2001): Building on PAT 10 London: DCMS 2001.

Emunah, Renee: Acting for Real Dramatherapy Process Technique and Performance. New York: Bruner Mazel 1994.

Gioffi, Kathleen M.: Out of Actions – between Performance and the Object. Thames and Hudson 1998.

Gomez-Pena, Guillermo: Dangerous Border Crossing. Routledge 2000.

Graham, J. and Bowling, B.: Young People and Crime. Home Office Research Study 1995.

Harbison, Robert: Eccentric Spaces. MIT Press 2000

Jermyn H.: Arts and Social Exclusion: A Review prepared for the Arts Council of England Arts Council of England 2001.

Jones, Phil: Drama as Therapy – Theatre as Living. Routledge 1996.

Kastner, Jeffery/Wallis, Brian (Eds.): Land and Environmental Art. Phaidon 1998.

Ladurie, Emmanuel Le Roy: Carnival in Romans. Penguin 1978.

Marranca, B./Dasgupta G. (Ed): Conversations on Art and Performance. John Hopkins 1998.

Mast, S.: Stages of Identity; A Study of Actors. Gower 1986.

Miles, A.: What Works in Offender Rehabilitation? Including the Arts Discussion. Paper prepared for the Institute of Public Policy Research Arts in Society Seminar Series, 11 Sept 2003.

http://www.a4offenders.org.uk/new/sections/research/pages/researchfr1.html (accessed April 2005)

Miles, Malcolm et al. (Eds.): The City Cultures. Routledge 2000.

Policy Action Team 10: A Report to the Social Exclusion Unit: Arts and Sport London: DCMS 1999.

Randell, N: Including the Arts - Preventing Youth Offending. Canterbury: The Unit for Arts and Offenders 2002.

Read, Alan: Theatre and Everyday Life. Routledge 1995.

Rogers, C.: On Becoming a Person. A therapists view of Psychotherapy. Houghton Mifflin 1961.

Smith, D.: 'How Much do we Really know about what Works?' in Information; The reality and the Potential', Proceedings of the 13th Annual Probation Information and Research Conference. 1997.

Turner, Victor/Edward Brunen: The Anthropology of Experience, University of Illinois Press 1986.

The Unit for Arts and Offenders (Sept 2003) Arts in Criminal Justice Settings: research and evaluation: 15 case studies http://www.a4offenders.org.uk/new/sections/research/pages/researchfr1.html (accessed July 2004).

Vennard, J. and Hedderman, C. : Effective Practice with Offenders, in 'Reducing Offending; An Assessment fo Research Evidence on Ways of Dealing with Offending Behaviour', Home Office Research Study 187, 1988.

Yalom, D., Irvin: The Theory and practice of Group Psychotherapy. Basic Books. LLC 1995.

Youth Justice: A Review of the Reformed Youth Justice System Audit Commission 2004.

Zlatko Bastašić, Jelena Sitar-Cvetko

Creative Models of Communication (KREMOK) Theatre Work with Children and Young People with Special Needs

Structure of the Module
KREMOK

Qualification on Completion of the Module:
Postgraduate Diploma in Theatre Work with Children and Young People with Special Needs

Format and Minimum Timeframe

The course consists of 15 workshops, 20 hours each
(Initially they take place on a monthly basis)

The workshops are comprised of the following:
- a theoretical component (lectures)
- practical theatre work (also connected with other branches of art)
- performances and video presentations

At the beginning of each workshop the participants / members report on the following:
- how they applied their learning and experience from the last workshop
- their personal responses concerning the events of the last workshop

Each workshop concludes with an obligatory feedback session on the current workshop.

Assessment Criteria

The knowledge and experience the KREMOK model offers is important for theatre pedagogues and also useful for any person who works with people professionally, particularly for social workers, teachers, work therapists, social pedagogues and artists who act as leaders of various workshops.

KREMOK can also be applied to different groups of volunteers: AA, cancer survivors, clubs, drug abusers, unemployed people, people in a life crisis, marriage and family counsellors. The KREMOK model can be directly applied to the work of a therapist as a part of a diagnostic or curative process. The KREMOK model can also be applied to work organisations or living communities where there is a desire for a better quality of life.

Admission Requirements

Participants should have knowledge of and experience in the theatre and / or in social fields. They also need to show some sensibility as regards psychosocial processes and human empathy. The personal growth of each participant is expected (and necessary).

Recommendations for Sequencing Courses

Courses on family dynamics (for theatre practitioners):
- The Family as a System
- Life Cycles of a Family
- Rituals in a Family
- Family Myths
- Legends and Scripts
- Alcohol in a Family
- Drug Abuse
- Sexually Abused Children
- Bulimia Nervosa and other eating disorders

- Gestalt Theatre
- Drama in Education
- Theatre Course: The value and use of the material on the scene (expression and poetic possibilities)
- Course: "3rd theatre"
- Art Therapy

Competencies and Learning Objectives of the Facilitators

1 Competencies: Aesthetics

Kremok is about making life aesthetic. Metaphor as one of the basic artistic tools is of key importance here. Position or relation can thus be observed without fear of revelation and without embarrassment, since we are inside the arena of aesthetics. Artistic expression (confession/declaration) is genuine only if it is real/true. Authentic confession/declaration is encouraged by creativity – within the artistic process the contents from personal history and reality become material for artistic creation. Conscious as well as subconscious positions, relations, feelings etc. designed artistically become valuable material for further observation and artistic design. By means of various artistic tasks, where different expressive techniques and observation points are present, we can test the accuracy of our observations.

Discovering new things about complex mechanisms of our existence in this way also work in the opposite direction i.e. not only is life melted into art but art is also melted back into life – and thus it enriches and changes it. As we search for various artistic techniques and tasks individual tasks are intertwined with group tasks. This way every individual member has a chance to go deeply into himself/herself and to share with the group. According to the principles of well-being in empirical group work the group accepts the experience emphatically and thus makes it stronger, whereby every individual enters the worlds of the others and thus tests his/her own position.

2 Competencies: Ethics

Aesthetics and ethics are extremely close. The category of Aesthetics always consists of ethics as well: what is beautiful is ethical. The life of every person and every family is specific. There are neither happy nor unhappy people, only happy or unhappy moments or periods, some of which are predictable while others are unexpected. They all have their reasons, their results and their functions. Ethical categories that develop within the group are: empathy, tolerance and sincerity. There is no place for moralizing in art, which is the process of the empirical group. There are also some ethical starting points that are relevant for KREMOK – as well as for other empirical workshops and processes – e.g. the principle of discretion. Tolerance and empathy achieved during workshops should also be practised outside the laboratory, in their own living and working environments.

3 Competencies: Methods

The members of the group gain knowledge of the systemic approach to social subjects, mainly family. This is obtained in three ways:
- Through lectures and discussions
- Through recommended and photocopied literature (recommended books, magazines, photocopied lecture notes, various articles, notes)
- As professional explanation of individual cases

With the help of empirical work the members of the group become more and more sensitive to the events of their personal as well as work environments.

The members of the groups gain knowledge of certain methods and tools of systemic dynamics and therapy (e.g. geneogram). Practical tasks are directly transferable to their personal and work environments. We discover, test and apply methodical innovations when applying elements of the theatre to work in social fields. This model is applied to and tested on different types of populations with whom members of the group work.

4 Competencies: Field-Related Knowledge

1. The system's approach to Family dynamics makes possible a modern approach to the family, which is a specific type of living experience. The main processes going on in a single family are identified and analysed. However, in each family these processes are happening in their own, original and different way.
2. Puppetry is a large and rich artistic field, far more interesting than one can imagine. The exploration of different techniques and approaches to this art involves many skills from other branches of art too (fine arts, literature, music, acting, directing, dance).

5 Competencies: Orientation

Members of the laboratory view their own life positions from a broader perspective. They can take more control and responsibility over their own lives and can achieve relationships of a higher quality in their lives and work. The personal experience and knowledge gleaned by participants / members helps them to act in a positive way within their field of work (social field or art). Empathy, tolerance, creativity and self-confidence are virtues every person working within social fields should fight for. Just as the fight for a higher quality of life is happening not only in the psychiatric surgery, so the fight for theatre processes of a higher quality and the results are happening in the theatre spaces. There are different forms of theatre all around us; KREMOK just offers one more possibility.

6 Competencies: Research and Communication

Information acquired on the course – experience, knowledge and the basic reading – from both fields (puppet theatre and family dynamics) makes it possible for members of the course to take part in a discussion or working process on one or both of the fields. The level on which they communicate depends on their previous knowledge and the serenity every participant develops in KREMOK.

7 Competencies: Interculturalism

At KREMOK workshop rituals have a place in maintaining identity and continuity. Identity – personal as well as family identity, belonging to a guild, profession etc. is of great importance. It is a well-known fact that identity is one of the criteria of maturity for an individual subject, an individual as well as family or even nation. Awareness of one's own identity is essential for respecting others, different forms of life on a national, religious and sexual basis.

Incidentally, KREMOK has a very interesting structure: citizens of Slovenia, Croatia and Italy are a part of the closest work group. However, some of the students in Graz, Austria, have also become familiar with certain KREMOK elements.

8 Competencies: Gender

Family as a system, which was at the centre of our laboratory findings, reveals all questions pertaining to gender roles and power, tasks and responsibilities within the partner relationship between a man and a woman. Family represents the most sensitive and at the same time the most fixed domain within which numerous social mechanisms are reflected as well as practically enacted. We can see two kinds of sexual discrimination within a family: one comes from the outside and the other, the inner one, the consequence of unwritten rules which every new generation as well as every new family is faced with. The latter is extremely interesting and far more 'effective' than the former.

To successfully solve questions pertaining to gender means successful functioning of the whole family system, since the whole family system is based on partnership. In the same way dysfunctional partnership leads to a dysfunctional family. Of special significance is the single-parent family which generates new questions about gender. In KREMOK the pair of the leaders are mixed gender. Distribution of responsibility and power is equal within the project as each of the leaders has his / her roots in a professional branch and is thus competent in his / her area. Communication between them is spontaneous, co-operative, complementary and based on mutual respect, which is basically a fortunate circumstance.

9 Competencies: Project Management

Project KREMOK is a good example of cooperation between different sectors of social life.
KREMOK is organised like a pyramid consisting of:
- Private surgery
- Club (nongovernmental organisation) – on a local level
- Fund (governmental organization) – on a national level
- International project – on an international level

The realization of the project is also in the shape of a pyramid:
- Work of the leaders with the facilitators
- Work of the facilitators in their environment, where transfer of experience and knowledge from the laboratory is vital
- Action in their home environment

In accordance with this concept connections were made on several levels: the most important contacts and support came from the areas where the members were able to apply their methods directly to their work: schools, clinics, centres for social work and homes for the elderly. These organisations have helped their members financially as well as giving them time off from work to attend laboratories.

The course content is balanced on three levels:
- If family dynamics is the research field, the puppet theatre is the methodology – the tool used to research it. Achieving the correct balance between the two branches is the responsibility of the project managers. Balance is achieved by choosing leaders who are experts within their own fields (family dynamics and/or puppet theatre) and by inviting participants who are "artists" and /or "workers in social fields". A new quality is generated by combining these two branches.
- Balancing experiential work and applied knowledge is very important in KREMOK.
- Balance must also be achieved between personal and professional experience and the growth of each participant.

Project Module: KREMOK
How the Project Progressed
Creative Models of Communication

It is said that theatre is the mirror of life. This is true, but it depends on where the mirror is placed – what we see in it depends on where it has been placed. Sometimes there are things we do not wish to see and we therefore place the mirror accordingly. But theatre is alive, its mirror does not stand still and it also reflects the other side. If puppets rather than people show us this, we do not hold any hard feelings against them. Faults in puppets are amusing, sometimes we can laugh at them. Our immeasurable and unnameable fears become wooden and tangible and are no longer frightening (a strict teacher is made smaller than the size of our hand. Looking like that we can tell her anything).

Anything can be done with puppets! They are not alive! Or maybe they are? This is why puppets have always been such a popular cure for fears of all of humanity. And what is more – they are fun! Children know this and that is why they like them so much. We, adults, should like them too. Let them be our partners for a better life!

The Title and the Content

Firstly, this is a play on words:
KREativni MOdeli Komunikacije (Creative Models of Communication)

Creative: (from Lat. creare – to create) Creativity is a basic element and a way of getting to know oneself, to express oneself and to realise oneself. Family psychotherapists like to say: If there is an interpretation of a certain position or relation that you like very much, try to think of two more straight away. Looking for new possibilities and more successful ways of communication calls for creativity. Let me remind you that creativity is also one of the key features of Gestalt and psychodrama as well. (Note1: Moreno wrote: "At the end of the nineteenth century, when all of the calculations had been made, it was considered that the idea of the subconscious and its amazing consequences was of the greatest importance to the mental and social sciences. When the twentieth century will draw to an end, I believe that its greatest importance will lie in the idea of spontaneity-creativity and in their indestructible and important connection. We can say that the domains of both centuries are complementary. If the nineteenth century was looking for the smallest unifying factor – subconscious, the twentieth century discovered its biggest unifying factor: spontaneity-creativity.")

Models (from modus, measure, fr. modelle): These are specific areas of interest from family dynamics expressed in a theatre-specific way. A collection of select creative tasks enables better understanding and insight into the situations we live in and the relations of which we are a part. Possibilities of transcending these are shown in the creative part, which consequently influences (positively) the quality of the lives of individuals and the group. The model is applicable and useful for various groups, in families as well as school classes, work organisations and when working with people with special needs.

Communication (Lat. communicatio): intercourse or connection – this speaks for itself.

The Background

At the heart of KREMOK — upon which its thinking and functioning are based – is systemic theory. Contemporary family psychotherapy has been developed out of this. Systemic theory has proved to be an excellent and effective way of treating the family as a basic form and some other forms of systems we live in. It is therefore used in its many forms today: the English school in Slovenia (also taught at the Faculty of Medicine) and a Dutch model – mainly accepted in counselling services. An American model, that has been disseminated by the Franciscan order from their family centre, is prevailing as far as family psychotherapy is concerned.

Zlatko Bastašić

Family as a System

Inspired by contemporary science, structural systemic-oriented family therapy sees each member of the family as a part of the family system. An individual makes only one part of the whole system. Each member of the system is in constant interaction with the other family members. Family therapists believe that the symptom is also a product of the interaction between family members.

Every person has his / her own characteristics. Most of them result from interpersonal interaction. Family is an open dynamic system. Its dynamic stability depends on internal and external factors. That relative stability is homeostasis. These properties are often emergent properties. They emerge when the system functions. It is impossible to understand a family system by looking into or analysing each segment of the system i.e. we must analyse family interaction as well. Each part of the family system makes an impact on the whole family system and vice versa. Family members behave in accordance with the general rules that are specific to every individual family. A lot of factors change the family system. There is something paradoxical in the fact that constant change produces instability and that this instability is very important for developmental progress.

Family balance is maintained by the family rules, myths, rituals, customs etc. Family interactions are regulated by family rules. How can we discover family structure? Family therapists discover family structure by studying family interaction. Transactions are interactions between the family members that are constantly being repeated. Family transactions are among the main basic family characteristics. Family stability depends on them. We can say that family transactions are the result of family history.

Each family has its hierarchy. The boundaries are vertical and horizontal. The most important subsystem in the nuclear family is father-mother system. They are powerful in the family and of course they have a lot of very difficult tasks. The family system consists of subsystems. They are formed on different bases, i.e. generation, gender, etc. At the same time every member can belong to different subsystems. In such cases we say that each active participant has many different roles. A person can at the same time have the role of father, brother, son, husband, grandfather etc. The number of subsystems depends on the number of family members. There are clear boundaries between the systems. Boundaries have to be clear, but not rigid. It is very important that the subsystems are connected together but with the boundaries made clear. When the responsibility, authority, and communication are not confused, the boundaries are clear, and the system is functioning well.

Which information is important when working with a family? The most important information is surely the one concerning the family's way of resolving everyday tasks, conflicts, how they organize free time, family connection with the members who live outside of the family circle and, finally, the way the family resolves problems of separation and individualization. In the therapy session special emphasis is put on the family transactions, family myths, and the way the family used to resolve tasks up until now as well as the dynamics of the communication among family members and among the subsystems.

Every family is confronted with different tasks. In puberty and adolescence the pressure is very strong. This pressure has a positive impact. All family members have to participate in the transformation, and each part of the family system has to accommodate a new situation. Today there is a lot of stress: migration, homelessness, discrimination, crime, drug and alcohol addictions, unemployment, poverty, etc. But the pressure on the family comes not only from the outside. Pressure emanates from the inside as well. Development in itself forces the family to adapt constantly.

Jelena Sitar-Cvetko

From the Surgery to the Puppet Studio

Moreno paid for his "flirting with God by means of theatre" with a heavy fall and a broken arm. He then came to a conclusion that theatre isn't reality, but that it can have real physical consequences. He later continued with theatre research and when working with children discovered (with their help) the concept of "culture tin".[1] Just like theatre, which he did not want to close into a "culture tin" (and instead fought for its spontaneity), Moreno saw psychotherapy mainly as a part of real life. Thus we can now understand his observation of Freud working "in vitro", inside the four safe walls of his surgery(while Moreno's surgery is action "on the field", among people):

So, Doctor Freud, we are going to start where you have stopped. You meet people in the artificial environment of your surgery, but I see them on the street, in their homes, in their natural environment. You analyse their dreams, I give them courage to dream again. I teach people how to play God. (J. L. In J. Moreno: skupine, njihova dinanika in psihodrama)2

These words can be understood as moving towards theatre in social fields. Just like Moreno many of us leave the surgery hoping that we can with theatre "give courage to people to dream again." (Moreno, J. L. and Zerka T. Moreno: Skupina, njihova dinamika in psihodrama, Inštitut Antona Trstenjaka, Ljubljana 2000, p. 164)

If the society in which we live and the relations within it is the basic topic of our research, the theatre form is the methodology or tool we use to research it. We have chosen the theatre of material and figure (puppets in a broader sense) out of numerous theatre forms. As God is an animator of humans (he breathes the soul into them), humans are animators of puppets. With puppets it seems that people can learn to play God.

Realizing this, however, is not the only value a puppet holds. Puppets have been demonstrating, for the past twenty years, to the authors of the laboratories what an amazing tool they are for a person's inner growth. Leaders experience puppets as a device of artistic expression that is closest to them. In his book

"Lutka ima srče i pamet" Zlatko Bastašić defines the puppet's place in empirical and therapeutic situations and also the characteristics of the content and methodology of its use:

> A puppet is close to the mythological world of magic and animism, typical for the childhood period of human kind and the individual. The belief that everything in this world possesses a soul, that everything is alive, is the first condition for the puppet show to happen. The puppet is led by a hand that units 'the body and the mind', since the hand takes up the largest space in the brain cortex beside mimic facial musculature. A resuscitated puppet enables, in a special way, blending of the intimate with the empirical and subconscious on the part of the animator as well as on the part of the audience. (Zlatko Bastašić: Lutka ima srče i pamet, školska knjiga, Zagreb 1986, p. 16)

Furthermore, there is the question of a synchronization of an art form that combines all other branches of art (visual, music, speech, literature, movement, animation). Another important argument for use of material on stage is its metaphorical value. Poetics of individual positions and relations created by means of the world of objects that functions as symbols or metaphors on stage, is revealing for the author and yet not directly threatening. This is also an expressive technique and its special value lies in the fact that there is no direct exposure in the sense of a mental striptease. There is instead "the dance of the seven veils", which – according to experience – is no less effective. In short: A puppet show thought of as a play with plastic metaphors offers a methodology for researching complex symbols and at the same time the joy of creation.

The Participants

The participants have been invited to KREMOK on the basis of their varying qualifications and / or interests. The KREMOK team consists of: psychologists (2), pedagogues (1), social pedagogues (1), work therapists from the field of psychiatry (psychiatric clinic) and those working with the elderly (home for the elderly) (2), a specialised pedagogue (for young people with impaired hearing) (1), teachers (2), directors and leaders of puppet theatre groups (4), Art teachers, kindergarten teachers from hospitals (1), visual arts and puppet artists (2). A neccessary requirement for participation is that each participant be connected to a work place in which the methods and skills obtained in the workshops can be applied.

Considering the fact that this is a combination of psychosocial work and theatres, the leaders of the workshops also originate from these fields:
Zlatko Bastašić from Zagreb, a neuro-psychiatrist and family psychotherapist, famous for his psychotherapies for children with puppets and also an author of two well-known books: "Lutka ima srče in pamet" and "Puberteta in adoloscenca". (The former has just been reprinted and is again sold out.) Zlatko Bastašić is a supervisor, an educator and a psychotherapist with 35 years of clinical experience. He puts a lot of his energy into prevention and protection of mental health. He is a lover of visual and puppet art and is also active in both fields.

Jelena Sitar is a dramaturg and a director, with experience of 25 professional shows in professional puppet theatres in Slovenia and abroad. She is an editor of the Lutka magazine, a founder and member of the Zapik theatre and programme manager of a children's cultural centre "Hiša otrok in umetnosti" in Ljubljana. Jelena Sitar has successfully completed her postgraduate studies in psychotherapy and family dynamics at the Faculty of Medicine in Ljubljana.

The Aims

The main aims of KREMOK as research is:
- To research the possibilities of applying the field of family dynamics to the art of the theatre of material and figures (puppets)
- To broaden as much as possible the reference space between theatre and psycho-social work
- To test the models practically
- To incorporate the feedback from practical application back into the system, to improve it and offer it as a **TWISFER** model.

The aims of KREMOK as an educational empirical laboratory are:
- The members improve their professional competencies for working with people.
- The members develop their human potential, research their own situations and relations and see the value of their work on themselves.

- The members gain new knowledge for working on themselves and for working with people.
- The members research and are exposed to new methods of creative work in the theatre, aimed not at the theatre show / performance but at the growth of the group and the individual.
- The members gather new information and experience as well as practical, immediately transferable guidelines for their own work.

And yet: KREMOK is not a collection of recipes, it is an approach.

The aim of KREMOK as a module is:
- To give pedagogues, therapists, theatre pedagogues and artists a new additional tool for interesting, expressive, creative and nevertheless entertaining work with their pupils or students. It should also make them see what a powerful tool they hold in their hands when they use art, or more accurately (puppet) theatre.
- As with other similar programmes it should help participants to understand the processes that are going on within groups and individuals and should help them to better understand their own role (of teacher, therapist etc.), to broaden its boundaries and to be more creative within it. Thus they can help their pupils to find the way that leads to themselves, to others and to the world. They can add in a small way to their findings and to the process of building responsible and satisfying relations; In other words they can find joy in interesting and creative tasks.
- Art should be happening to them here and now and every day. Theatre can also be a way of life and not just an important building with golden doorknobs, boxes and tapestries etc. But the only one who can teach you to realise that is the one who has a deep understanding of this, something that is not merely a coincidence for the majority of our teachers.

KREMOK helps artists to be better artists. A combination of life and art - research into the representative forms of each, the widening of the reference space within art as well as raising awareness of its real power over a person's mentality - these are topics that are of great interest to an artist, for he / she goes through them empirically. Thus he / she looks for deeper meanings and new forms and becomes more lively in his / her plays and more responsible in his / her responsibility.

The aims of KREMOK as a strategy are:
- To discover, research and test new, successful methods and to design a model, using art, for systematic work and intervention with various groups and communities.
- To apply the model to the public in the following ways:
  - In the targeting individual users by educating their leaders using the pyramid form
  - In the form of workshops organised by the two leaders and members who have been educated in this approach
  - In the form of a suitable publication
  - As part of the curriculum when educating suitable members
  - In educating a certain number of people in Slovenia this way

Structure of the Workshops and Timeframe

So far 15 workshops, each consisting of 20 pedagogic hours, have been carried out. The first one took place in September 2002 and the last one in March 2005. All workshops took place in Ljubljana, only three took place in Grad Snečnik. Obligatory elements of each meeting are:

- Supervision: what and how the elements from past workshops were used in practice on professional and personal levels. We try to fill in the gaps i.e. the time during which we have had no contact with each other, to find out what personal and professional experience each member brings to the group, essentially to establish our current common reality. An important element of such introductory conversations is to show how the KREMOK elements were used in practice and to report on the results or the effects. At first the idea was to test the elements used in the previous workshop, but the most interesting moment was when the events started to 'resound', to interconnect and to function as individual 'tasks' turned into a process. Since this is an empirical laboratory the process happens simultaneously on personal and professional levels.

- Warm-up (connected to the main topic):
  For the warm-up we combine exercises from theatre and puppet training, improvisation, social games, DIE, Boal, Gipius, Viola Spolin and others. We make up certain exercises ourselves. The choice of exercises depends on the

aims of the specific workshop and on the type of group. As far as this is concerned we are probably no different to most other laboratories and schools of a similar nature.

- Presentation of the Topic
  A short introduction (which is different every time): a practical assignment, experience, theoretical lecture etc..

    - Development of the topic through a creative process, where the tasks are set on three levels:
    - Creative challenge
    - Becoming familiar with or testing a specific expressive technique
    - A topic from systemic (family) dynamics (which includes facing the topic and working on empirical material, letting a synergy occur that is made possible by a creative and dynamic group and poeticisation of the material.)

- "Cheering up" and going through the topic in a humorous way.
- Meditation, massage etc.
- Feedback, evaluation:
  As far as time management is concerned, all the important questions are addressed in the afternoon, so that "secondary processing" can take place during the night. The most difficult tasks take place the following morning. The closing of the workshop is also very important: It involves cheering up, humour and a final connection of the group before the end.
  We always function as a semi-open group with an agreement to be discrete outside of the group where personal material is concerned. The core of the group forms into a special brotherhood/sisterhood; the closeness of the members is very intense, which is typical for therapeutic groups. Creativity, on the other hand, is what makes them different. Individual creative tasks done well ensure mutual respect as well as emphatic reception of the members. Creativity (in which play is immanent!) also guarantees a relaxed and pleasant working atmosphere.

Exemplary Working Instructions

Unit 1: Family as a System and Theatre of Object – from Installation to Animation

Activities
- Presentation of the project and the participants
- Guided fantasy: A TREE
- Setting up a FAMILY from logs / sticks (positions, closeness, eye direction…)
- Making the puppets from logs - focusing on one family member.
- Presentation and animation of the newly designed puppet
- Lecture

Workshop Aims
Getting to know a family within the context of the theory of the system; creative work on participants' own family systems; gaining insight into different family systems and their variety; getting to know the theatre of objects as a form of artistic expression and the possibilities it offers for social intervention.

Unit 2: Family Tree and Various Puppet Techniques

Supervision

Activities
- Theatre: I am a tree; individual and group work by means of creative movement
- Visual arts expression: Visual creation of a conjoined tree
- Paper puppets: On the tree
- Theory: Genogram, lecture, dealing with individual cases, participants own genograms
- Empirical work: Hellinger's setting up of a family system within space
- Final cheering up: A play with puppets with humorous inserts from family biographies
- Feedback
- A film "about a man who was planting a tree" – a cartoon

Workshop Aims:
Experiencing and experimenting with a genogram as a tool for becoming aware of the family system, working on their own genograms, presentation of Hellinger's method, overall artistic expression, and animation of the drawing.

Unit 3: Life Cycle of a Family, Love, a Young Childless Couple, a Wedding

Supervision

Activities
- Annual rings on a tree
- Visual arts work on the set topic
- Opening of the visual arts exhibition, role play
- Massage in a circle
- The meaning of transfer, a task in pairs
- Winnicott's "Blots" - making up a story connected with this
- Travelling around the life spiral of the family (creative movement with music)
- Love story in a literary form
- Shadow puppets, becoming familiar with technology, theoretical starting points and possibilities of use, creativity with shadow puppets
- Lecture on communication, the cycle of family development and love
- Group play involving the actors and material (newspapers)
- Feedback

Workshop Aims
The idea of transfer – theoretically and practically – getting to know the life cycle and the main features of family system formation, theatre of shadows; its technology and poetics.

Unit 4: A Young Couple and a Young Baby, Finger Puppets

Supervision

Activities
- Guided fantasy on childhood
- Making a small finger puppet – presentation and interaction
- Messages from the puppet and to the puppet
- Comments
- A performance of the Zapik Theatre: 'Mi ka ka ko kuhala' (Slovene children's finger games); Lecture on a small child within the context of the family; the two leaders and a guest, Igor Cvetko, M.A. lecture on finger puppets
- Puppet vignettes with puppets on the hands
- Final discussion
- Feedback

Workshop Aims
Getting to know a period of a family cycle (a young couple with a child), a child during the first three years of his/her life (development at psychology; context and meaning), presentation of the meaning of and testing the finger theatre technique.

Unit 5: Adolescents and Masks

Adolescents and Masks

Supervision

Activities
- Guided fantasy on the topic of youth
- Two profiles of the same person in two different age periods of life; a dialogue between them: a puppet show with flat puppets
- Lecture: definition of adolescent period and its features and development at tasks of a family with an adolescent
- Flat puppets and masks; lecture on both theatre forms of expression

- Making the masks
- A play with masks, use of the requisites
- Feedback

Workshop Aims

Developmental tasks of the family during adolescence, theoretical and practical work, introduction to and experimentation with the flat puppet and the mask as a form of theatre expression.

Unit 6: Rituals and Time, Hand Puppets

Supervision

Activities
- Making of small wooden hand puppets
- Definition of the term SELF; a short lecture
- Making of the auto-portrait; heads of hand puppets made of artificial clay
- Arrangement of the hand puppets around the tree as a symbol of workshops
- Logs and puppets: used and raw material meet; improvisation with puppets.
- Feedback

Unit 7: Chaos and Order

Chaos, organised disorder; a part of the whole

Supervision

Activities
- Warming up, group building
- Group drawing with background music
- Interpretations
- Deciding on the title for the picture
- Role-play

- Division of the picture into small parts
- Emergence of a new picture through a dialogue with part of the big picture
- Exhibition, confrontation and comments
- Lecture: A part and the whole within the systemic whole
- Lecture: Texture and structure as artistic categories
- Feedback

Workshop Aims
Defining connection and interaction between separate parts and the whole - theoretically and empirically – as well as connections between organisation and disorganisation; becoming familiar with the categories of structure and texture while creating a piece of art (theatre, visual arts, music etc.).

Unit 8: Object and Movement, Stories and Adventures of Wooden Families

Supervision

Activities
- A game with logs
- Setting up a family using logs; some members wished to set up their families again because certain changes had taken place.
- Dynamics (shifts) within families looking for balance
- Lecture: Subsystems, closeness, distance etc.
- Animation as input for movement and possibilities for change
- Visual art's interpretation of the setting
- Exhibition of the paintings with comments by the authors and a lively discussion within the group (role play - in the gallery)
- Constructing: a hanging mobile; the task of balancing the system and putting it in motion at the same time
- System and homeostasis
- Lecture: The meaning of balance in dramaturgy and directing theatre performance
- Feedback

Workshop Aims
Getting to know a family as a system in constant motion, which threatens it and

at the same time offers it possibilities for further development. Getting to know the principle of homeostasis and the laws of connection involved in building it up. To understand the principle of balance as an aesthetic and technical category important in the production of an art work.

Unit 9: Speech and Animation of Photography, Family in Time

Supervision

Activities
- Sorting random photographs as excerpts from life into a meaningful whole with a clear message
- Animating the composition and the message
- Lecture: on the life cycle of a family based on photographs
- Associative story telling of the members based on selected photographs
- Frozen scenes: motifs from photographs
- Theatre improvisation as a continuation of what is going on in the picture (animating the picture)
- Comics as part of visual arts, films and theatre
- Puppet scenes, picture animation
- Feedback

Workshop Aims
Becoming familiar with time as a co-player in the life of a family; time in art, time and rhythm, time as a condition for animation.

Unit 10: Evaluation

- Festival of Possibilities (see Evaluation)

Particularly Successful Segments

An Example of a Workshop

Family as a System and the Theatre of Object – From Installation to Animation

Setting up a family from logs
The participants make an installation of their own families. They choose specific pieces of wood to represent family members. Even though instructions are not given the participants usually try to find logs with some characteristics (tall, thick, narrow, round etc.) which represent specific people. Their task is to set up the logs in a way that forms the family system in which they live. The logs are cut in such a way it possible for them to "look" in a certain direction depending on the way they are turned. When the systems are ready, participants present them to the group. An installation of a "group sculpture" made of pieces of wood has rather limited possibilities and expression. In spite of this we can collect basic information about the family system which is placed in front of us.

> ... we gave them logs as unstructured material. Each participant played with them for a while, making various sculptures. After that we suggested that the logs be changed into family members. They are of different heights, the ends are cut off and the oval part of the log represents a face. We asked each of them to show (set up) their own family of three generations. The logs could be placed close together or far away from each other and the faces could be turned in any direction. An experience of one's own family in a given moment was frozen / stopped and symbolically represented by the sculpture. Some participants also included their pets. They were denoted by a log lying down. Then a discussion followed, first in pairs then in groups. Families came to life in front of our eyes. Every participant was able to recognize the structure of either his /her or someone else's family. Such sculptures enable an individual to identify exact relations among members of their own family no matter how close or distant they are, to recognize family alliances and hidden problems like, for example, grieving. In some of the structures certain family members had no place (e.g. the divorced partner). This representation of an inner picture of a family served for further research. Zlatko Bastašić, diary

Than we go a step further: how do we animate pieces of wood to develop live interaction amongst the wooden family members? The solution is rather simple

– act as Maestro Geppetto in Pinocchio and turn pieces of wood into live beings
– puppets.

How to do it?
Follow these tasks:
- Saying one sentence that each member of the family would say (his/her typical sentence in a specific situation). We don't need to move the logs yet. We can create little dialogues.
- Placing the system in the before and after position. What happened before and what comes next. (We introduce time as an important factor)
- Finding out who will be the first to leave the system and why.

Which positions will the other members take after that has happened. This task is already very complex. It has to be checked before the "performer" and the group is ready for it. There are lots of other tasks which can be suggested by the trainer or the group.

Afterwards participants make their own log – puppets, just one, the "auto portrait" or the whole group. Participants create faces, sew dresses, make hair etc. They use sticks and ropes for manipulation etc. The time used for "manual work" is very important. Puppets are decorated in a specific way. Humorous approaches are always welcome. The creator of the puppet has an opportunity to get in touch with the person he/she is presenting in a creative way. He/she even has the possibility of changing that person. At the end there is the obligatory puppet play. There are plenty of possibilities: it can be played in a certain system (family), there can be some visitors going around or it can be a fantasy play where different puppets are involved.

After this process the positions of the members within their systems are no longer their destiny, but simply the momentary situation in which they find themselves and which can be changed with a single move... And that's the point! The process is very simple: pieces of wood as dramatis personae playing the roles of family members, and acting out the family dynamics in front of us.

The theme can be realised in different settings and according to different time schedules. The group and the aims of the workshop dictate the time spent on it. Hours could be spent on this but so too could a week or even a month.

...With the exception of group work, a family sculpture is an effective diagnostic and therapeutic method of working with individuals. We can use it instead of psychodrama and it can also act as introduction to designing a living sculpture (V. Satir, B. Hellinger). It is also useful at supervision when we are dealing with the dynamics of the relations within an institution. When our group reached homogeneity we also used logs to represent personal family relations/events (when an individual participant wished to do so). Zlatko Bastašić

We did not suggest any exercises at the beginning as the exercises depend on different circumstances – who the members of the group are, what the aim of their work is, the age of participants, how well they know each other, how big the group is etc. (We have also used "a fantasy trip" for the beginning of the unit where we came in touch with our own trees.)

Jelena Sitar-Cvetko

Lecture: Puppetry – Object Theatre

Object theatre within puppet theatre is a type of puppet show where a puppeteer does not use a scene puppet but instead objects for everyday use. It is a radical form of puppet theatre in which the useful and the poetic value of the object must be clearly distinguishable. The object on stage is animated in such a way that all its qualities are employed – the form, the material it is made of, the colour, size and its purpose. Usually the latter is of vital importance: WHO the object is. On the basis of this other answers to questions LIKE WHAT are added (old, clumsy, shiny). The animator first closely observes the object and lets it 'talk' about itself. Then the awakening time arrives: what will he think, what will he want, where would he go and how will he do it. The answers to all these questions in movement are already an ANIMATION. Its success depends on the skill of the animator and even more, on his/her ability to adopt the part of the other being, the latter being either a school bag or a teacup. Then the process is similar to playing a musical instrument. A musician can either play the notes or the music. An instrument in the hands of a good musician is a LIVING BEING. Think of, let's say, a flute player walking behind his flute while it leads him around the stage and determines his steps. A similar thing happens to the puppet and the puppeteer, music in this case is our animation. But still, a school bag remains a school bag and a teacup remains a teacup. The main rule of good object theatre is that the audience are part of the transformations from a school bag as a useful object to a school bag as a living being. This is a magic moment of 'birth' and it would be wrong to deprive the audience of this magical moment of transformation.

The greatest experts in object play are children. In their hands everyday objects lead the lives of people. Children in their play teach the puppeteers. This is probably the reason why children and puppeteers get along so well. In many puppet schools (e.g. productions by Wroclaw and Bialystok High School for puppeteers – where the author of this contribution is based) future puppeteers must first be able to play with the object. When they have mastered this, they can start using scene puppets involving various techniques and technologies. According to one of the leading puppet theorists Henry Jurkowski "playing with an object is going back to times of animism" (Lutka 37, ZKOS Ljubljana p. 5, 1983), and this is where most probably the puppet was born. After everything that has been written so far it is of no surprise that play with an object is what started the chain of our KREMOK laboratories.

Zlatko Bastašić

Lecture: The Family System as an Installation in Family-Therapy

There are numerous methods that can help us gather information on family structure and relations within a family. Basic constellations at different times in the connection between a problem and family interaction are researched. An idea of a family sculpture refers, above all, to a live sculpture, but here however, we are interested in the methods used with wooden sculptures. The most famous is surely the family board introduced by Ludewig and Kvebeak test-sculpture (see: Cierpka, M.: Handbuch der Familiendiagnostik, Springer Verlag, Berlin, Heidelberg, New York, 1996). They all have in common the use of wooden figures for setting up a family. Working on a sculpture encourages the family members to interact and so the relations are expressed in symbolic relationships between figures. The sculpture can represent the family as it was in the past or what it might be like in the future. This enables the individual and the family to smooth past actions creatively. Even the process of setting up functions as feedback for the family. Within the set-up / sculpture aspects of space are analysed: closeness, distance, direction of face and eyes. The key role is the one of social distance and intensity of relations. A circle and a semi-circle express harmony and a mutual sense of belonging.

S. Neil (Neil, S. E.: The Family Chess Board and Projective Genograming: The Two Tools for Exploring Family System, Journal of Family Psychotherapy 15, (1, 2), 2004, str. 173 - 186) describes the use of chess pieces in a project genogram. The figures are widely accepted in individual, marriage, family and group therapy and also in counselling. Chess pieces also enable a symbolic representation. Looking at it from the systemic point of view, working on a sculpture enables a new communicative reality to be formed through communication with the others and, what is more, it allows the past to be seen in a new light.

Target Groups: Aims and Competencies

The KREMOK model has a pyramid structure: the participants of the KREMOK group are at the same time leaders of their own groups and pass their experience on and adapt them to these groups. In supervision, with which every laboratory begins, members and leaders discuss the effects of individual contents and work methods on various target groups (children at school, children, members of puppet theatres, high school students in boarding houses, families, adolescents - patients of psychiatric clinics, children in hospitals (the neurology ward), children and teenagers with impaired hearing, senior citizens in homes for the elderly). These are the effects of the KREMOK laboratory on a relatively large number of different people.

1   Competencies: Aesthetics

In KREMOK we see a person and their essence in creativity rather than perceive them merely as 'homo sapiens'. Aesthetisation of life is one of the fundamental aspects of the work in KREMOK. A shift onto an artistic level gives a particular situation much needed distance and change in the sense that the situation becomes identifiable and recognizable but not threatening. Certain features of this process can be compared to dreams. In order for that to happen a certain amount of creative effort is required. It is accompanied by satisfaction, which is an integral part of every creative process. It is for these reasons that the KREMOK workshops are always fulfilling.

2   Competencies: Ethics

Work in KREMOK is not possible without empathy and tolerance - virtues, which every individual tries to develop and set in relation to other members. The support of the group gives an individual value and dignity and the creative product gives them self-confidence and self-respect. All of these are of great importance, since, in many, cases members of groups have fewer opportunities. When the authentic essence of one human being touches another human being his possible 'defect' is only of a secondary importance.

3   Competencies: Action

The members of target groups try to accomplish the following by applying a selection of contents from KREMOK:

- Creative processes show that no rigid forms are successful - neither in art nor in life. Creativity opens up numerous possibilities and ways in which individual cases can be solved, no matter in which area they appear.
- Dealing with one's own situation and relationships and confrontating others through the medium of art leads to a deeper understanding of certain rules in family life and art as unique and thus the value of each separate life form.

4   Competencies: Field-Related Knowledge

Expressions of theatre, literary, painting and puppetry involve becoming familiar with and using knowledge from these areas. They encourage similar behaviour in other situations as well.

A successful connection between artistic area and social activities and help has stirred interest in individual artists (puppet theatre, festival, cultural-artistic societies, Public Fund for Cultural Activities of the Republic of Slovenia - JSKD) as well as in those from the field of social work and health care (Faculty of Education - the department of social education, Psychiatric clinic, Children's hospital, Homes for the elderly, Fund for those with impaired hearing and for those working with them). The successful project has created greater interest in making connections between the two fields.

5 Competencies: Orientation

To make sure the users understand that their own situation can be influenced or can be accepted with understanding and the best made of it. To use one's own creative potential and to encourage creativity within others for a richer and better life. Confrontation, awareness, acceptance of similarity and difference; we are all different and we are all similar; we are all unique originals and thus each in our own way creative. Creativity – it is innate in all of us. KREMOK's practice and all the individuals show this to themselves and to the group.

KREMOK therefore fights against social exclusion.

6 Competencies: Gender

Considering the fact that family is the subject matter of artistic and research activities in KREMOK, we focus strongly on the issue of partnership as the basic bond in a family. Good partnership and therefore a functional family system consists of appropriately solved gender issues. (In every family!)

7 Competencies: Organization

Practical tasks are set into time frameworks from one meeting to the next, which is approximately one month. The realization of this is up to individual leaders: some wish to use the novelties in their own environment while still 'hot', others wish to sleep on them... It also depend on the groups since not all topics and tasks are appropriate for all users.

Overall the activities were well accepted by the target groups as well as by the leaders of the organizations from which the members came from. The organizations, for the most part, managed to find a substitute for the member(s) of the group during the KREMOK laberatories as they believed are saw this as a valuable investment. In the case of a more intensive programme of participation – that would probably become an obstacte to participation for some.

Evaluation

In KREMOK the action takes place on two levels: Personal experience and in gaining new knowledge and competencies. This is why evaluation also took place on these two levels:

In the form of discussions:
- during workshops (when meeting again e.g. in the morning - regular discussions on personal experience)
- at the end of a workshop (mainly personal experience)
- when meeting again (the successful or unsuccessful application of certain methods to living and work environments)
- exchanging authors' opinions at the end of individual topics, workshops, cycles so that the programme could be adapted to the group (as a rule more material than was actually needed was always prepared, mainly due to the experiential nature of the work)

In the form of creative tasks:
- within an individual workshop
- at the end of each cycle (e.g. looking for a KREMOK logo, brainstorming about KREMOK, a mysterious note on a piece of paper in a hole in a tree that is then sent into space etc.)

At the End of KREMOK: Festival of Possibilities
The members of the group each lead their own workshop for a chosen target group. They choose a topic they find particularly interesting, the most appropriate or closest to their concerns and they go through it in the form of a workshop. The topic is not put forward directly but in accordance with KREMOK's creativity principles – the leader adapts and improves it in accordance with these – KREMOK material can only be a part of his / her own workshop; it can be a starting point or even its greatest part.

In accordance with this the Festival of Children's Creative Workshops (Festival otroških ustvarjalnih delavnic) was carried out in Snežnik.

Titles of some of the workshops include:
- From Winnicott's blotches to a puppet scene
- Coloured stones, our family in its favourite place (at home, on holiday etc.)
- The crest of our family
- Stones of courage for my family members (for each their own and designed for them)
- Family picture of the Flintstones in a valuable frame decorated with magic dust.

All workshops were innovative. The group members showed immense skills as far as group work was concerned; they proved to be skilled in methodologies and sensitive to the work with content related to the inner world. They also demonstrated a great deal of knowledge in visual art, theatre and puppetry.

During the time of KREMOK workshops most members also improved their own quality of life (finished their studies, started with postgraduate studies, got married, had children, became independent, experienced an improvement in relations within families and work environments). Certain topics from KREMOK have also been used by the leaders as material for work with various groups (Psychology students, young people with limited opportunities, creative theatre workshops, psychiatric surgery) and has been proved to be very successful. Flexibility of the model, however, also means something else: the concept and the scheme of the workshops can be used for numerous other topics.

Footnotes

1 J. L. Moreno i Z. Moreno, Skupine, njihova dinamika in psihodrama, str. 278-280
2 J. L. Moreno i Z. Moreno, Skupine, njihova dinamika in psihodrama

Bibliography

Andolfi, M., Angelo, C., De Nichilo, M.: Der Mythos von der Last der Schultern. Heidelberg 1997.

Bandler, R., Grinder, J., Satir, V.: Mit Familien reden. München 1987.

Barker, P.: Basic Family Therapy. Oxford London Edinburgh Boston Palo Alto Melborne 1968.

Zlatko Bastašic, Zlatko: Pubertet i adolescencija, Zagreb 1995

Zlatko Bastašic: Lutka ima i srče i pamet, Zagreb 1990

Boal, Augusto: Games for Actors and Non- Actors, London, New York 1992.

Bolton, Gavin: Acting in Classroom Drama, A Critical Analysis. London 1998.

Boscolo, L., Bertraando, P.: Die Zeiten der Zeit. Eine neue Perspektive in systemischer Therapie und Konsultation. Heidelberg 1994.

Boszormenyi-Nagy, I., Spark, M.G.: Unsichtbare Bindungen. Die Dynamik familiärer Systeme. Stuttgart 1981.

Bregant, Leopold: Psihoterapija 14, Katedra za psihiatrijo medicinske fakultete, Ljubljana 1986.

Cierpka, M.: Handbuch der Familiendiagnostik. Berlin, Heidelberg, New York 1996.

Džukanivic, Boro M.: Kultura psihiatrija psihologija, Sarajevo 2002.

Gledališki besednjak, Mestno gledališče Ljubljansko, Ljubljana 1981.

Gordon, T. : Familienkonferenz. München 1989.

Haley, J.: Direktive Familientherapie. München 1985.

Hare, A. Paul and June Rabron: J.L. Moreno, London 1996.

Hellinger, B.: Ordnungen der Liebe. Heidelberg 1997

Imber-Black, E.: Geheimnisse und Tabus in Familie und Familientherapie. Freiburg im Breisgau 1995.

Imber-Black, E., Whiting, A.R.: Rituale in Familien und Familientherapie. Heidelberg 1993.

Kralj, Vladimir: Dramaturški vademekum, Ljubljana 1964.

Lutka 2000, tematska Stevilka: Lutka v vzgoji in terapiji, tematski del zbrala in uredila Jelena Sitar, Ljubljana 2000.

McGoldrick, M.,Gerson, R.: Genograme in der Familienberatung. Bern, Göttingen, Toronto, Seattle 2000.

Minuchin, S.: Familie und Familientherapie. Theorie und Praxis struktureller Familientherapie. Freiburg im Bresgau 1987.

Minuchin, S., Rosman, L. B., Barker,L.: Psychosomatische Krankheiten in der Familie, Stuttgart 1986.

Moreno, Jakob Levy in Zerka Teoman Moreno: Skupine, njihova dinamika in psihodrama, Inš titut Antona Trstenjaka za psihologijo, logoterapijo in antropohigijeno, Ljubljana 2000.

Moskau, G., Muller, F. G.: Virginia Satir – Wege zum Wachstum. Paderborn 1992.

Neil, S. E.: The Family Chess Board and Projective Genogramming: Two Tools for Exploring Family System. Journal of Family Psychotherapy, 15, 2004 (1,2), p. 173-186.

Nerin, F.W.: Familienrekonstruktion in Aktion. Paderborn 1989.

O'Connor, J., Mc Dermott: The Art of Systemy Thinking. London 1997

Pedopsihiatrija 4, Katedra za psihiatrijo Medicinske fakultete in Univerzitetna psihiatrič na klinika. Ljubljana 1982.

Piercy, F.P., Sprenkle, D.H., Wetchler, J.L.: Family Therapy Sourcebook. New York London 1996.

Reiter, L. Brunner, J.E., Reiter-Theil, S.: Von der Familientherapie zur systemischen Perspektive. Berlin, Heidelberg, New York 1997.

Satir, V.: Selbstwert und Kommunikation. München 1988.

Satir, V., Englander-Golden, P.: Sei direkt. Paderborn 1994.

Sauber, S.R. ‚L'Abate, L., Weeks, G.R.: Family Therapy. Basic Concepts and Terms. Rockville, Maryland 1985.

Selvini-Palazzoli, M., Cirillo, S., Selvini, M., Sorrentino, A.M., Die psychotischen Spiele in der Familie, Stuttgart 1996.

Sitar, Jelena: Gledališki proces kot psihoterapevtska tehnika (diplomska naloga, tipkopis), Medicinska fakulteta, Ljubljana 2004.

Sprenkle, D.H., Moon, S.M.: Research Methods in Family Therapy. New York London: Guilford Press 1996.

The Puppet, What a Miracle, The UNIMA Puppets i Edication Commission, Zagreb 2002.

Tomm, K.: Die Fragen des Beobachters. Schritte zu einer Kybernetik zweiter Ordnung in der systemischen Therapie. Heidelberg 2001.

Walsh F.: Normal Family Processes. New York, London 1993.

Wall, K., Ferguson, G.: Rituale für Lebenskrisen. München 1999.

Watzlawick, P., Beavin, H.J., Jackson, D.D.: Menschliche Kommunikation. Bern, Göttingen, Toronto, Seattle 1996.

Wynne, L.C., McDaniel, S.H., Weber, T.T.: Systems Consultation. New York, London 1986.

Watzlawick, P. Weakland, H.J.: Interaktion. Bern, Stuttgart, Wien 1980.

Weber, G. Zweierlei Glück. Die systemische Psychotherapie Bert Hellingers. Heidelberg 1995

Welter-Enderlin, R., Hilderbrand, B.: Gefühle und Systeme. Heidelberg 1998.

Welter-Enderlin, R., Hilderbrand, B.: Rituale – Vielfalt in Alltag und Therapie. Heidelberg 2002.

Appendix

List of Authors and Editors

Ann Barry holds a B.A. in Applied Psychology /Sociology, an M.A. in Counselling Psychology and an M.A. in Drama & Theatre Studies from University College Cork. She also holds performance diplomas in Speech & Drama from Trinity College London. Ann has taught and continues to teach with a variety of departments within UCC including the Centre for Adult Continuing Education and the Department of Applied Psychology. She also works as a drama workshop facilitator with a variety of community groups and as a Special Needs drama teacher with children and teenagers with learning disabilities. In addition she is employed in the Cork School of Music (Cork Institute of Technology) where she is currently involved in designing a degree in Drama Studies. Current research interests include: The body and bodily experiencing in Therapy /Counselling and in drama, various acting processes and the use of drama with students with special needs.

Zlatko Bastašić was born in Croatia and studied in the Faculty of Medicine, University of Zagreb, Croatia, with a specialization in neuropsychiatry and sub-specialization in child and family psychotherapy. She holds an MSc in psychiatry (therapy using dolls) and has worked at the Centre of Medial Care at the Clinic Hospital Rebro in Zagreb. For over 15 years she has had a private practice in psychotherapy. Publications include: The Doll has Ears and a Mind (published by _kolska knjiga Zgreb/Croatia); Puberty and Adolescence (published by _kolska knjiga Zagreb/Croatia)

Matthias Bittner studied German Literature, Media Studies and Sports and holds a teaching qualification in Sports; He has free-lanced since 1998 in the areas of Theatre, Performance, New Media, Film, theatre work with handicapped people. Institutions he has worked with include: the University of Hannover, "Gesellschaft für Theaterpädagogik", a variety of different schools, "Schauspielhaus Hannover" – NDR (German TV-Channel), other free production studios for film and BSN (Behindertensportbund Niedersachsen).

Bernadette Cronin teaches in the German Department and the Department of Drama and Theatre Studies at University College Cork. She is a member of the Board of Drama and Theatre Studies, in which capacity she was involved in setting up the undergraduate degree programme in Drama and Theatre Studies in UCC. She is also a performer and researcher and her current field of interest is Austrian experimental theatre. She holds an MA in German Studies and a diploma in Education from University College Cork, a diploma in translation from the London Institute of Linguists and a performance diploma from the London Academy of Music and Dramatic Art. She is currently writing a doctoral dissertation in Theatre Studies for the University of Exeter, UK.

Katharina Grilj was born in Graz and studied psychology and Theatre Work in Social Fields at the University of Graz. She works as theatre pedagogue with children, adolescents and elderly people.

Jennie Hayes is a writer, researcher and arts practitioner with a background in community and participatory arts practices. She is currently AHRB Research Fellow in Creative and Performing Arts at Dartington College of Arts, Devon, England, researching community based arts practices in the UK.

Henrietta Ireland holds a postgraduate diploma in drama therapy and a diploma in counselling and psychotherapy. She has trained up to intermediate level as a Systemic Family Therapist and has qualified as a teacher in adult education. She has been working within the Youth Justice sector for six years as a parent and family support coordinator and is currently also managing an early intervention project with young people to prevent anti-social-behaviour.

Gerd Koch is professor for Sociocultural Studies at the Alice-Salomon-Fachhochschule (University of Applied Sciences) Berlin. He is co-editor of KORRESPONDENZEN (Theatre Pedagogy News Journal), head of the German Society for Theatre Pedagogy and is director of the editing centre of Dictionary of Theatre Pedagogy (Arbeitsstelle Wörterbuch der Theaterpädagogik).

Roberto Mazzini holds a degree in psychology; he is a teacher and theatre practitioner and is the founder of the Giolli association. His main field of practice is in street and political theatre. Working with many different social groups, he uses Boal's method inspired by Freire's framework. His publications include articles and books on theatre and conflict resolution or intercultural education.

Annetta Meißner holds a degree in social work from the ASFH-Berlin and an MA in Theatre Pedagogy (Universität der Künste – Berlin). She has carried out projects based on theatre pedagogical methods, art and performance with children, adolescents and elderly people for social, cultural and christian institutions in Berlin (e.g. KREATIVHAUS e. V., Kunstverein ACUD; Jüdisches Museum, Murkelbühne e.V.). Since 1999 she has engaged in theatre work with mentally handicapped persons as director of the theatre group "Confetti" (Diakonisches Werk Berlin Oberspree). She currently works as theatre pedagogue in a day-care facility for children and is a trainer for educators in this field (Diakoniewerk Hamburg).

Martina Pusterhofer is a theatre pedagogue, a teacher and researches in the field of biography. She has carried out theatre projects both with elderly people and young people.

Sieglinde Roth was born in Graz and studied German Literature, Philosophy and Pedagogy at the University of Graz and Theatre Pedagogy at the Universität der Künste Berlin. She has worked as a theatre pedagogue and dramaturg at the Deutsches Theater Berlin, at the Landestheater Linz and as a freelancer. Since 2002 she has been head of Theatre Work in Social Fields at uniT-Cultural Association at the University of Graz, Austria. Within this framework she is coordinator of the Grundtvig1-projects: "Spielend Leben Lernen" (2001-2004), "TWISFER: Theatre Work in Social Fields – European Research" (2003-2005), coordinator of the Grundtvig2-learning partnership: "Performing Life: Site Specific Performance as a Means of Active Citizenship" (2004-2006).

Armin Ruckerbauer is an artist who is concerned with the use of art forms (theatre and fine arts) in social contexts. He is artistic director of the art gallery 'Zwischenbilder' located in the social welfare office, Graz; social-cultural projects since 2000.

Manfred Schewe studied German, English, History, Political, Social and Educational Sciences at Carl von Ossietzky Universität Oldenburg from 1975-81. He held a position as DAAD-Lektor/lecturer in German at University College Cork (UCC) from 1982 until 1987 after which he returned to Oldenburg University to complete a drama-based DPhil-research project and a special Drama/Theatre training course. There he also lectured in Drama/Theatre Pedagogy from 1988 until 1994. He has been back at UCC ever since and holds a position as Senior Lecturer in the Department of German. Numerous publications focus mainly on aspects of Applied Drama and Theatre.

Roger Sell helped to pioneer the Theatre and Education movement in the UK during the 60's and 70's. He moved to the University sector and became Director of Theatre at Dartington College of Arts. At present he is Director of International Development at Dartington and tutor and coordinator of the MA in Performance and Cultural Location in Contemporary Europe.

Jelena Sitar-Cvetko is a qualified dramaturg, a theatre director and pedagogue, puppeteer and freelance artist. She was was chief editor of the journal Lutka (puppet) from 1983 to 1993 and together with Igor Cvetko she founded the puppet theatre Zapik (puppets and music in games, education and therapy) in 1996. She is programme manager of the Children and Arts House in Ljubljana (SI) since 2001. Her publications include many professional and scientific articles on the place and role of puppets in education and therapy.

Gabriele Skledar studied drama, acted in some films then retired to the countryside to become a farmer for 7 years. Back in the city she married, gave birth to four children and once again escaped to the countryside and began to study. She completed a university course in "Theatre work in social fields" and is currently completing her course in cultural studies. She has carried out theatre work in social fields with young people, elderly people and prisoners and is also a member of Inter*ACT*, Werkstatt für Theater und Soziokultur in Graz (studio for theatre and sociocultural activities).

Florian Vaßen studied German, French, philosophy and history at the universities of Frankfurt, Aix-en-Provence and Marburg where he was awarded a DPhil in 1970. He formerly held a post as assistant lecturer at the University of Gießen and in 1982, he took up his current position as Professor for German Literature at the University of Hanover where he is director of the "Arbeitsstelle Theater/ Theaterpädagogik" (Centre of Theatre/Theatre Pedagogy) and co-editor of "Korrespondenzen. Zeitschrift für Theaterpädagogik" (Correspondences. Journal for Theatre Pedagogy). His research interests include drama and theatre, theory and practice of theatre pedagogy, literature of the "Vormärz", Bertolt Brecht and Heiner Müller.

Martin Vieregg is a pedagogue with a special interest in adult education and social pedagogy. He is also a theatre pedagogue, participating in theatre work in social fields and works with Inter*ACT* – studio for theatre and sociocultural activities, Graz.

Tina Wellmann holds a Masters degree in German Literature and Philosophy. She has worked as theatre pedagogue (BuT) and in mediation. Since 1996 she has freelanced on various theatre projects and as director of a variety of projects: "Theatre and School", Theatre in Conflicts, Theatre and Sport (Improvisation), Theatre with handicapped people. Institutions she has worked for include the University of Hannover, BuT (Bundesverband für Theaterpädagogik), Bundesverband für Mediation, Theaterwerk Albstedt and Aue-Kreativschule.

Michael Wrentschur holds a post as assistant lecturer at the University of Graz, Institute of Education, Department of Social Pedagogy. His fields of teaching and research include: Theatre Work in Social Fields; social/cultural and community work. He is artistic director of Inter*ACT* – Werkstatt für Theater und Soziokultur in Graz (studio for theatre and sociocultural activities, Graz) leading workshops, projects and productions in social and political theatrework. Co-leader of the first universitary theatre course at the University of Graz.

Special thanks to Monika Austermühle, Katrin Adolph, Wolfgang Rappel, Robert Roth

TWISFER Partner Institutions

The Alice-Salomon-University for Applied Sciences: The history of the Alice Salomon University of Applied Sciences (ASFH) is closely connected with the development of modern professional social work and social reform. The roots of the University extend back to the 19th century when one-year social training courses in Germany began. In the context of the educational reforms of the 60s, the school was expanded in 1971 as the University for Applied Sciences for Social Work and Social Education. In 1994, a second degree program in Nursing/Nursing Management was established. Today, the University of Applied Sciences for Social Work/Social Education and Nursing/Nursing-Management is one of the largest educational institutions in the social work field in Germany. There is an obligatory education in theory and practice of social cultural work (theatre, creative writing, video, foto, dance/movement, music, arts) in the basic study period. In the advanced study period: project study in social cultural work.

Artemisszió was founded in 1998 in order to favour intercultural relations and the integration of disadvantaged social groups. The founders were young anthropologists looking for possibilities to connect scientific research and social activities. The Foundation is a civil organisation independent of governments and political parties. On the one hand, through its activities, Artemisszió aims at promoting cultural, scientific and personal relations between Hungary and other European countries; on the other hand, it intends to create equal opportunities for disadvantaged groups in Hungary.

Charles University Prague: The Department of Primary Education of the Faculty of Education at the Charles University has a focus on a basic drama in education-training for all students. There is the possibility to specialise on Drama in Education within the teacher's qualification. For these students the subject is part of their bachelor or master degree. At least two terms of Drama in Education, with the focus on personal and social development, are obligatory for all students. Experience in EU-projects through many Sokrates-Exchange-programmes, through an annual summer course at the university of Prag and through participating in several Lingua-, Comenius- and other Sokrates-projects.

CONCEPT Foundation (www.concept.ro) is a non-governmental, non for profit and non-partisan organization, which mission is to help strengthen an open society by developing effective partnerships between culture and other fields. Our objectives are to develop projects which enable cultural, educational and social policies to become interrelated and to empower various societal actors to build participatory initiatives through developing effective partnerships. CONCEPT Foundation manages programs in the cultural, educational, social and media fields by developing projects and services which enable the convergence among them: access to information, social campaigns, participatory arts, surveys, assistance and consultancy, etc.

Dartington College of Arts is one of just a few specialist arts colleges in the UK – a university sector higher education institution offering a range of opportunities for BA, MA, Mphil and PhD awards. All our energies are devoted to the study and performance of contemporary arts and to the development of the artist's role in society. Our studios are set in rich and inspirational countryside, but we stand solidly on the world's stage and at the centre of an extensive network of international practice and live connections. We encourage collaboration and experiment across artforms, between languages and cultures, and beyond existing social and cultural boundries. The invention of new work and an intense curiosity regarding emerging disciplines and forms are at the heart of everything we do. We celebrate diversity at Dartington.

Giolli Centro Ricerche su Teatro dell'Oppresso e Coscientizzazione works since 1992 in Italy and abroad by using especially the Boal's method called Theatre of the Oppressed in several social and educational fields. Its roots are also in the so-called Community Approach, in No- Violence and in Freire's thought that is "conscientization". Giolli has a democratic structure with a sovereign assembly 4 times a year and a range of roles that take care different aspects of its life: realizing of projects, practitioners' education, training and supervision, relation with outer people, theatre production, planning and evaluating intervention, and so on. Giolli intervene wherever a conflict, an oppression, a problem exists and give its contribute in order to improve the situation of voiceless people; in this sense it has been working with drug addicts, homeless, psychiatric patiences, students, youth at risk, teachers, parents, social workers, prisoners and so on.

Institute for Education Science, University of Graz, department for social pedagogyThe institute contributes in an important way to the theory of the project and is carrying out theatre pedagogical practical work in the usual curriculum. The pilot course "Theaterpädagogik / Theatre Work in Social Fields" was situated at this institute, especially at the department für Social Pedagogy, which concerns itself both in scientific research and theory with suggestions, social support and help in the organization and coping of everyday life of people of different age groups and situations in life. At the same time it is oriented towards a multitude of theoretical positions, forms of intervention and institutions. Since it refers to man as a whole in social life, it includes a claim of social participation.

"Theatre pedagogy" is offered to the students in the institute/department since more than ten years but it also plays an increasing role in scientific research. Especially questions about possibilities of application and modes of action of theatre pedagogic in social, educational and sociocultural fields are discussed. In addition, a new branch – in theory and research-is being established which tackles the relationship of art, cultural and social work / socioculture thoroughly.

Inter*ACT* – Werkstatt für Theater und Soziokultur is a non-profit association, developing theatre work in social fields in several ways; workshops, projects and productions using means of theatre for a culture of living together. In order to stimulate solutions in fields of social problems and conflicts, we produce – as ensemble and / or directors – true to life and interactive theatre. The aims are activation, empowerment, participation and change. We take up "hot" topics and open a playful – creative and aesthetic – entertaining access to them. We think that all human beings have the right to actively and independently use the creative, aesthetic and powerful potential of theatre as a form of art and understanding. In our theatrework the methods and forms of the "Theatre of the Oppressed" after A. Boal are of a particular importance, especially: Image Theatre, Forum Theatre, Legislative Theatre. Our work is orientated on socio-politically relevant themes and conflicts and is starting from subjective points of view, experiences and wishes of the involved persons. Target groups relevant for the project are refugees, homeless people, prisoners and theatre work in communities and urban districts.

JSKD has expert and administrative personnel at its headquarters in Ljubljana and 58 local offices in all major urban centers in Slovenia. Program of local offices is coordinated in 10 regional subdivisions. Network organization of Fund enables multidirectional interactions between cultural societies and local communities through local offices and central expert unit to state institutions. Such organizational structure allows easier access to cultural goods. Fund also organizes reviews and promotional events on local, regional, and national level for all arts (music, theatre and puppet theatre, folklore, film, dance, fine arts, literature, and intermedia projects), thus allowing interactive comparison and evaluation of achievements and stimulating innovation and creativity.

uniT is the cultural association at the university of Graz (www.uni-t.org). It was founded in 1998 to implement cultural work at the university. The aim of the work of uniT is to build up a creative space and to foster cross-over-projects connecting people from different cultural, social, economic and scientific fields. Objectives are: to develop a variety of national and international cultural programs bringing together artists, members of the university business people and people dealing with social work; to organize different kinds of cultural events, e.g. theatre and dance presentations, exhibitions; to build up international relationships; to work out curricula for special courses in cultural fields such as drama writing and theatre work in social fields; to offer a variety of workshops for students because we think culture should be a part of the general education of the university just as sport uses to be; to try to foster communication and to build up networks between artists students and people from economy. So we try to construct a space of creativity at the university.

University College Cork participated in the TWISFER-project with the Department of German in cooperation with the interdisciplinary Board of Drama and Theatre Studies. There have been for a long time cooperations with the institute for german literature and language at the University Hannover, the institute for dramatics at the university Bern, the Goethe Institutes in Berlin and Munich in the field of drama /theatre and professionals on leading theatres in Berlin; organisation of international drama/theatre conferences in cooperation with the National Association of Youth Drama, Irland; cooperation with Meridian Productions and Graffiti Theatre (TiE-company); project experience through agreements in the Sokrates framework amongst others with the University Hannover.

The **workplace Theaterpädagogik / Theater at the University Hannover** has been working in a scientific and theatrepractical way in the fields of theatre pedagogics and theatre science since the end of the seventies. On the one hand it is organising within the university the education of the students with the focus theatre pedagogics and "Darstellendes Spiel", on the other hand it is doing work outside of the university with conferences, workshops and cooperations, e.g. with the Gesellschaft für Theaterpädagogik and the National Theatre Hannover. It has edited several publications and its head, Prof. Dr. Florian Vaßen, is co-editor of the Korrespondenzen. Zeitschrift für Theaterpädagogik.

Photos

InterACT (p. 13, 128)
Jennie Hayes (p. 41, 185)
Katharina Grilj (p. 42)
Matthias Bittner (p. 75)
Andrej Štular (p. 222)

Translations
from the original languages of the authors by:

Nora Bauermann, Ditte Bellettre, Anja Ambrož Bizjak, Bernadette Cronin, Andrea Gardner, Martin Kroissenbrunner, Maureen Levis

Reiner Steinweg
Lehrstück und episches Theater
*Brechts Theorie und
die theaterpädagogische Praxis
2. Aufl., Pb., 192 S., ISBN 3-86099-250-3*

Das Buch bietet eine Überprüfung und Weiterentwicklung der von Reiner Steinweg Anfang der siebziger Jahre entdeckten »Theorie des Lehrstücks« bei Brecht und setzt sie in Beziehung zu den Praxiserfahrungen, die seither durch den Autor und viele andere gemacht wurden. Mit einem Nachwort zur 2. Auflage.

*Florian Vaßen/Gerd Koch/
Gabriela Naumann (Hrsg.)*
Wechselspiel: KörperTheaterErfahrung
216 S., Pb. mit Fotos, ISBN 3-86099-150-7

Für eine körperorientierte theaterpädagogische Praxis. Unterschiedlichen Arbeitsweisen werden anschaulich verknüpft und dargestellt. Das Buch versteht sich als Reise zu Körper, Theater und Erfahrung, das zu neuen Erfahrungen anstiften will.

Fe Reichelt
Tanz der Wandlungen
144 S., Frz. Br., mit zahlr. Fotos und Zeichnungen, ISBN 3-86099-809-9

Es geht in diesem Buch um die tanztherapeutische Entschlüsselung des tänzerischen Ausdrucks. Gleichzeitig gibt das reich illustrierte Werk dem schöpferischen Tanz neue Impulse für die Gestaltung. Hinzu kommen Renerationsübungen für den Alltag sowie Übungen für den Einstieg in Improvisationen. »Morgenübungen« sorgen für Ganzheit, für die Stärkung des Ich.

Gerd Koch
Sieglinde Roth
Florian Vaßen
Michael Wrentschur (Hrsg.)
Theaterarbeit in sozialen Feldern/ Theatre Work in Social Fields
Ein einführendes Handbuch

Pb., 304 S.
ISBN 3-86099-325-9

Das Werk fundiert eine künstlerische und soziale Arbeit, die sich immer mehr durchsetzt.

Die konzeptionellen und theoretischen Grundlagen sowie die Lern- und Lehrpraxis werden ausführlich beschrieben. Es wird bewusst exemplarisch argumentiert, um den Übergang in weitere Praxis durch die LeserInnen zu erleichtern. Eingehalten wird die im europäischen Kontext erprobte Theorie-Praxis-Verbindung.

Zahlreiche Künstler und Praktiker aus mehreren europäischen Ländern kommen zu Wort.

Bitte fordern Sie unser kostenloses Gesamtverzeichnis an.
Brandes & Apsel Verlag · Scheidswaldstr. 33 · D-60385 Frankfurt am Main
Fax 069/957 301 87 · E-Mail: brandes-apsel@doodees.de